INDIAN MANUFACTURING SECTOR IN LIBERALISED ERA

INDIAN MANUFACTURING SECTOR IN LIBERALISED ERA

Dr. A. Vijayakumar

Prints Publications Pvt Ltd

New Delhi

Published by

Prints Publications Pvt Ltd
Viraj Tower-2, 4259/3, Ansari Road,
Darya Ganj, New Delhi-110002
Tel. : +91-11-45355555
Fax: +91-11-23275542
E-mail : contact@printspublications.com
Website : www.printspublications.com

First Edition : 2022 (Hardbound)

ISBN: 978-93-936743-0-2

Price: ₹ 1495/-

Published and Printed by Mr. Pranav Gupta (Director) on behalf of Prints Publications Pvt Ltd, New Delhi.

CONTENTS

PART III
LIQUIDITY ANALYSIS

PART IV
PRODUCTIVITY ANALYSIS

PART V
PERFORMANCE APPRAISAL

PART VI
SOCIAL PERFORMANCE

PART VII

IMPACT OF LIBERALISATION, PRIVATISATION AND GLOBALISATION

FELICITATION

I am very much happy to note that **Dr. A. Vijayakumar**, Reader in Commerce, Erode Arts College (Autonomous), Erode is publishing a book entitled **"Indian Manufacturing Sector in Liberalised Era"** which contains 25 research papers published by him in leading journals both in India and abroad on various occasions.

This book provides various aspects of performance appraisal such as Profitability, Working capital, Liquidity, Productivity, Social performance and impact of LPG measures with special reference to Indian manufacturing sector during post-liberalization period. I am quite confident that this book will greatly help the academics, research scholars, financial executives and students.

I wish him every success in all his future endeavour.

23rd July 2008.

Erode Arts College
Erode

K. K. Balusamy
Secretary & Correspondent

FOREWORD

Globalization which is a more romantic word indicating the desire to integrate nation-states within a overall frame work of WTO, is nothing but a modern version of the "Theory of Comparative Cost Advantage; Globalization and its major paths privatization and liberalization are considered as an important element in the reform package of any community.

The Indian Industrial manufacturing sector, which posses a relatively high marginal propensity to save and invest contributes significantly to the eventual achievement of a self-sustaining economy with continued high levels of investment and rapid rate of increase in income and industrial development.

At this juncture, this new comprehensive book "Indian Manufacturing Sector in Liberalized Era" authored by Dr. A.Vijayakumar, Reader in Commerce, Erode Arts College, Erode, comprises of various factors, which have always dodged our mind in comprehending its real sense.

This book exemplifies implication of better financial management in the manufacturing sectors of the present environment apart from clearly explaining the very subject. The illustrations of different manufacturing industries are self-explanatory and the explanatory notes are real boon for the learners.

I congratulate Dr. A.Vijayakumar, for his indepth study on the subject and coming out with a very concise and precise book.

BHARATHIAR UNIVERSITY
COIMBATORE - 641 046.

Dr. G. THIRUVASAGAM
VICE-CHANCELLOR

PREFACE

Manufacturers from across the world are transforming India- which has all the required skills in process, product and capital engineering, thanks to its long manufacturing history and higher-education system – into a potential manufacturing powerhouse. Every major company has India on its radar screen. And the number of companies, spanning diverge industries, planning to make India their global hub for host of operations has only been increasing by the day. Taking the advantages of vast domestic market and availability of low-cost workers with advanced technical skills, several multinationals operating in skill-intensive industries requiring advanced technical expertise have set up their shop in India. India is all set to threaten China as the world's backyard for manufacturing in the next three to five years. It says companies are planning to offshore manufacturing activities primarily to India, that will surpass its IT and BPO activities. Thus, India will become the hub for world manufacturing industry.

It is well recognized fact that there exists a wide gap in the research being done getting published in journals and included in the books. It is difficult for most people to consult professional and academic research oriented journals regularly. The benefits which the society may derive from such research remain untapped and the findings based on hard labour and serious efforts to researchers decorate the columns of professional and academic research journals which in turn either pile dust in some obscure corners of the libraries or decorate the offices of senior professors.

To fill this gap, I have attempted to include all my articles of interest relating to Indian service sector published in well known journals both in India and abroad.

This book contains 25 research papers to focusing six important areas of performance appraisal viz, Profitability, Working capital, Liquidity, Productivity, Social performance and Impact of LPG measures. Further, in order to cater to the needs of research scholars, teachers and financial executive, the subject matter in the book has been treated in a conceptual - cum-analytical manner.

The book is intended to be useful for practicing managers, financial executives working in the service sectors, students of M.Com, MBA, MFC and other banking professional examinations. Further, this book is of special interest of Ph.D and M.Phil scholars of various universities, colleges and research institutions. The contents of the book may be much useful to researchers pursuing research in the field of service sector.

I earnestly hope that it would serve its purpose and meet the market needs. However, I would gratefully welcome suggestions and feedback from colleagues, students and practitioners. Any constructive criticism will undoubtedly help me greatly to enhance my research capability.

In the preparation of this book, I have received help and encouragement from different sources. I shall forever cherish the kind permission and encouragement given to me by **Thiru. K. M. Dhandapani**, President, The Mudaliar Educational Trust. I am grateful to **Thiru. K. K. Balusamy**, our most beloved Secretary and Correspondent, Erode Arts College, for his encouragement and inspiration given to me. I would like to thank **Thiru. K.N.Murugesan**, Vice-President, **Thiru. U. N. Murugesan**, Vice-President, **Thiru. L. Kumaravel**, Treasurer and other management committee members for their encouragement. I would like to thank **Dr. V. Venkateswaran**, Principal, Erode Arts College, Erode and **Thiru. N. Senthamari**, Professor of Commerce (Retired), C. N. College, Erode for the necessary help I required in completing this work. I also express my deep sense of gratitude to **Dr. G. Thiruvasagam**, Vice-Chancellor, Bharathiar University, for so kindly providing me foreword to this book.

I am thankful to all my co-authors and the editors of the various journals viz., Management Accountant, Management and Labour Studies, Tamil Nadu Journal of Co-operation, Indian Banking Today and Tomorrow, Southern Economist, Journal of Marketing, for granting me necessary permission most generously to include these research articles in this book. I am grateful to my colleagues and friends for their help and support in the completion of this book.

My thanks would remain incomplete if I fail to pay my gratitude to my beloved wife **Mr. Ponne Vijay Kumar**, Lecturer in Nutrition and Dietetics, Vellalar College for Women, Erode, my son **Mr. V. Sudhirkumar** and my daughter **Miss V. Sruthi**, for the co-operation, understanding and the sacrifice of the time which belonged to them which in no measure I would ever be able to compensate. I also express my thanks and gratitude to my sister, brother-in-law, co-brother, father-in-law, mother-in-law, and sister-in-law for encouraging me to complete the work. I also extend my profound thanks to Prints Publication Pvt. Ltd., New Delhi, for giving shape of my ideas by publishing this book in a record time.

Finally, and most importantly, many thanks to my parents for their affectionate blessings and loving co-operation at all moments of this academic venture. To them, I will be grateful forever

Dr. A. VIJAYAKUMAR

PART - I

PROFITABILITY ANALYSIS

1

STRUCTURE OF PROFIT RATES IN INDIAN AUTOMOBILE INDUSTRIES—A COMPARISON

Profitability of various industries would hardly diverge in a world of perfection, because, future can easily be predicted. However, real world is far from perfection. A number of dynamic forces (e.g., changes in income, technology, population, etc.) operate simultaneously in a real imperfect and uncertain world, consequently, profitability of different concerns and industries gets greatly affected. Rate of profit which is one of the most used and popular financial measure of performance of a concern and an industry, plays a pivotal role in the growth process of the concern, the industry and the whole economy. It reflects the financial stability and also enhances the earning capacity of the concern. It plays dual role in the investment process of the economy by attracting fresh investment on one hand, and generating internal source of finance on the other hand. However, low rate of profit or loss repels any fresh inflow of investment and induces existing capital to quit towards the fields of higher rates of profit. It thus reflects investor's and lenders need of knowing financial indicator of performance and is a key factor in determining the commercial viability of the concern and the industry[1].

Issues Explored

The current rate of profit is an indicator and source of and a need for the expansions of business through re-investment and through attracting and observing new capital in the industry. Hence, investors and lenders are interested in knowing the profitability of a concern and industry over time or at a point of time. The celebrated tendency of rates of profit to fall over long period of time had been theoretically developed by classical economists like Adam Smith, David Ricardo, etc., their critic Karl Marx and also by neoclassical writers like Alfred Marshall. The study therefore intends to empirically examine whether the rate of profit in Indian Automobile Industry have a tendency to rise or fall over a period of 1991-92 to

2003-04. The objective is not to test the validity of classical hypothesis, as the economic conditions as assumed by classical writers do not prevail in the country. However, knowledge about whether profitability is raising or falling over the period 1991-92 to 2003-04 would throw interesting results for formulation of future policies.

Methodology

An attempt has been made in this study to examine the trends in rates of profit of selected Indian Automobile Industries over the period 1991-92 to 2003-04. Further an attempt has also been made to capture the industry wise variations in the series of profit rates, which reveals the dispersion of the series for each industry over the study period. In this study a ratio of profits to capital employed and express it in percentage terms has been used for this purpose. The rate of profit on capital employed indicates the earning power of capital of long term nature and thus examines long-term profitability better. The Linear regression model fitted is as follows:

$$P = \alpha + \beta t + e$$

where P is rate of profit, t is the time and α and β are the parameters (intercept and co-efficient respectively) and e is the error term. The results of the application of above stated model to the profitability of Indian Automobile Industries are presented in Table 1.0 and 1.1.

Table 1.0

Results of Regression of Rates of profit on Time for Indian Automobile Industries: 1991-92 to 2003-2004

Sl. No.	Industry	$P = \alpha + \beta t + e$			
		α	β	R^2	F value
1.	Ashok Leyland Ltd	10.124 (4.813)	0.340 (1.283)	0.13	1.65
2.	Tata Motors Ltd	20.174 (3.017)	-0.501 (2.595)*	0.47	35.41
3.	Bajaj Tempo Ltd	24.326 (2.815)	-1.113 (1.022)	0.09	1.05
4	Eicher Motors Ltd	5.300 (0.867)	-2.514 (3.265)*	0.49	10.66
5.	Swaraj Mazda Ltd	-10.312 (-1.313)	-5.096 (5.147)*	0.71	26.50
	Commercial vehicles sectors	14.182 (2.700)	-0.862 (3.303)*	0.51	31.45

6.	Hindustan Motors Ltd	14.682 (3.208)	-0.993 (2.723)*	0.46	29.69
7.	Mahindra & Mahindra Ltd	19.261 (5.016)	-0.370 (0.765)	0.05	0.59
8.	Maruti Udyog Ltd	42.541 (3.293)	-1.990 (3.223)*	0.40	34.15
9.	Daewoo Motors India Ltd	3.541 (0.996)	-0.246 (0.550)	0.03	0.30
	Passenger cars and Multi utility vehicles sectors	17.112 (2.802)	-0.477 (0.621)	0.03	0.39
10.	Bajaj Auto Ltd	39.047 (6.420)	-1.540 (2.010)	0.27	4.04
11.	LML Ltd	22.676 (2.768)	-1.596 (1.546)	0.18	2.39
12.	Maharastra Scooters Ltd	40.083 (17.393)	-3.194 (11.001)*	0.92	121.03
13.	TVS Motors Company Ltd	44.803 (4.378)	-0.553 (2.429)*	0.39	24.16
14.	Kinetic Motors Company Ltd	20.817 (2.601)	-0.761 (0.754)	0.05	0.57
15.	Hero Honda Motors Ltd	6.892 (1.253)	-6.526 (9.419)*	0.89	88.72
16.	Kinetic Engineering Ltd	26.508 (6.914)	-1.877 (3.885)*	0.58	15.09
17.	Majestic Auto Ltd	23.189 (6.057)	-1.824 (3.781)*	0.57	14.30
18.	Scooters India Ltd	5.344 (0.771)	0.375 (0.429)	0.02	0.18
	Two and Three wheelers sectors	25.512 (8.442)	-0.487 (3.280)*	0.43	36.38
	Whole Automobile Industry	18.935 (5.030)	-0.234 (3.072)*	0.48	51.26

Notes: 1. Figures in brackets are t values

2. * Indicates at estimate is significant at 5 per cent level.

Source: Computed

Table 1.1
Industry wise variations in profitability of Indian Automobile Sector (1991-92 - 2003-2004)

S. No.	Industry	Mean	S.D	CV
1.	Ashok Leyland Ltd	12.50	3.70	0.30
2.	Tata Motors Ltd	16.66	11.06	0.66
3.	Bajaj Tempo Ltd	16.54	14.71	0.89
4.	Eicher Motors Ltd	22.89	13.95	0.61
5.	Swaraj Mazda Ltd	25.36	23.61	0.93
	Commercial vehicles sectors	**20.21**	**9.18**	**0.45**
6.	Hindustan Motors Ltd	7.73	8.39	1.09
7.	Mahindra & Mahindra Ltd	16.67	6.41	0.38
8.	Maruti Udyog Ltd	28.61	22.41	0.78
9.	Daewoo Motors India Ltd	1.82	5.86	3.22
	Passenger cars and Multi utility vehicles sectors	**13.77**	**10.11**	**0.73**
10.	Bajaj Auto Ltd	28.27	11.57	0.41
11.	LML Ltd	11.50	7.00	0.61
12.	Maharastra Scooters Ltd	17.72	12.99	0.73
13.	TVS Motors Company Ltd	40.99	16.86	0.41
14.	Kinetic Motors Company Ltd	15.49	13.36	0.86
15.	Hero Honda Motors Ltd	52.58	26.95	0.51
16.	Kinetic Engineering Ltd	13.37	9.61	0.72
17.	Majestic Auto Ltd	10.42	9.45	0.91
18.	Scooters India Ltd	7.97	11.38	1.43
	Two and Three wheeler sectors	**22.10**	**5.27**	**0.24**
	Whole Automobile Industry	**18.69**	**6.12**	**0.33**

Source: Computed from annual reports of the respective industries

Trends in Profit Rates

Table 1.0 reveals that the linear model of time trend of profitability has proved to be a "good fit" in case of ten out of eighteen industries, i.e., 55.55 per cent of the industries examined. This reveals from value of R^2, the co-efficient of determination. All these ten industries, viz., Tata Motors Ltd, Eicher Motors Ltd, Swaraj Mazda Ltd (Commercial vehicles), Hindustan Motors Ltd,

Maruti Udyog Ltd (Passenger Cars & Multiutility vehicles), Maharastra Scooters Ltd, TVS Motors Company Ltd, Hero Honda Motors Ltd, Kinetic Engineering Ltd and Majestic Auto Ltd (Two and Three wheelers), experienced a strong tendency in profitability to decline over the study period. The negative values of β, the time trend co-efficient, confirms this as these are observed to be statistically significant. Statistically significant negative values of β indicate strong negative relationship between profitability and time over the study period. Table 1.0 further reveals that β assumes different values (negative) for different industries and ranges in value from -0.50 for Tata Motors Ltd to -6.50 for Hero Honda Motors Ltd during the study period. This implies that profitability of different industries declined at different rates over this period.

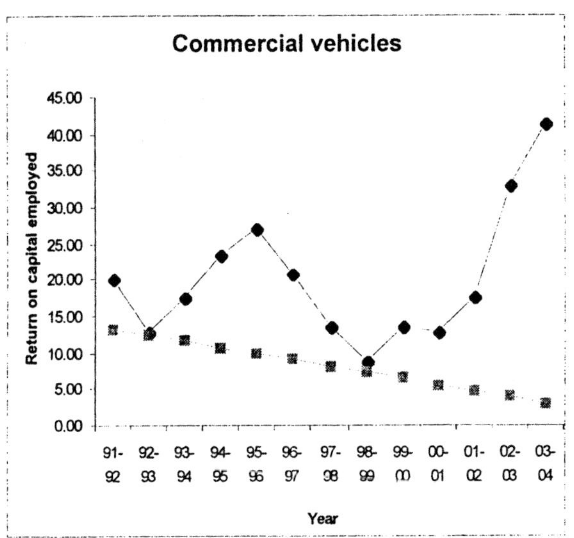

Only in case of two industries viz., Ashok Leyland Ltd and Scooters India Ltd, the sign for β, the time trend co-efficient is positive, implying a tendency of profit rate to rise over time. However β being statistically non-significant, the result are not discussed. In case of eight industries, no definite trend could be observed as the results are statistically insignificant. The value of co-efficient of determination, R^2, varied in case of industries having strong declining tendency of profit rate over time, from 0.39 for TVS Motors Company Ltd to 0.92 for Maharastra Scooters Ltd. Such great variation in the value of R^2 implies that time explain profitability variation of different industries in different degree over the time. This means that time explains variations in profitability of the above two industries to the *extend* of 39 per cent and 92 per cent respectively over the study period.

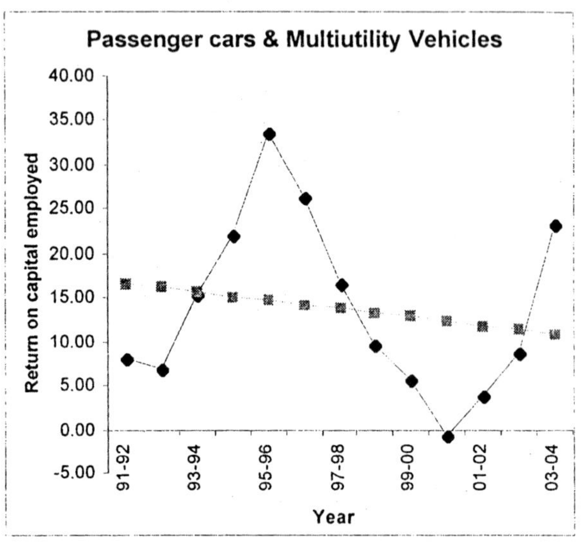

Sector wise time trend regression results are also presented in Table 1.0. It may be noted from the table that out of three sectors shown, Commercial vehicles and Two and Three wheelers sectors, as well as Whole Automobile Industry, all had a strong tendency for profit rate to fall over the study period as the results for R^2 and β, are statistically significant, while results are non-significant for Passenger cars and Multiutility vehicle sectors. The value of R^2 varianced between 0.03 (Passenger cars & Multiutility vehicle sector), to 0.51 (Commercial vehicles sector) indicating that time explain profitability variation of these sector to the tune of 3 per cent and 51 per cent respectively. For whole Automobile Industry time explain variations in profitability to the extend of 48 per cent over the study period. β the time trend co-efficient also varies in value from -0.234 (Whole Automobile Industry) to -0.862 (Commercial vehicles sector), indicating that as time increases, profit rates of sector fall between this range.

Dispersion in rate of profit

The industry wise dispersion in rates of profit of Indian Automobile Industry over the study period is achieved through estimation of mean, standard deviation and co-efficient of variation.

The estimates are presented in Table 1.1. It is observed from Table 1.1 that on an average, Hero Honda Motors Ltd experienced highest profit rate (52.58 per cent), while Daewoo Motors India Ltd experienced lowest rate of profit (1.82 per cent) over the study period. The Whole Automobile industry, on an average, enjoyed 18.69 per cent rate of profit. Amongst the sector, Commercial vehicles (20.21 per cent), and Two and Three wheelers (22.10 per cent) on an average, had a profit rate above the whole Automobile Industry, while Passenger cars and Multiutility vehicles (13.77 per cent) had below it. Out of total eighteen industries, six industries, i.e., (33.33 per cent industries) viz., Eicher Motors Ltd, Swaraj Mazada Ltd (Commercial vehicles sector), Maruti Udyog Ltd (Passenger cars and Multiutility vehicles sector), Bajaj Auto Ltd, TVS Motors Company Ltd and Hero Honda Motors Ltd (Two and Three wheelers sectors), enjoyed, on an average, a higher rate of profit than whole manufacturing sector. Another important observation from Table 1.1 is that mean rates of profit vary greatly in case all the industries, irrespective of the sector of which these belong.

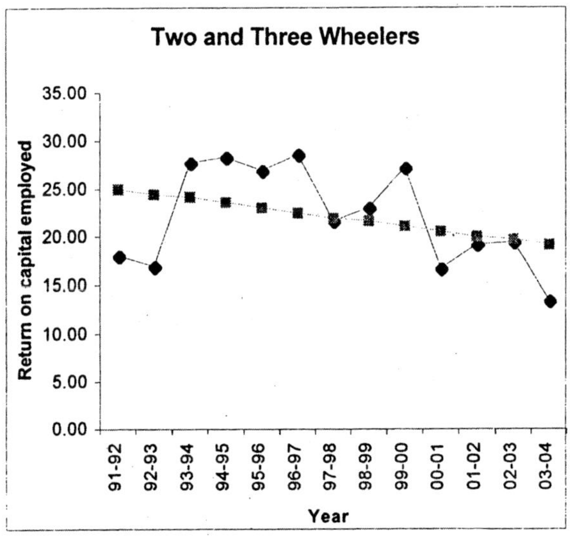

In order to study year to year variation in the profit rates over the study period, the estimates of standard deviation and co-efficient of variation for profit rate series of selected Indian Automobile Industries are worked out and presented in Table 1.1. These measures reveal the extend of variation of actual values of profit rate of each industries from its mean value of the series. The higher values of co-efficient of variation indicate larger dispersion among the profit rate series of respective industries and vice-versa. Ashok Leyland Ltd, with co-efficient of variation being 0.30 experienced lowest variation in profit rates over the study period while Daewoo Motors Ltd, with lowest mean profit rate suffered from largest dispersion, co-efficient variation assuming value equal to 3.22. Among the sector, Two and Three wheelers sector had lowest variations in profit rates (Co-efficient of variation = 0.24) while Passenger cars and Multiutility vehicle sectors suffered from largest variation (co-efficient of variation = 0.73) during the study period.

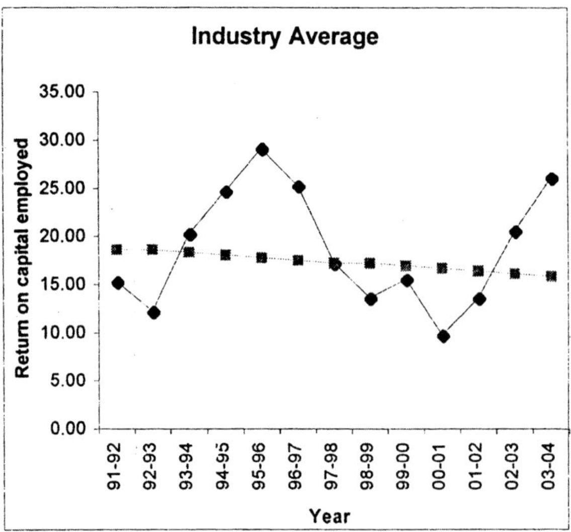

The selected Automobile Industries are divided arbitrarily divided into Relatively stable (CV with value up to 0.25), Moderately fluctuating (CV laying between 0.251 and 0.500), Highly fluctuating (CV laying between 0.501 and 0.750 and Erratically fluctuating (CV above 0.750), then it is observed from Table 1.1 that majority of the industries, eight out of eighteen industries (44.44 per cent) experienced erratically fluctuating variations in profit rate series. These industries are Bajaj Tempo Ltd and Swaraj Mazda Ltd (Commercial vehicles), Hindustan Motors Ltd, Maruti Udyog Ltd and Daewoo Motors India Ltd (Passenger cars & Multiutility vehicles) and Kinetic Motors Company Ltd , Majestic Auto Ltd and Scooters India Ltd (Two & Three Wheelers). Six out of eighteen industries (33.33 per cent) experienced highly fluctuating variations in profit rate series. These industries are Tata Motors Ltd and Eicher Motors Ltd (Commercial vehicles) and LML Ltd, Maharastra Scooters Ltd, Hero Honda Motors Ltd and Kinetic Engineering Ltd (Two and Three Wheelers). Four out of eighteen industries (22.23 per cent) experienced moderately fluctuating variations in profit rate series. These industries are Ashok Leyland Ltd (Commercial vehicles) Mahindra & Mahindra Ltd (Passenger Cars & Multiutility vehicles) and Bajaj Auto Ltd and TVS Motors Company Ltd (Two and Three wheelers). As per as the whole Automobile industry variations are concerned, it experienced moderately fluctuating series of profit rates over the study period.

In sum, the profitability trends in Indian Automobile Industry reveal that most of these industries have a tendency for rates of profit to fall over a long period. Moreover, time explains this fall in profitability at various degrees. Further, most of the industries, 44.44 per cent experienced erratical fluctuations in profitability series while 33.33 per cent had highly fluctuating series.

Policy Implications

The declining trend in profitability of ten out of eighteen industries (55.55 per cent) Indian Automobile industries studied here is a very big cause of concern. The falling tendency of profit rate of these industries is a proof of adverse effect of various controls on prices, output, expansion, and investment etc., exerted by government on these industries over time. If the country aims at speedy growth, the results of this study suggest that the liberalization measures should be further strengthened in Indian Automobile industry. Again the policy of opening up of private and public sector for competition, both domestically and internationally, so that it would enhance efficiency, productivity and profitability of all the concerns in the Automobile industry, and in turn, of other industries and of economy at large.

References

1. Lata Arun Rede, (1998) Profitability Trends and Business/ Cycles, Discovery Publishing House, New Delhi, (1998).
2. Rede, L. A. (1988), Business cycle and Rate of profit in Indian Manufacturing Industries: 1950-51 to 1977-78, Artha-Vijnana, Vol.30, No. 3, September, pp.106-128.
3. Vijayakumar, A. (2002), Determinants of corporate size, growth and profitability – The Indian Experiences, in Edited Book "Research Studies in Commerce and Management", Classical Publishing Company, New Delhi.

4. Debasish Sur (1999), Inter – company profitability analysis of Indian general insurance industry, The Management Accountant, July 1999, pp.495-501.
5. Mahammad Rafiqul Islam (2000), Profitability of Fertilizer industry in Bangladesh, The Management Accountant, May 2000, pp. 338-345.
6. Dutta S. K. (1999), An analysis of Profitability Trend in the Indian Cotton Mill Industry, Asian Economic Review, Vol.41, No.2, pp.294-307.

2

WORKING CAPITAL AND PROFITABILITY—AN EMPIRICAL ANALYSIS

In conventional production function approach for determination of relationship between output and profit, fixed capital is taken into account as explanatory variable amongst others: the role of working capital is ignored. It is therefore felt that there is the need to study the important role of working capital in profit generating process. Sarkar and Saha have aptly observed the management of working capital as an important bearing on the profitability of an enterprise. Generally the higher the working capital, the less the rate of return on capital employed while a lower value of working capital yields a higher rate of return. Hence, in this study an attempt is made to study the association of profitability with working capital. The impact of working capital on profitability has been examined by computing coefficients of correlation and regression between profitability ratio and working capital ratios, viz., Current Ratio (CR) Liquid Ratio (LR), Working Capital Turnover Ratio (WTR), Inventory Turnover Ratio (ITR), Cash Turnover Ratio (CTR), and Receivables Turnover Ratio (RTR).

Sampling Design

There are about 31 sugar industries operating in Tamil Nadu of which 14 are under co-operative sector, 14 are under private sector and 3 are under public sector. Since this study has been directed towards assessing the problem over a period of time, all these sugar industries are not taken because most of them are just a few years old leading to the absence of data for the last ten years. In order to select the industries for the purpose of study first of all the list of those industries which were established before 1975 and having crushing capacity of 2000 MT (per day) or more has been prepared which shows 13 such industries, 6 under co-operative sector and 7 under private sector. Thus, 13 industries selected for the study form the important industries and seem to have represented the sugar industries of Tamil Nadu as a whole.

Working Capital and Profitability – Correlation Analysis

The co-efficient of correlation between working capital ratios and profitability ratio for the selected sugar industries of Tamil Nadu as a whole are presented in Table 2.0. It is evident from the table that the co-efficient of correlation between profitability ratio and current ratio is [-]0.78. It reveals a moderate degree of negative correlation between the variables. The value is also found to be significant at 5 per cent level of significance. Similarly, the co–efficient of correlation between profitability ratio and liquid ratio stands at [-]0.31. It indicates that there is a low degree of negative correlation between these two variables. At 5 per cent level of significance, the value of co-efficient of correlation is found to be not significant. Both the ratios, current and liquid ratios confirms with the assumption that larger amount of current and liquid assets decreases risk as well as profitability.

Table 2.0

Impact of Working Capital Ratios' on Profitability-Simple Correlation Analysis (Total Industry)

Year	Working Capital Ratio						PBT to Total
	CR	LR	WTR	ITR	RTR	CTR	Asset Ratio
1982 - 83	2.24	0.43	2.87	1.97	11.88	44.32	0.087
1983 - 84	2.13	0.91	3.88	3.58	10.21	10.45	0.079
1984 - 85	1.98	0.83	3.84	3.28	7.61	13.21	0.100
1985 - 86	2.18	0.66	3.62	2.81	10.35	19.28	0.100
1986 - 87	2.21	1.02	4.17	4.24	8.99	11.56	0.092
1987 - 89	1.94	0.60	4.19	2.94	11.48	16.26	0.116
1989 - 90	1.97	0.96	4.03	3.87	6.03	13.19	0.115
1990 - 91	2.80	0.99	1.67	1.66	3.67	18.77	0.073
1991 - 92	2.78	1.02	2.00	2.02	4.44	17.53	0.081
Co-efficient of Correlation							
(r)	-0.78	-0.31	0.72	0.49	0.33	-0.18	
	(3.29)*	(0.86)	(2.75)*	(1.49)**	(0.93)*	(0.48)	

Figures in bracket show t value

* Significant at 0.05 level

* Significant at 0.10 level

Source : Computed from annual report of the respective units.

Thirdly, the co-efficient of correlation between profitability and working capital turnover ratio is +0.72. It shows that there is a high degree of positive correlation between the two variables, as five percent level of significance, the value of co-efficient of correlation is found to be significant. Fourthly, the co-efficient of correlation between profitability ratio and inventory turnover ratio is found to be +0.49 which is found to be significant at 10 percent level of significance. It shows a moderate degree of positive correlation between the variables. Fifthly, the co-efficient of correlation between profitability ratio and debtors turnover ratio indicates positive association of +0.33. It shows low degree of positive correlation is very insignificant. All these three turnover ratio confirms with the assumption that higher the turnover increases the profitability of the selected sugar industry of Tamil Nadu as a whole.

Lastly, the co–efficient of correlation between profitability and cash turnover ratio is [-]0.18. This correlation is very insignificant. Thus the study of the impact of working capital ratios on profitability showed both negative and positive impacts. Out of the six independent working capital components ratio three ratios, namely CR, LR and CTR, have shown negative correlation with profitability ratio. Among these three ratios, the co-efficient of correlation between profitability ratio and current ratio is found to be significant at five per cent level of significance, and LR and CTR have no such significant association with profitability. The remaining three ratios, namely WTR, ITR and RTR, have shown positive co-efficient of correlation with profitability ratio. Among these three ratios, the co-efficient of correlation between profitability ratio and WTR and ITR are found to have significant association with profitability ratio, while CTR is not found to have such significant association with the profitability ratio.

Impact of Working Capital Ratios on Profitability – Multiple Regression Analysis

For the purpose of establishing defenite relationships between working capital ratios and profitability ratio, Karl Pearsons' correlation co-efficient can be applied. It implies the interdependence of the set of variables upon each other in such a way that changes in

Table 2.1

Correlation Matrix (Total Industry)

	CR	LR	WTR	ITR	RTR	CTR	PBT/TA
CR	1.000						
LR	0.399	1.000					
WTR	-0.935	-0.175	1.000				
ITR	-0.702	0.292	0.873	1.000			
RTR	-0.658	-0.776	0.613	0.252	1.000		
CTR	0.156	-0.729	-0.374	-0.614	0.342	1.000	
PBT/TA	-0.779	-0.305	0.716	0.489	0.330	-0.181	1.000

Source: Computed

the one are in sympathy with changes in the other. In this section, in order to identify that influence on profitability, a linear multiple regression model were used. In the analysis, working capital ratios VIZ, CR, LR, WTR, ITR, RTR and CTR are taken as the independent variables and profit before tax to total assets ratio is used as dependent variable.

For the purpose of selection of variables for the model, the co – efficient of correlation between the independent variables can be computed and presented in Table 2.1. It is evident from the table that there is a high degree of correlation between CR and WTR ([-]0.935) and ITR and WTR ([-]0.873). Therefore, current ratio and working capital turnover ratios are omitted for the analysis. The model used in this study is

$$PBT/TA = b_0 + b_1\ LR + b_2\ ITR + b_3\ RTR + b_4\ CTR$$

Where b_0, b_1, b_2, b_3, and b_4 are parameters to be estimated.

Table 2.2

Estimated Regression Results of Impact of Working Capital Ratios on Profitability (Total Industry)

(PBT/TA = $b_0 + b_1$ LR +b_2 ITR + b_3 RTR + b_4 CTR)

Variables	Beta Co – efficient	t Value	
Constant	0.2456 (0.0501)	4.90	Significant *
Liquid Ratio (LR)	-0.1591 (0.0405)	-3.93	Significant *
Inventory Turnover Ratio (ITR)	0.0195 (0.0061)	3.20	Significant *
Receivables Turnover Ratio (RTR)	0.0075 (0.0025)	2.94	Significant *
Cash Turnover Ratio (CTR)	-0.0009 (0.0005)	-1.64	Significant *
R^2 = 0.8529			
Adj R^2 = 0.7058			

** Significant at 0.05 level

* Significant at 0.10 level

Source : Computed

The pooled regression results of the models showing impact of 'orking capital ratios on profitability for the total industry are presented in Table 2.2. The table indicates that the impact of liquid ratio, inventory turnover ratio, receivables turnover ratio and cash turnover ratio were statistically significant as seen from the values of regression co–efficient. For a unit increase in liquid ratio, profitability decreased by 0.16 unit which was statistically significant at 5 per cent level. When inventory turnover ratio increased by one unit, profitability increased by 0.02 unit which was statistically significant at 5 per cent level of significance. When receivables turnover ratio increased by one unit, profitability increased by 0.08 unit which was statistically significant at 0.05 level of significance. For a unit increase in cash turnover ratio, profitability decreased by 0.001 unit which was significant at 0.10 level of significance. The four independent variables contribute 85 per cent of the variations in the profitability of the selected sugar industries of Tamil Nadu. Thus, the over – all results presented in the table are encouraging. The signs of all the co-efficients are as expected. The co-efficients are also statistically significant.

Conclusion

It is inferred from this study that liquid ratio, inventory turnover ratio, receivables turnover ratio and cash turnover ratio influenced the profitability of the selected sugar industries of Tamil Nadu.

References

1. Vittorio et al. (1979), "The Translogy Production Function: Some Evidence from Establishment Data". Journal of Econometrics, Vol.10, pp 193 – 99.
2. Sarkar and Saha, (1987), "Profitability crises and working capital management in the public sector in India." The Management Accountant, p. 329.

3

FIRM SIZE AND PROFITABILITY; AN EMPIRICAL TESTING-INDIAN PUBLIC SECTOR MANUFACTURING INDUSTRIES, 1981-2001

In a perfectly competitive market, profit rates tend to equality. As imperfect markets are taken into account the size of a firm must be considered as a factor in producing profits. Baumol (1967) suggested that the larger firm might be in a position to earn a higher rate of return on its investment than the smaller firm because it has all the options of a smaller firm open to it and in addition can undertake projects, which are of large scale and are denied to smaller firms. A similar argument had earlier been put forward by Steindl (1945). A counter argument is that size breeds inefficiency and that, accordingly, large firms cannot undertake the options open to a small firm as efficiently as the small firms and hence profitability may decline with size of firms. Benishay (1961) argued that the stock market would tend to favour large firms so that there will be a negative relationship between profitability and equity. Thus we find that some theoretical arguments suggest that profitability should increase with firm size, others suggest a negative relationship. It is in view of these contradictory suggestions, that it becomes necessary to study the relationship between size and profitability of firms in selected Indian Public Sector Manufacturing Industries during the 1981-2001.

Further, the analysis of this relationship is also important from another angle, i.e. if profitability increases on average, with the size of the firm. This will suggest that profitability is not constrained by size; in fact, in this case it is a positive inducement to further growth. If profitability does not vary systematically with size it will not be a constraint on future growth, but neither will be a positive inducement to growth.

One may also be interested in the relationship between profitability and size for other two broad reasons, (1) Its likely effect on industrial concentration and (2) Its possible implications for returns to scale and monopoly power. A positive relationship between average profitability and size would suggest that industrial concentration is likely to be increased by large firms growing at a faster average rate than the small firms. This will reinforce the tendency for concentration to increase as result of the inter-firm dispersion of growth. The implications of relationship between profitability and size for economies of scale and monopoly power are ambiguous, because the two effects are not identified separately (though profitability can be expected to be directly related to the monopoly power and increasing returns to scale.) Economies of scale will affect the cost structure of firms of different size, whereas monopoly power will affect revenue (through decisions as to price and quantity of output). Monopoly power may also enable a monopolistic firm to operate inefficiently, so that it is not forced towards its production possibility frontier and does not take full advantage of economies of scale. Therefore, clear inferences about either economies of scale or monopoly power from the above relationship cannot be made.

Empirical Studies on Relationship between Profitability and Size

Stigler,G. J. (1963) in "Capital and Rates of Return in Manufacturing Industries," pointed that very small firms produced a small proportion of the output of concerted industries than of unconcerted industries; such firms, particularly in unconcerted industries were more likely to absorb profits in the firm of large implicit salaries for owner-manager showing thereby a lower profit rate. He found a negative and significant relationship between the rate of profit and significant output of smaller firms. By adjusting the profit rates for such accounting discrepancies between larger and smaller firms, he by and large found no relationship between profitability and four firm's concentration ratio in the three digit U.S. manufacturing industries for the years 1947 to 1954.

Stekler (1964), in his research study entitled 'The Variability of Profitability with Size of Firms 1947-1958', tested several hypotheses about the relative profitability and growth possibility of firms of various sizes. Each hypothesis is designed to perform a specific task. Interest is added to profit to avoid bias that could result due to variations in the ratio of equity to debt financing. The study concludes that variation over a period of time of average profitability for small and large firms was less than that of medium size firms.

Bates (1965) in "Alternative Measures of Size Firms" emphasized that all possible measures related, to size of firm's determination have both advantages and disadvantages. It is argued that there is high degree of correlation between different measures of size. Apart from the above study Hall and Weiss (1967), in 'Firm Size and Profitability' found firm size as the major determinant of profitability. They hypothesized that large enterprises should earn higher profit rates even in the long run and even in the absence of barriers to entry other than those directly associated with availability of capital. Using data of 341 firms for the years 1956-1962, they concluded that size tends to result in high profit rates.

Baumol (1967) in 'Business Behaviour, Value and Growth' has emphasized that there is a positive relationship between firm size and profits. He states that "increased money capital will not only increase the total profits of the firm but because it puts the firm in a higher echelon of imperfectly computing capital groups, it may also increase its earnings per dollar of investment." Besides large firms have an advantage over smaller firms as they can enter in variety of product lines which gives them the benefits of both the scale and the size. Generally these firms are in a position to take full advantage of technical and pecuniary economies in manufacturing, marketing, supervision and in raising capital. Also bigger firms being more efficient in research and development (R&D) which together with their ability to spend large sums on advertising, substantially raise the cost of entry to a new corner. This creates powerful monopoly position, giving large firms a degree of independence in pricing and output decisions.

Marcus and Wilson (1967) in their study entitled 'Advertising, Market Structure and Performance' tried to re-evaluate the hypothesis that the rate of return increases with the size of the firm, against new data within an improved analytical frame work. Their conclusion was that the hypothesis did not perform uniformly in all the industries and it cannot therefore be viewed as having general validity whereas other authors (like Hall and Weiss) restricted their investigation only to the very large firms. The findings of the study suggested that the size of a firm influences profitability in some but not in all industries, in 74 out of 118 industries the null hypothesis that the size has no effect on the rate of return could not be rejected at 5 per cent level. Since profitability was ultimately determined by several complex factors – product lines, factor costs, the production function whose relationship to the size of the firm might vary among industries in a manner, which could not be readily identified.

Samuels and Smyth (1968) in 'Profits, Variability of Profits and Firm Size' took the cross-section data of annual observation (1959 to

1963) of profits and net assets for 186 United Kingdom companies. These companies engaged in manufacturing distribution and mining were classified, into ten size classes according to their assets in 1954. Net assets were used as measure of firm size and the ratio of profits (after depreciation but before taxation) to net assets was the measure of profitability. They calculated average profit rates over the ten-year period and applied analysis of variance. There was some evidence that firm's size was a significant factor in the determination of its mean profits over the ten-year period. The analysis did not indicate whether the higher profit rates were associated with large or small firms. But the mean rate of return for each size group for each year and also the average for the whole ten-year period, suggested that the higher profit rates were associated with the smaller firms. Further, it was observed that the difference in the profit rates of large, and small firms were becoming more marked over time. In order to examine the variability of profit rates, the hypothesis tested was that large companies are more able to withstand fluctuations in the level of activity and are usually the more diversified so that they can offset losses in one activity against profits in another. Time variability of profit rates was thus inversely related to firm size. There was greater variability among profit rates of firms of the same size for small firms than for larger firms. Further, the relationship between the degree of competition in an industry (as measured by concentration ratio) and time variability of profits was investigated. The hypothesis examined was that firms in the more highly concentrated industries have less variable profits than firms in less highly concentrated industries.

Singh, Ajit and Whittington (1968) in 'Growth, Profitability and Valuation,' conducted an empirical study of the relationship between the growth, size and profitability of the firm, growth being the main dependent variable for 450 U.K. public quoted companies, existing over the period 1948-60 or at least for 6 years. The balance sheet or the book value of 'net assets' was used as a measure of size of the firm and the difference between the values of net assets had represented differences in size of firm. The results exhibited that the average growth rate measured in terms of net assets was independent of the opening size of the firms. The same was also true of profitability. But the variability of the growth rates and the profit rates as between firms did change with the size to a significant extent. In both cases it tended to decrease as size increased. Large firms had a more predictable rate of growth and rate of profits, but not a higher one. The small firms studied include both the fastest growing and fastest shrinking companies, but the large firms rarely shrinked in size or made losses. The examination of persistence of growth and profitability exhibited that firms having above average growth rates in the period 1948-54 also tended to have above average growth rates in the period 1954-60.

Marcus (1969), in 'Profitability and Size of Firm: Some Further Evidence' tried to reevaluate the hypothesis that the rate of return increases with the size of the firm, against new data within an improved analytical framework. His conclusion was that the hypothesis did not perform uniformly in all the industries and that it cannot therefore be viewed as having general validity.

Shepherd's first study (1972) in 'The Elements of Market Structure,' examined the effects of market share, four firm concentration ratio, absolute size of firm, advertising, sales ratio and estimated barriers to entry on after rax return on equity of 231 large U.S. corporations for the period 1960-69. He found that the rates of return closely related to the market shares of the firms rather than concentration and entry barriers. The second study examined the relationship between price cost margin and concentration ratios, size of the firms (sales) and advertising intensity for all four digit U.S. manufacturing industries. The margins were found positively associated with concentration and advertising intensity.

Gale (1972) in 'Market Share and Rate of Return,' states the effect of market share on the rate of return of selected firms operating in different market environment using data of the 106 firms. He found that high market share is associated with high rates of return and that the effect of share on profitability depends on other firm and industry characteristics such as degree of concentration and rate of growth in the industries in which the firm competes and on the absolute size of the firm. He also found that the relation between rate of return on equity and the equity to capital ratio (a measure of risk in an inter-industry of sample of firms) to be positive and significant.

Dalton and Penn (1976), in 'The Concentration-Profitability Relationship: Is there a Critical Concentration Ratio?' tried to examine whether or not there was a level of concentration which separated groups of industries earning significantly different profit rates and if it was, then how concentration and profitability were related within the separated groups. The basic model employed firm profit rates as a function of product differentiation, industry growth, absolute firm size and market share as well as seller concentration. The sample consisted of 97 large food manufacturers. Concentration for each firm was computed by taking the 1954 four-firm concentration ratio in each of the firm's product classes and multiplying it by the firm's shipments in that product class and then summing overall of the firm's product classes and dividing by the company's total value of shipments. The measures of firm profit were the rate of return on equity, as measured by the ratio of net income after taxes to owner's equity average over the period 1949-54. The empirical results suggested that there was a threshold level of concentration. On the average profit rates in the group with concentration exceeding 45 per cent for the top four times and 60 per cent for the top eight were greater than profit rates for those with concentration less than 45 and 60 per cent respectively. The results also suggested that changes in concentration were not having a significant impact on profit rates within concentration groups. The coefficient for the market share variable was positive and significant in each of concentration group. Advertising was significant only in the high concentration group, which was indicative of the coincidence of higher entry barriers and higher concentration. The positive and significant association between size and profitability in the low concentration group was puzzling.

Whittington (1980) in 'The Profitability and Size of United Kingdom Companies: 1960-1964' extended his investigation further covering the period 1960 to 1974 and found that average profitability was largely independent of firm size. The relationship between inter company dispersion of profitability and variability of profits through time tended to decline with firm size. There were managerial reasons for large firms exhibiting less dispersion of profitability between firms or through time, in so far as they tended to be more bureaucratic, managed by employees rather than owners with great risk aversion, and perhaps less entrepreneurial motivation but a higher level of competence. He also found that the average profitability margins and Sales/Assets ratio did not vary systematically with firm size and also profitability margins of large firms tended to be relatively stable through time whereas their Sales/Assets ratio did not. Thus the relative stability through time of rates of return of large firms was due to relative stability of their profits, rather than the stability of their capacity utilization. Profitability was not an incentive for large firms to grow at a relatively higher rate.

Nagarajan and Burthwal (1990) in their research work entitled 'Profitability and Structure: A Firm Level Study of Indian Pharmaceutical Industry,' intensively examined the relationship between profitability and structure, using a sample of thirty eight pharmaceutical firms in India for the period 1970-1982. Two measures of profitability i.e. ratio of net profit to total sales revenue and the ratio of net profits to total assets, have been used to find out the determinants of profitability. The analysis demonstrated that under the condition of price controls the most significant determinant of the profitability of firms in this industry is vertical integration. Size and advertising intensity did not appear to be major determinants. This was perhaps due to the inability of firms to translate their market power into prices, because of controls. The Co-efficient of growth rate of sales was positive and significant, suggesting that factors on the demand side of a firm had a greater impact on profitability than on the supply side.

Vijayakumar (2002) in his study entitled 'Determinants of Corporate Size, Growth and Profitability. The Indian Experience' focussed on the relationship between size and profitability, growth and size of firms etc. For this study Indian public sector industries were selected. The study covers the period from 1980-81 to 1995-96. The techniques of average, correlation, linear and multiple regression analysis have been used in the study. The findings conclude that growth is found to be significantly associated with profitability. Moreover, profitability explains considerable part of the growth of the firms in the Indian Public Sector Industry.

Statement of the Problem

In general, profitability is expected to increase with size because of certain economies of scale associated with large firms. Many earlier empirical studies have confirmed this relation Robinson (1958), Baumol (1967), Hall and Weiss (1967) Comanor and Wilson (1967), and Whittington (1971). It also came to be recognized that with the growth of corporate enterprise the objective of the firm had changed. Each firm now has several objectives and decides its own policies. Thus, an attempt has been made to study the relationship between size, profitability as well as growth.

METHODOLOGY

Selection of Sample

As on March 31st, 2001 there were 236 public sector undertakings (PSU), divided into manufacturing and service sector under central government control. While the manufacturing sector contains 13 categories of industries with 165 units, service sector contains 8 categories of industries with 71 units. Among the 13 manufacturing industries, only 9 industries viz. steel, minerals and metals, coal and lignite, power, petroleum, chemicals and pharmaceuticals, heavy engineering, medium and light engineering and transportation equipment have continuous data for twenty year period of time. Within this list only six industries viz. steel, minerals and metals, coal and lignite, power, petroleum and chemical and pharmaceuticals have been selected based on simple random technique. The total investment made by the central government in all the selected industries under study accounted for 53.57 per cent. Hence an attempt has been made over these industries, which may be helpful, in making a general assessment about the overall industries.

Sources of Data

The necessary data related to profitability and other variables used in this study have been collected mostly from the consolidated annual reports of the selected enterprises, published by Bureau of Public Enterprises (BPE), Ministry of Finance, Government of India, New Delhi. For analyzing, certain information was collected through various reports prepared by the various committees. Apart from these, various other Journals, reports by individual enterprises, Business magazines and Newspapers were referred to.

Model Specification

The relationship between corporate size and profitability of selected industry are presented with the help of regression analysis obtained through different equation models which are explained as under.

With a view to estimating the relationship between the size and profitability, this study uses Semi-logarithmic specification. For this purpose, four different models using varying concepts of size and profitability are considered. This helps in analysing changes in the results due to different measures of profitability and size. Two different measures of size are used viz. Sales and Total Assets. Profit is defined in terms of Gross Profit. The concept of Gross Profit is employed for calculating profitability as ratio to sales and ratio to Total Assets.

Profitability ratio is calculated in two different ways by using sales as well as profit margins as indicated below.

(a) Profit on Total Assets (PR)

This concept uses Gross Profit as a percentage of Total Assets. Total Assets are defined as share capital plus reserve plus borrowings.

(b) Profit Margin (PM)

This concept follows Gross Profit as a percentage of Sales turnovers.

Between the two concepts, the Profit Margin (PM) is a flow concept while the Profit Ratio (PR), is a stock concept.

Using the above concepts, to investigate the relationship between size and profitability the following models are used.

PR = b0 + b1 log size 1 + U1 ....(i)

PR = b0 + b1 log size 2 + U2 ....(ii)

PM = b0 + b1 log size 1 + U3 ....(iii)

PM = b0 + b1 log size 2 + U4 ....(iv)

Where

PR = ratio of gross profit to Total Assets

PM = ratio of gross profit to sales turnover

Size1 = size measured by Total Assets

Size 2 = size measured by sales turnover

U = random disturbance term

b0, b1 = parameters

After taking into account the above said concepts in mind an analysis has been made. The results of the regression analysis are discussed in the following paragraph.

Steel Industry

The pooled regression results of the model, regressing Profit Rate (PR) with Total Assets (size) and sales for the Steel Industry are presented in Table 3.0. The overall results presented in the table are encouraging. The co-efficient is also statistically significant and the goodness of fit of the model is also satisfactory.

The results of regression equation given show that degree of explanation of profitability by size is 36 per cent and 45 per cent respectively. The result also shows the positive relationship between the size and profitability. It is evident from the results that one unit increase in assets has resulted in 2.94 unit increase in profitability and this is significant at 1 per cent level of significance. Similarly one unit increased in sales will lead to 3.55 unit increase in profitability, which is significant at 1 per cent level of significant. The pooled regression results of the model regressing Profit Margin (PM) with Total Assets and Sales for the Steel Industry are presented in the table are encouraging. The co-efficient is also statistically significant and goodness of fit of this model is also satisfactory. These results show more and less similar findings to the result of regressing Profit Rate (PR) with total assets and sales. However, the explanation capacity of Size and Sales on profit margin improved in this model. It explains 51 per cent and 57 per cent variations in profit margin respectively. It is evident from the results

Table 3.0
Size and Profitability - Regression results (a) PR = $b_0 + b_1$ log size (b) PR = $b_0 + b_1$ log sales

	Constant	Co-efficient	R^2	Adj.R^2	F-Value	DW
Steel Industry						
(a)	-10.243	2.94	0.36	0.32	9.91	1.50
		(3.15)**				
(b)	-11.472	3.55	0.45	0.42	14.84	1.50
		(3.85)**				
Minerals and Metals						
	Constant	Co-efficient	R^2	Adj.R^2	F-Value	DW
(a)	-52.09	14.64	0.64	0.62	32.4	1.54
		(5.69)**				
(b)	-30.444	10.58	0.84	0.83	92.62	1.66
		(9.62)**				
Coal and Lignite						
	Constant	Co-efficient	R^2	Adj.R^2	F-Value	DW
(a)	-26.241	7.23	0.50	0.47	18.05	1.01
		(4.25)**				
(b)	-25.520	7.76	0.59	0.57	25.75	1.09
		(5.07)**				
Power						
	Constant	Co-efficient	R^2	Adj.R^2	F-Value	DW
(a)	-13.613	4.51	0.58	0.56	23.62	0.40
		(4.86)**				
(b)	-4.974	3.16	0.63	0.61	28.69	0.40
		(5.36)**				
Petroleum Industry						
	Constant	Co-efficient	R^2	Adj.R^2	F-Value	DW
(a)	43.635	- 6.60	0.42	0.39	13.11	0.31
		(-3.62)**				
(b)	36.883	-5.09	0.18	0.14	4.01	0.26
		(2.00)*				
Chemicals and Pharmaceuticals						
	Constant	Co-efficient	R^2	Adj.R^2	F-Value	DW
(a)	-20.449	6.71	0.19	0.14	4.21	0.97
		(2.05)**				
(b)	-25.985	9.07	0.33	0.29	8.87	0.99
		(2.98)**				

Figures within parentheses indicate '*t*'-values

** Significant at 1% level

Source : Computed

that one unit increase in assets has resulted in 8.62 increases in profitability and this is significant at 1 per cent level. Similarly one unit increase in sale will lead to 9.71 unit increase in profitability, which is also significant at 1 per cent level.

Minerals and Metals Industry

The pooled regression results of the model, regressing Profit Rate (PR) with Total Assets (Size) and sales for the minerals and metals industry are presented in Table 3.0. The results of regression equation given show that degree of explanation of profitability by size is 64 per cent and 84 per cent respectively. The results also show the positive relationship between the size and profitability. It is evident from the result that one unit increase in assets has resulted in 14.64 unit increase in profitability and this is significant at 1 per cent level of significance. Similarly, one unit increase in sale will lead to 10.58 units increase in profitability which is significant at 1 per cent level of significance. The pooled regression results of the model regressing Profit margin (PM) with Total Assets and Sales for the minerals and metals Industry are presented in Table 3.1. The overall results presented in the table are encouraging. The co-efficient is also statistically significant and goodness of fit of this model is also satisfactory. These results show almost similar findings to the result of regressing Profit Rate (PR) with total assets and sales. However, the explanatory capacity of the size on profit margin has improved whereas sales on profit margin remain the same. It explains 67 per cent and 84 per cent variations in profit margin respectively. It is evident from the results that one unit increase has resulted in 36.41 increases in profitability and this is significant at 1 per cent level. Similarly 1 unit increase in sales will lead to 25.83 unit increase in profitability, which is also significant at 1 per cent level.

Coal and Lignite Industry

The pooled regression results of the model, regressing Profit Rate (PR) with Total Assets (size) and sales for the coal and lignite industry are presented in the Table 3.0. The overall results presented in the table are encouraging. The co-efficient is also statistically significant and the goodness of fit of the model is also satisfactory.

Table 3.1

Size and Profitability - Regression results (a) PR = $b_0 + b_1$ log size (b) PR = $b_0 + b_1$ log sales

	Constant	Co-efficient	R^2	Adj.R^2	F-Value	DW
Steel Industry						
(a)	-31.188	8.62	0.51	0.48	18.76	1.40
		(4.33)**				
(b)	-32.099	9.71	0.57	0.54	23.59	1.39
		(4.86)**				
Minerals and Metals Industry						
	Constant	Co-efficient	R^2	Adj.R^2	F-Value	DW
(a)	-128.585	36.41	0.67	0.65	37.06	1.14
		(6.09)**				
(b)	-73.099	25.83	0.84	0.84	97.91	1.12
		(9.90)**				
Coal and Lignite Industry						
	Constant	Co-efficient	R^2	Adj.R^2	F-Value	DW
(a)	-58.484	16.12	0.44	0.41	14.1	1.29
		(3.76)**				
(b)	-54.710	16.74	0.48	0.45	16.84	1.38
		(4.10)**				
Power Industry						
	Constant	Co-efficient	R^2	Adj.R^2	F-Value	DW
(a)	83.131	-9.90	0.31	0.27	7.77	1.03
		(2.79)**				
(b)	62.449	-6.42	0.29	0.25	6.98	1.02
		(-2.64)**				
Petroleum Industry						
	Constant	Co-efficient	R^2	Adj.R^2	F-Value	DW
(a)	13.555	-0.47	0.02	– 0.03	0.40	1.05
		(0.63)				
(b)	36.883	-0.54	0.02	- 0.03	0.39	1.04
		(0.63)				
Chemicals and Pharmaceuticals						
	Constant	Co-efficient	R^2	Adj.R^2	F-Value	DW
(a)	-51.324	16.58	0.28	0.24	6.89	0.88
		(2.63)*				
(b)	-56.600	19.95	0.38	0.35	11.15	0.68
		(3.34)**				

Figures within parentheses indicate '*t*'-values

* Significant at 5% level, ** Significant at 1% level

The results of regression equation given show that degree of explanation of profitability by size is 50 per cent and 59 per cent respectively. The result also shows the positive relationship between the size and profitability. It is evident from the results that one unit increase in assets has resulted in 7.23 unit increase in profitability and this is significant at 1 per cent level of significance. Similarly one unit increase in sales will lead to 7.76 units increase in profitability, which is significant at 1 per cent level of significance. The pooled regression results of the model regression Profit Margin (PM) with Total Assets and Sales for the Coal and Lignite Industry are presented in Table 3.1. The overall results presented in the table are encouraging. The co-efficient is also statistically significant and goodness of fit of this model is also satisfactory. This results show more and less similar findings to the result of regressing Profit Rate (PR) with total assets and sales. However the explanation capacity of sales on profit margin have reduced in this model. It explains only 44 per cent and 48 per cent variations in profit margin respectively. It is evident from the results that one unit increase in assets have resulted in 16.12 increases in profitability and this significant at 1 per cent level. Similarly 1 unit increase in sales will lead to 3.76 unit increase in profitability, which is also significant at 1 per cent level.

Power Industry

The pooled regression results of the model, regressing Profit Rate (PR) with Total Assets (size) and sales for the power industry are presented in Table 3.0 The overall results presented in the table are encouraging. The co-efficient also statistically significant and the goodness of fit of the model is also satisfactory.

The results of regression equation given shows that degree of explanation of profitability by size is 58 per cent and 63 per cent respectively. The result also shows the positive relationship between the size and profitability. It is evident from the results that one unit increase in assets has resulted in 4.51 unit increase in profitability and this is significant at 1 per cent level of significance. Similarly one unit increase in sales will lead to 3.16 units increase in profitability, which is significant at 1 per cent level of significant. The pooled regression results of the model regression Profit Margin (PM) with Total Assets and sales for the power industry are presented in Table 3.1. The overall results presented in the Table are encouraging. The co-efficient is statistically significant and however, goodness of fit of this model is not satisfactory. This result shows different findings to the results of regressing Profit Rate (PR) with total assets and sales. It explains 31 per cent and 29 per cent variations in profit margin respectively. It is evident from the results that one unit increase in assets has resulted in –9.90 decreases in profitability which has 1 per cent level of significance. Similarly 1 unit increase in sales will lead to (-) 6.42 decrease in profitability, which is also significant at 1 per cent level.

Petroleum Industry

The pooled regression results of the model, regressing Profit Rate (PR) with Total Assets (size) and sales for the petroleum industry are presented in the Table 3.0. The overall results presented in the table are not encouraging. The results of regression equation given shows that degree of explanation of profitability by size is 42 per cent and 18 per cent respectively. The result partly supports the positive relationship between the size and profitability. It is evident from the result that one unit increase in assets has resulted in –6.60 unit decrease in profitability, this is significant at 1 per cent level. Similarly 1 unit increase in sales will lead to –3.62 decreases in profitability which is found to be insignificant.

The pooled regression results of the model regression Profit Margin (PM) with Total Assets and Sales for the Petroleum Industry are given in Table 3.1. The overall results which appear in the table are not satisfactory. The co-efficient is also statistically insignificant. This result shows reverse findings to the results of regressing Profit Rate (PR) with total assets and sales. The explanatory capacity of size and sales on profit margin has almost failed in this model. It explains only 2 per cent variations in profit margins while regressing profit margin with total assets and sales. It is evident from the results that one unit increase in assets has resulted in –0.47 decrease in profitability, which is found to be insignificant. Similarly 1 unit increase in sales will lead to –0.54 decrease in profitability which is also insignificant.

Chemicals and Pharmaceuticals Industry

The pooled regression results of the model, regressing Profit Rate (PR) with Total Assets (size) and sales for the chemicals and pharmaceuticals Industry are presented in the Table 3.0. The overall results presented in the table are encouraging. The co-efficient is also statistically significant.

The results of regression equation given shows that degree of explanation of profitability by size is 19 per cent and 33 per cent respectively. The results also show the positive relationship between the size and profitability. It is evident from the results that one unit increase in assets has resulted in 6.71 unit increase in profitability and this is significant at 1 per cent level of significance. Similarly, one unit increase in sales will lead to 9.07 units increase in profitability which is significant at 1 per cent level of significance. The pooled regression results of the model regression Profit Margin (PM) with Total Assets and Sales for the chemicals and pharmaceuticals Industry are presented in Table 3.1. The overall results presented in the table are encouraging. The co-efficient is also statistically significant. These results show more or less similar findings to the result of regressing Profit Rate (PR) with total assets and sales. However, the explanation capacity of size and sales on profit margin value has improved in this model. It explains 28 per cent and 38 per cent variations in Profit Margin respectively. It is evident from the results that one unit increase in assets has resulted in 16.58 increases in profitability and this significant at 1 per cent level. Similarly 1 unit increase in sales will lead to 19.95 increases in profitability, which is also significant at 1 per cent level.

Conclusion

The above analysis clearly shows that the average profitability is largely independent of firm size. However, the explanatory capacity of size on profitability has varied between industries. The result of the regression also shows both positive and negative relationship between profitability and size of the selected industries during the study period. The positive relationship between profitability and size is observed in steel industry, mineral and metals, coal and lignite, power industry and chemicals and pharmaceuticals industry. This supports the findings of Baumol (1967), Hall and Weiss (1967), Samuel and Smith (1968), Gale (1972) and Shepherd (1972). However, the negative relationship between profitability and size is observed in petroleum Industry. It supports the findings of Bain (1951), Dyckman and Steklar (1964), Marcus (1969), Singh, Ajit and Whittington (1971) and Dalton and Penn (1976). Thus the study indicates that selected industries have made efforts to increase profitability through various means including increasing size .through diversification and moving into higher technology. While some of the industries have succeeded in their efforts, others have to intensify their efforts.

References

Baumol, W.J. (1967). Business, Behaviour, Value and Growth, (Revised Ed). New York: Harcourt Brace and World.

Steindl, J. (1944). Small and Big Business: Economic Problems of the size of firms, Oxford University Press, pp. 33-35.

Benishay, Haskel (1961). "Variability in earnings – price ratios of corporate equities". American Economic Review. Vol.51, pp.81-94.

Stigler, G.J. (1963). *'Capital and Rates of Return in Manufacturing Industries,"* Princeton: Princeton University Press.

Stekler, H.O. (Dec. 1964). 'The variability of Profitability with Size of Firms 1947-1958", *Journal of American Statistical Association.* Vol. 59, pp. 1183-1193.

Bates, J. (1965). "Alternative Measures of Size Firms" in P.E. Hart, *"Studies in Business Savings and Investment in the United Kingdom 1920-1962".* vol-1, Part-II, London, Allen Unwin.

Hall, M. and Weiss, L. (Aug, 1967). "Firm Size and Profitability", *Review of Economics and Statistics*, vol.49, pp.319-331.

Baumol, W.J. (1967). Op.cite.,

Marcus Comanur, W.S. and Wilson, T.S.(1967)."Advertising, Market Structure and Performance" *Review of Economics and Statistics.* Vol.49 pp.423-440.

Samuels, J.M. and Smyth, D.J.(1968). "Profits, Variability of Profits and Firm Size". *Economica*, vol.35. 1968, pp.127-139.

Singh, Ajit and Whittington, G. (1968). *"Growth, Profitability and Valuation*, D.A.E. occasion paper 7, Cambridge, Cambridge University Press.

Marcus, M. (1969). "Profitability and Size of firm: Some further Evidence" *Review of Economics and Statistics.* vol. 51, pp.104-107.

Shepherd, W.G. (Feb, 1972) "The Elements of Market Structure", Review of Economics and Statistics, p.54.

Gale, B.T. (Nov, 1972). "Market Share and Rate of Return" *Review of Economics and Statistics* vol.54. pp.412-423.

Dalton, James. A., and David, W.Penn. (Dec,1976). "The Concentration-Profitability Relationship: Is there a Critical Concentration Ratio?". *The Journal of Industrial Economics*, vol.25. No.2. pp.133-140.

Whittington, G. (1980). "The Profitability and Size of United Kindom Companies 1960-1964". *The Journal of Industrial Economics*, vol.28. pp.335-342.

Nagarajan, M. and Burthwal, R. R. (Oct-Dec,1990). "Profitability and Structure: A Firm Level Study of Indian Pharmaceutical Industry". *The Indian Economic Journal.* No.2. vol.38, pp.-84.

Vijayakumar, A. (2002). "Determinants of corporate Size, Growth and Profitability-The Indian Experience". In the book "Research Studies in Commerce and Management". Classical Publishing Company. New Delhi. pp.75-80.

Vishnu Kanta Purohit, Profitability in Indian industries, Gayatri Publications House. New Delhi.

Kuldip Kaur, Size, Growth and Profitability of Firms, Gyan Publishing House, New Delhi.

Sahu R.K., Analysis of Corporate profitability. Anmol Publications Pvt. Ltd. New Delhi.

Stekler, H. (Dec, 1964). "The Variability of Profitability with Size of Firms 1947-1958" *Journal of American Statistical Association*. vol. 59, pp. 1183-1193.

4

DETERMINANTS OF CORPORATE SIZE, GROWTH AND PROFITABILITY—THE INDIAN EXPERIENCE

It is recognized that the size of the firm has assumed importance with regard to economies of scale. Given that the larger the size of the firm, the greater the efficiency in terms of cost and, therefore, profits. There exists potentially a powerful incentive for continuous expansion of the firm and consequently, increased concentration, and monopoly. In the context of a planned and regulated economy like India where there is government controls on capital size, expansion, output etc., some questions come up. What is the relationship between size and profitability? Is it true that a firm can expand continuously or are there any limits? What are the implications of the above for the growth of different sizes of firms? These are some of the concerns of this paper with the experience of Indian public sector industry.

Statement of the problem

According to traditional theory, the increase in size of firm is defined in terms of an increase in output. The objective of the firm was profit maximization and the firm, which expanded its output, earned the highest profit and was, therefore, considered the optimum firm. By implication, it is meant that firms either bigger or smaller than the optimum were ruled out as improbabilities. But, a firm can't grow continuously or make abnormal profits. The small firms can never (in the long run) earn higher profit rates than big firms because all the technical advantages are not open to them, whereas big firms may earn higher rates of profit than small firms because some advantages open to them are not open to small firms. Thus, a hierarchy of profit rates will be established with a smooth increase of profit rates as size of enterprise increases.

It also came to be recognized that with the growth of corporate enterprise the objectives of the firm had changed. Each firm now had several objectives and each decided its own policies. Firms functioned in imperfect markets, diversified and showed no signs of ceasing to grow. The concept of growth itself underwent a change from a mere concern with the increase in output. The concern had shifted from the optimum size of the firm to the optimum rate of growth. Thus, an attempt has been made in this paper to study the relationship between the size, profitability and growth.

Concepts and measurements

In this study net assets (in current prices) is used as a size variable. Return on net worth (RNW) is used as measures of profitability. For calculating the return on net worth, the numerator is defined as gross profits (after deducting depreciation and interest charges from trading profits) less taxation. Net worth is equal to share capital plus reserves. For measuring the growth, growth of assets has been used. Growth has been calculated by taking the simple arithmetic average of annual changes for the specified time period.

Data and methodology

To meet the objectives of the study, Indian public sector industries were selected. The data relating to size, growth and profitability were collected from their annual reports published by the Bureau of Public Enterprises (BPE), Government of India. The study covers the period from 1980 – 81 to 1995 – 96. The techniques average, correlation and linear and multiple regression analysis has been used in this study.

The following regression models have been estimated:

$$g = a + bP + e \ldots\ldots\ldots\ldots (1)$$

where g denotes growth rate of the firm and P refers to profitability. Equation (1) indicates that the growth rate of the firm is a linear function of profitability. Further, in analyzing the determinants of growth, since profitability does not explain the entire variation in growth rate, this study also examines whether the rate of growth of a firm is related to certain other financial factors like retention, long – term borrowings etc., Thus determinants of growth are looked at in an integrated way by multiple regression analysis. For this purpose the following multiple regression model have been estimated. The main indicators used for this purpose are size, profitability, retention, and long-term borrowings/ net assets, which would cover internal and external sources of finances.

$$g = a + b_1\,SIZE + b_2\,RNW + b_3\,RET + b_4\,LTF + e \ldots\ldots\ldots\ldots (2)$$

where g - Growth rate of total net assets, SIZE – Average size measured by total net assets, RNW – Return on net worth, RET – Retention ratio defined as per cent of net profits and LTF – Long term finance defined as the debentures + long term loans as per cent of total net assets.

The relations described in the equation (1) and (2) are estimated for all public sector enterprises and six major industrial groups – Steel, Power, Petroleum, Fertilizer, Chemicals and Textiles. The results are presented in Tables 4.0 to 4.2.

Results and discussion

The results presented in Table 4.0 indicates that growth is negatively associated with the profitability of Indian public sector industry during the study period. Further, the association between these two are insignificant. The better explanation of corporate growth is obtained when applied to industry groups as compared to the results for all firms. This suggests significant inter – industry difference in the growth process of the firms under study. This is probably due to the fact the economies of scale, monopoly power and government controls vary significantly in different industries. Further, the relative profitability varies from industry to industry because of different demand conditions in various industries. It is evident from the Table 4.0 that growth is positively associated with the profitability in case of steel, power, and chemicals whereas negatively associated in the case of petroleum, fertilizer and textiles. Further, the association between growth and profitability are significant in case of power, petroleum, chemicals and textiles.

Table 4.0

Correlation between profit rates and growth in the Indian Public Sector Industry (1980 – 96)

Industry	Correlation Coefficient
Steel	0.117
Power	0.518*
Petroleum	-0.881*
Fertilizer	-0.159
Chemicals	0.563*
Textiles	-0.742*
All Industry	-0.367

* - Significant at 5 per cent level **Source :** Computed

The results presented in Table 4.1 shows a linear relationship between profitability and growth for all selected industry groups and public sector industry (total) in India. It is evident from the table that in the case of Fertilizer and Textiles, the coefficient of profitability are negative and insignificant. The coefficient of profitability implies that if the growth rate of assets increase by 1 per cent, the rate of profitability will rise by 1.46 per cent in petroleum, 1.39 per cent in power, 1.15 per cent in chemicals and 1.07 per cent in steel, which has been found to significant at 5 per cent level in the petroleum, power and chemical group. It is also seen from the Table that in the case of all public sector industry, the value of profitability coefficient (-0.487) is negative and statistically insignificant. This is probably due to the existence of a considerable number of firms with a high growth rate of assets and low profitability. The degree of explanation is the highest in case of petroleum (R^2 = 0.76), followed by power, chemicals, steel, textiles and fertilizer.

Table 4.1

Results of regression of growth on profit rate in the Indian Public Sector Industry (1980 – 96)

(g = a + bP + e)

Industry	Constant	Correlation of Profitability	R^2	F Value
Steel	2.57	1.07	0.25	6.58
		(0.81)		
Power	-0.86	1.39	0.68	28.56
		(2.40)*		
Petroleum	1.28	1.46	0.76	91.26
		(3.08)*		
Fertilizer	2.05	-1.06	0.18	4.23
		(0.71)		
Chemicals	1.06	1.15	0.56	20.85
		(2.15)*		
Textiles	2.16	-0.48	0.27	8.52
All Industry	1.09	-0.48	0.31	9.26
		(1.37)		

*- Significant at 5 per cent level

Figures in parentheses denote "t" Value.

It is important, however, to see if growth is associated with other financial variables like size, retention, long-term borrowings etc., i.e., both internal and external. The results of multiple regression analysis of growth on all these variables i.e., size, return on networth, retention and long term borrowings/ net assets are presented in Table 4.2. The results shows that a significant R square, a significant and positive association between growth and size and growth and long-term borrowings/ net assets, a significant but negative association of growth and profitability and growth and retention in the Indian public sector industry during the study period.

Table 4.2

Results of Multiple Regression Analysis of growth on Size, RNW, Retention and Ltb/ Net Assets in the Indian Public Sector Industry

$(g = a + b_1 \text{ SIZE} + b_2 \text{ RNW} + b_3 \text{ RET} + b_4 \text{ LTF} + e)s$

Industry	Constants	Regression Coefficients				R^2	F Value
		SIZE	RNW	RET	LTF		
Steel	-1.05	0.42	0.008	0.392	1.15	0.65	26.57
		(3.12)*	(2.24)*	(0.96)	(1.26)		
Power	3.21	1.45	0.208	-0.321	-4.40	0.86	32.68
		(7.19)*	(2.56)*	(0.98)	(2.16)*		
Petroleum	-2.71	1.86	0.731	0.781	-2.81	0.72	30.45
		(3.63)*	(2.25)*	(0.89)	(0.72)		
Fertilizer	-0.95	1.36	-1.572	1.213	-1.71	0.56	22.56
		(7.65)*	(0.96)	(0.87)	(1.65)		
Chemicals	-0.98	1.86	0.112	-0.109	0.721	0.62	28.70
		(7.12)*	(1.91)*	(2.86)*	(1.55)		
Textiles	-0.76	1.26	-0.007	-0.165	0.651	0.45	9.86
All Industry	-1.08	0.786	-0.581	-1.123	0.485	0.65	25.56
		(2.45)*	(1.95)*	(1.19)*	(2.12)*		

* - Significant at 5 per cent level

Figures in parentheses denote "t" Value.

Source : Computed

Inter – industry analysis reveals that the growth is positively and significantly associated with the size in all the industry groups except textiles. Further, the growth is positively associated with the retention in case of steel, petroleum and fertilizer and negatively associated in case of remaining industry. Similarly, the growth is positively associated with long-term borrowings/ net assets in the case of steel, chemicals and textiles and negatively associated in case of remaining industry. From this analysis, it is concluded that in the Indian public sector industry growth does seem to be associated with profitability and other financial variables but is negatively associated with profitability variables like RNW and retention.

Conclusion

It can be concluded from the above analysis that growth is found to be significantly associated with profitability during the study period. The findings at the aggregate level, i.e., for all the firms, bring out the importance of various factors in the growth of the firms in the Indian corporate sector. The outstanding influence of size, return on network, retention and long – term borrowings/ net assets is highlighted. There are some inter – industry variations in the relative importance of factors affecting corporate growth. This is probably because different industries face varying degrees of demand conditions, competition and government controls.

It may also be noted that profitability explains considerable part of the growth of the firms in the Indian public sector industry. The sinews of growth seem to have come from other sources. It seems that the commitment to growth and the ability to perceive growth opportunities and exploit them fully exert an important influence on the growth performance of the firm's display an overriding commitment to growth and have a high degree of accumen to their ability to perceive a business opportunity and exploit it.

References

1. J. Steindl (1994), Small and Big Business, Economic problems of the size of firms – Basil, Blackwell, Oxford.
2. Donald A. Hay and Derek J. Morris, Industrial Economics, Oxford University Press, 1989.
3. R.N. Agarwal, Profitability and Growth in Indian Automobile Manufacturing Industry, Indian Economic Review, vol. XXVI, No. 1, 1991, pp. 81 – 97.
4. Prem Kumar, "Determinants of Corporate Growth – The Indian Experience". Margin, April – June 1987, pp.55 – 67.
5. E.T. Penrose (1996), The Theory of the Growth of the Firm, Basil, Blackwell, Oxford.

5

PROFITABILITY DETERMINANTS IN INDIAN AUTOMOBILE INDUSTRY— AN ECONOMETRIC ANALYSIS

The question of determination of profit is of great importance. The profit of a business may be measured by studying the profitability of investment in it. Profitability is a relative term and its measurement can be achieved by profit and its relation with the other objects by which the profit is affected. It is the test of efficiency, powerful motivational factor and the measure of control in any business. Actually profitability is highly sensitive economic variable which is affected by a host of factors operating through a variety of ways. Some of them affect product prices and quantities, some affect the cost of production while others make changes in capital stock, size, market share and growth of the firm. Further, corporate policy relating to various functions will affect profitability. Some of them are relevant in short run while others have impact in the long run. It is doubtful to build a theory of profitability, which accounts for all such factors. Because of these difficulties, it is quite natural to analyse the variation in profitability by taking the partial approach i.e., to find the effect of certain major variables, ignoring the implications of other left out independent variables at a time. The present study is a step towards this direction.

There are a number of cross sectional studies which provide direct evidence about the determinants of profitability. These studies include Shepherd (1972), Agarwal V.K. (1978), Newmann, Bobel and Haid (1979), Asha Jain (1981), Bothwell (1982), Das (1998) and Vijayakumar (2002).

The review of above empirical works facilitates to understand various structural and non-structural variables that determine profitability. It gives an idea of extensive and diverse works on determinants of profitability.

The objective of this study is to examine determinants of profitability of Indian automobile industry during the period 1991-92 to 2003-04. Determinants of profitability are analysed using the technique of ordinary least squares. Based on existing theories and relevant econometric empirical works, variables are selected. The variables occurring in the models and their measurement are described in methodology. While using the regression technique, efforts are made to reduce the problem of multi-collinearity and auto correlation.

METHODOLOGY

Selection of variables

In this study at hand, a number of key financial variables have been identified for the purpose of analysis. The computation of these variables has been made for a period of 13 years. An epigrammatic explanation of the selected variable is outlined below.

Profitability

Return on assets and return on sales are widely used measures of profitability. It is assumed that management may be concerned with effective utilisation of all resources and these two measures could be proper in this line of arguments. The review includes Samuels and Smyth (1968), Neumann, Bobel and Haid (1979), Deepak Chawala (1986), Narayanan and Barthwal (1990), Amit Mallick and Debasish Sur (1998), and Vijayakumar (2002) which provide direct evidence of using return on assets and return on sales as a measure of profitability. The profit rates measured by sales will give a short-term perspective of profitability because sales are annual flows. On the other hand, the return on assets will give us long-term perspective of profitability. In this study, ratio of profit margin on sales is used as dependent variable.

Size

One of the very important structural characteristics of the industry which is commonly used to explain profitability in applied research is the size of the firm. Many researchers have employed firm size as a variable in their study of determinants of profitability. The big firms have been considered to be endowed with certain advantages such as lower costs and higher returns on accounts of access to capital market (Hall and Weiss, 1967) and economies of scale (Sidhu and Bhatia, 1993). Hence, generally a positive hypothesis is set for size-profitability relationship. The size - profitability relationship is more likely to be curve-linear and after reaching a certain stage, the advantage of scale economies may cease and beyond that the relationship may even reverse due to the problems of large scale. Due to the expected curve-linear size performance relationship, size variable is generally employed in long term. Though the positive relationship between size and profitability has been found to be significant, after a point of time, profitability increases at a rate with proposal increase in size. This could arise when (i) other firms in the market follow similar strategies (ii) diseconomies and inefficiency due to in manageable size, and (iii) increased possibility of public criticism of excessive profits as firm becomes larger. Therefore, impact of firm size on profitability cannot be determined a priori.

Generally two sizes measures are employed, they are assets and sales turnover. Assets express amount of resources utilised for producing output whereas sales is an output variable. Sales are an annual flow depending upon output produced and sold in the market. Further sales needs to be adjusted for excise payment to more meaningful comparison. Therefore, in this study the log of total assets as the measure of size has been employed .

Leverage

A firm with high leverage ratio represents greater financial risk than a firm with relatively less risk. If competition equalises earnings, then high debt should result in higher return on net worth. It is argued that firms have low debt because they operate in industries with high degree of business risk and thus expect a negative relations between leverage and profitability, it owners are risk averse. It seems that the relationship between leverage and rate of return is indeterminate a priori. In an intra industry study, business risk is assumed to be same and leverage must be a better measure of risk. The debt equity ratio as the measure of leverage has been employed in this study.

Current ratio

The management of working capital involves decisions about the amount and composition of current assets and how they are financed. Such decisions involve a trade off between solvency and profitability. In inter-firm comparison, the firm with higher current ratio has better liquidity. A high ratio of current assets to current liabilities may be indicative of slack management practices, as it might signal poor credit management in terms of over-extended accounts receivables. A low ratio is also not desirous since there will be an inadequate margin of safety.

Inventory turnover ratio

Another variable, which can influence the profitability is the inventory turnover ratio. It is the ratio of sales to inventory which indicates the number of times inventory is replaced during the year. Instead of taking year-end stock of inventory, an average of the opening and closing stock of inventory is considered. A high ratio implies good inventory management. But low inventory will adversely affect the ability of a firm to meet customer demand and in turn will affect profitability. On the other hand, a very low inventory turnover ratio signifies excessive inventory or over investment in inventory and high carrying cost. The sign of inventory coefficient is ambiguous.

Fixed assets turnover ratio

Another variable influencing the profitability of the industry is fixed assets turnover ratio which is defined as the ratio of sales to fixed assets. It indicates the relationship between the amount invested in fixed assets and the results in accruing in terms of the sales. It is expected that an increase in this ratio would result in increase in profitability. The capital employed of a firm includes both current and fixed assets. The fixed assets provide the productive base and earning capacity for the firm. But an efficient utilisation of the earning capacity calls for an optimum use of working capital.

Operating expenses to sales ratio

Apart from the above-discussed factors operating expenses ratio is included as an explanatory variable in this study. A low operating ratio is by and large a test of operational efficiency. The implication of low operating expenses ratio is that relatively a high percentage share of sales is available for meeting financial liabilities like interest, taxes and dividends. Therefore, a negative relationship is expected with operating expenses and profitability.

Vertical integration

Firm-specific vertical integration motivated by considerations such as the avoidance of costs incurred in using the market of organized production, government policies and also consideration of market power is an important determinant of profitability. The costs of using the market alternatively known as transaction costs include search cost, cost of drawing up contracts, monitoring costs, etc., In our context government policies assume an important role in determining vertical integration. The degree of vertical integration is sought to be measured by the value added to sales ratio in the analysis. Value added is defined as total sales revenue less costs of purchased inputs, repair charges and customs and excise duty.

Past profitability

In operational terms it would mean the current level of business success measured in terms of profitability should, to a large extent, depend on the success achieved in the preceding years. The implicit assumption underlying the postulate is that under normal situation a firm in a given year tries to achieve at least the profitability level of the preceding year. Past profitability of a particular year of a firm has been taken on the profitability in the respective previous year of that firm.

Growth rate of assets

The other variable, which is considered, is growth of firm. Growth is essential to a firm even if it is not among the firm's major objectives. The reason is that growth helps in providing the firm finances for attaining its objective by increasing the size of its profit growth, by providing room for initiatives and exercise managerial ability, stimulates managerial efficiency leading to a lower capital output ratio and consequently higher profit rate. It is thus, likely to have positive association with profitability. Growth rate is measured in this study by the ratio of simple growth rate of assets.

Specification of profitability model

In order to explain the profitability of selected sectors of Indian automobile industry, the model specified for estimating profitability function is as follows:

$$P = b_0 + b_1 S + b_2 L + b_3 CR + b_4 ITR + b_5 FATR + b_6 OESR + b_7 VI + b_8 PP + b_9 GRA$$

Where,

S	-	**Size**
L	-	**Leverage**
CR	-	**Current Ratio**
ITR	-	**Inventory Turnover Ratio**
FATR	-	**Fixed Assets Turnover Ratio**
OESR	-	**Operating Expenses to Sales Ratio**
VI	-	**Vertical Integration**
PP	-	**Past Profitability**
GRA	-	**Growth Rate of Assets**

The model was estimated using ordinary least square method, while estimating, checks were made for model violation such as multicollinarity.

Research Design

Keeping in view the scope of the study, it is decided to include all the companies under Automobile Industry working before or from the year 1991-92 to 2003-04. But, owing to several constraints such as non-availability of financial statements or non-working of a company in a particular year etc., it is compelled to restrict the number of sample companies to 18. Therefore, this study is expost facto based on survey method making a survey of eighteen companies in Indian Automobile Industry. There are 26 companies operating in the Indian Automobile Industry. The companies under Automobile Industry are classified into three sectors namely; Commercial Vehicles, Passenger Cars and Multiutility Vehicles and Two and Three wheelers.

For the purpose of the study all the three sectors have been selected. The selected sectors include 26 companies. Out of 26 companies, 5 are under commercial vehicles, 8 under passenger cars and multiutility vehicles and 13 under two and three wheelers sector. Out of 26 companies of the selected sectors, 13 years data is available for 18 companies only. Therefore, all the 18 companies are included in the sample (Table 5.4). It accounts for 69.23 per cent of the total companies available in the Indian Automobile Industry. The selected 18 companies include 5 under commercial vehicles, 4 under passenger cars and multiutility vehicles and 9 under two and three wheeler sectors. It is inferred that sample company represents 98.74 percentage of market share in Commercial Vehicles, 89.76 percentage of market share in Passenger Cars and Multiutility Vehicles and 99.81 percentage of market share in Two and Three Wheelers. Thus, the findings based on the occurrence of such representative sample may be presumed to be true representative of Automobile Industry in the country.

Period of study

The period 1991-92 to 2003-04 is selected for this study of Indian Automobile Industry. This 13 years period is chosen in order to have a fairly long, cyclically well balanced period, for which reasonably homogeneous, reliable and up-to-date financial data would be available. Further, the span chosen for the study is the period of the beginning of liberalization measures introduced by the Government of India. Hence, the period 1991-92 to 2003-04 is an era of growth of corporate performance in the manufacturing sector, particularly Automobile Industry and has got genuine economic significance of its own.

Source of Data

The study is mainly based on secondary data. The major source of data analysed and interpreted in this study related to all those companies selected is collected from "PROWESS" database, which is the most reliable on the empowered corporate database of Centre for Monitoring Indian Economy (CMIE). Besides prowess database, relevant secondary data have also been collected from BSE Stock Exchange Official Directory, CIME Publications, Annual Survey of Industry, Business newspapers, Reports on Currency and Finance, Libraries of various Research Institutions, through Internet etc. The study required variety of data; therefore, websites like http://indiainfoline.com, www.indiastat.com and www.google.com have been comprehensively searched.

Analysis of results

The model described above has been estimated for all the selected sectors of automobile industry and whole industry and the results are presented in Table 5.0 to 5.3. It presents beta co-efficient and t values of the variables.

Whole industry

For the whole automobile industry, model explains 99 percentage of variation in profitability of firms included in the industry (Table 5.0). The analysis shows that all the variables except past profitability are found to be statistically significant in explaining profitability of Indian automobile industry. It is evident from the results that size is stronger determinant of profitability followed by vertical integration, current ratio, growth rate of assets, past profitability, leverage, inventory turnover ratio, fixed assets turnover ratio and operating expenses to sales ratio. As expected size, leverage, operation expenses to sales ratio, vertical integration and growth rate of assets did support our hypothesis with the expected sign. However the co-efficient of current ratio, inventory turnover ratio, fixed assets turnover ratio and post profitability did not support our hypothesis rather these appear with opposite sign.

It is evident from the result that co-efficient of size shows the increase of 16.48 per cent in profitability as a result of one per cent increase in size, which is statistically significant at 5 per cent level. The co-efficient of leverage indicates that a decrease of 0.49 per cent

Table 5.0

Determinants of profitability in Indian automobile industry - Multiple Regression Model

[Dependent Variable: Ratio of profit margin on sales (P)]

[P = 32.59 + 16.48 S-0.49 L + 10.79 CR – 0.71 ITR – 3.57 FATR – 9.76 OESR + 13.05 VI – 0.07 PP + 0.20 GRA]

Variables	Beta Co-efficient	t value	Significant / Not significant
Constant	32.59	2.878	
Size (S)	16.48	3.625*	Significant
Leverage (L)	-0.49	1.648**	Significant
Current Ratio (CR)	10.79	3.472*	Significant
Inventory Turnover Ratio (ITR)	-0.71	3.215*	Significant
Fixed Assets Turnover Ratio (FATR)	- 3.57	4.416*	Significant
Operating Expenses to Sales Ratio (OESR)	-9.76	4.316*	Significant
Vertical Integration (VI)	13.05	5.759*	Significant
Past Profitability (PP)	-0.07	0.705	Not significant
Growth Rate of Assets (GRA)	0.20	6.054*	Significant
R^2 = 0.99			
Adj R^2 = 0.95			
F = 27.30			
D.W = 2.03			

D.W - Durbin - Watson statistics; * - Significant at 0.05 level; ** - significant at 0.10 level

Source: Computed

in profitability as a result of one per cent increase in leverage which is significant at 10 per cent level. It is appeared from the result that value of one per cent increase in current ratio resulted in 10.79 per cent increase in profitability, which is significant at 5 per cent level. Further, one per cent increases in inventory turnover ratio, fixed assets turnover ratio and operating expenses to sales ratio shows 0.71 per cent, 3.57 per cent and 9.76 per cent decrease in profitability respectively during the study period. All these co-efficient are statistically significant. It is also apparent from the table that co-efficient of vertical integration and growth rate of assets show 13.05

per cent and 0.20 per cent increases in profitability as the result of one per cent increase, which is significant at 5 per cent level. However, the co-efficient of past profitability shows that 0.07 per cent decrease in profitability as a result of one per cent increase in past profitability. This is not statistically significant.

The overall explanatory power of regression appears to be good. This may be inferred from the co-efficient of determination (R^2) which is the measure of extent of movement in the dependent variable that is explained by the independent variables. It is 99 per cent and the adjusted explanation is around 95 per cent.

Commercial vehicles

For the commercial vehicles, model explains 94 percentage of variation in profitability of firms included in the industry (Table 5.1). The analysis shows that all the variables except current ratio and growth rate of assets are found to be statistically significant in explaining profitability of commercial vehicles sector. It is evident from the results that size is stronger determinant of profitability followed by vertical integration, fixed assets turnover ratio, past profitability, growth rate of assets, inventory turnover ratio, leverage, current ratio and operating expenses to sales ratio. As expected size, leverage, current ratio, fixed assets turnover ratio, operating expenses to sales ratio, vertical integration and past profitability did support our hypothesis with the expected sign. However the co-efficient of inventory turnover ratio and growth rate of assets did not support our hypothesis rather these appear with opposite sign.

It is evident from the results that co-efficient of size shows the increase of 16.11 per cent in profitability as a result of one per cent increase in size, which is statistically significant at 5 per cent level. Further, one per cent increase in leverage, current ratio and inventory turnover ratio shows 0.98 per cent, 14.38 per cent and 0.18 per cent decrease in profitability respectively during the study period. All these co-efficient are statistically significant except current ratio. The co-efficient of fixed assets turnover ratio shows the increase of 5.27 per cent in profitability as a result of one per cent increase in fixed assets turnover ratio, which statistically significant at 5 per cent level. The co-efficient of operating expenses to sales ratio decrease in 30.63 per cent in profitability as a result of one per cent increase in operating expenses to sales ratio which is significant at 5 per cent level. Further one per cent increase in vertical integration and past profitability shows 13.32 per cent and 0.38 per cent increase in profitability respectively during the study period. All these co-efficient are statistically significant at 10 per cent level. However, the co-efficient of growth rate of assets shows that 0.02 per cent decrease in profitability as a result of one per cent increase in growth rate of assets. This is not statistically significant.

Table 5.1

Determinants of Profitability in Commercial Vehicles Sector - Multiple Regression Model

[Dependent Variable: Ratio of profit margin on sales (P)]

[P = - 26.09 + 16.11 S – 0.98 L - 14.38 CR – 0.18 ITR + 5.27 FATR - 30.63 OESR + 13.32 VI + 0.38 PP - 0.02 GRA]

Variables	Beta Co-efficient	t value	Significant / Not significant
Constant	-26.09	2.275	
Size (S)	16.11	2.922*	Significant
Leverage (L)	-0.98	2.611*	Significant
Current Ratio (CR)	-14.38	1.398	Not significant
Inventory Turnover Ratio (ITR)	-0.18	2.062*	Significant
Fixed Assets Turnover Ratio (FATR)	5.27	3.154*	Significant
Operating Expenses to Sales Ratio (OESR)	-30.63	3.276*	Significant
Vertical Integration (VI)	13.32	1.967**	Significant
Past Profitability (PP)	0.38	2.331**	Significant
Growth Rate of Assets (GRA)	-0.02	1.226	Not significant
R^2 = 0.94			
Adj R^2 = 0.77			
F = 15.38			
D.W = 2.16			

D.W - Durbin - Watson statistics; * - Significant at 0.05 level; ** - Significant at 0.10 level

Source: Computed

The overall explanatory power of regression appears to be good. This may be inferred from the co-efficient of determination (R^2) which is the measure of extent of movement in the dependent variable that is explained by the independent variables. It is 94 per cent and adjusted explanation is around 77 per cent.

Passenger cars and Multiutility vehicles

For the passenger cars and multiutility vehicles, model explains 95 percentage of variation in profitability of firms included in the industry (Table 5.2). The analysis shows that all the variables except past profitability are found to be statistically significant in explaining profitability of passenger cars and multiutility vehicles sectors. It is evident from the results that size is the strongest determinant of profitability followed by current ratio, fixed assets turnover ratio, past profitability, growth rate of assets, leverage, inventory turnover ratio, vertical integration and operating expenses to sales ratio. As expected size, leverage, fixed assets turnover ratio,

Table 5.2

Determinants of profitability in Passenger Cars and Multiutility Vehicles sector - Multiple Regression Model

[Dependent Variable: Ratio of profit margin on sales (P)]

[P = 256.59 + 84.36 S - 2.63 L + 20.89 CR - 3.35 ITR + 9.01 FATR - 497.41 OESR - 482.28 VI + 0.13 PP - 0.98 GRA]

Variables	Beta Co-efficient	t value	Significant / Not significant
Constant	256.59	2.488	
Size (S)	84.36	2.682*	Significant
Leverage (L)	-2.63	1.683**	Significant
Current Ratio (CR)	20.89	1.787**	Significant
Inventory Turnover Ratio (ITR)	-3.35	2.843*	Significant
Fixed Assets Turnover Ratio (FATR)	9.01	2.369*	Significant
Operating Expenses to Sales Ratio (OESR)	-497.41	3.062*	Significant
Vertical Integration (VI)	-482.28	2.992*	Significant
Past Profitability (PP)	0.13	0.274	Not significant
Growth Rate of Assets (GRA)	-0.98	3.046*	Significant
R^2 = 0.95			
Adj R^2 = 0.79			
F = 11.02			
D.W = 1.93			

D.W - Durbin - Watson statistics ; * - Significant at 0.05 level; ** - Significant at 0.10 level

Source: Computed

operating expenses to sales ratio and past profitability did support our hypothesis with the expected sign. However the co-efficient of current ratio, inventory turnover ratio, vertical integration and growth rate of assets did not support our hypothesis rather these appear with opposite sign.

It is evident from the results that co-efficient of size shows the increase of 84.36 per cent in profitability as a result of one per cent increase in size, which is statistically significant at 5 per cent level. The co-efficient of leverage indicates that a decrease at 2.63 per cent in profitability as a result of one per cent increase in leverage which is significant at 10 per cent level. It is appeared from the result that value of one per cent increase in current ratio resulted in 20.89 per cent increase in profitability, which is statistically significant at 10 per cent level. Further, one per cent increase in inventory turnover ratio, operating expenses to sales ratio, vertical integration and growth rate of assets shows 3.35 per cent, 497.41 per cent, 482.28 per cent and 0.98 per cent decrease in profitability respectively during the study period. All these co-efficient are statistically significant. It is evident from the result that value of one per cent increase in fixed assets turnover ratio resulted in 9.01 per cent increase in profitability, which is significant at 5 per cent level. However, the co-efficient of past profitability shows that 0.13 per cent increase in profitability as a result of one per cent increase in past profitability. This is not statistically significant.

The overall explanatory power of regression appears to be good. This may be inferred from the co-efficient of determination (R^2) which is the measure of extent of movement in the dependent variable that is explained by the independent variables. It is 95 per cent and adjusted explanation is around 79 per cent.

Two and Three wheelers

For the two and three wheelers, model explains 94 percentage of variation in profitability of firms included in the industry (Table 5.3). The analysis shows that all the variable except leverage and growth rate of assets is found to be statistically significant in explaining profitability of two and three wheelers sector. It is evident from the results that size is stronger determinant of profitability followed by inventory turnover ratio, past profitability, growth rate of assets, leverage, vertical integration, fixed assets turnover ratio, operating expenses to sales ratio and current ratio. As expected size, leverage, current ratio, inventory turnover ratio, operating expenses to sales ratio and past profitability did support our hypothesis with the expected sign. However the co-efficient of fixed assets turnover ratio, vertical integration and growth rate of assets did not support our hypothesis rather these appear with opposite sign.

Table 5.3
Determinants of profitability in Two and Three Wheelers sector
- Multiple Regression Model
[Dependent Variable: Ratio of profit margin on sales (P)]
[P = 70.63 + 23.53 S – 1.41 L – 37.66 CR + 3.72 ITR – 5.53 FATR - 29.34 OESR – 3.71 VI + 1.33 PP - 0.03 GRA]

Variables	Beta Co-efficient	t value	Significant / Not significant
Constant	70.63	2.112	
Size (S)	23.53	1.998**	Significant
Leverage (L)	-1.41	0.634	Not significant
Current Ratio (CR)	-37.66	2.364*	Significant
Inventory Turnover Ratio (ITR)	3.72	2.268**	Significant
Fixed Assets Turnover Ratio (FATR)	-5.53	1.667**	Significant
Operating Expenses to Sales Ratio (OESR)	-29.34	1.639**	Significant
Vertical Integration (VI)	-3.71	1.652**	Significant
Past Profitability (PP)	1.33	3.682*	Significant
Growth Rate of Assets (GRA)	-0.03	0.647	Not significant
R^2 = 0.94			
Adj R^2 = 0.75			
F = 11.65			
D.W = 2.12			

D.W-Durbin -Watson statistics; * - Significant at 0.05 level; **- significant at 0.10 level

Source: Computed

It is evident from the results that co-efficient of size shows the increase of 23.53 per cent in profitability as a result of one per cent increase in size, which is statistically significant at 5 per cent level. The co-efficient of leverage indicates that a decrease of 1.41 per cent in profitability as a result of one per cent increase in leverage. This is not statistically significant. It is appeared from the result that a decrease of 37.66 per cent in profitability as a result at one per cent increase in current ratio, which is statistically significant at 5 per cent level. It is also apparent from the table that co-efficient of inventory turnover ratio and past profitability shows 3.72 per cent and 1.33 per cent increase in profitability as the result of one per cent increase, which is statistically significant. Further, one per cent increase in fixed assets turnover ratio, operating expenses to sales ratio and vertical integration shows 5.53 per cent, 29.34 per cent and 3.71 per cent decreases in profitability respectively during the study period. All these co-efficient are statistically significant at 10 per cent level. However, the co-efficient of growth rate of assets shows that 0.03 per cent decrease in profitability as a result of one per cent increase in growth rate of assets. This is not statistically significant.

Table 5.4

List of sample companies included in the present study

Sl. No.	Sectors / Companies	Year of Incor poration	Ownership	Market share (%)	Total market share (%)
	Commercial Vehicles (5)				
1.	Ashok Leyland Ltd	1956	Hinduja Group	35.62	
2.	Tata Motors Ltd	1956	Tata Group	34.22	
3.	Bajaj Tempo Ltd	1958	Firodia Group	11.50	
4.	Eicher Motors Ltd	1982	Eicher Group	10.65	
5.	Swaraj Mazder Ltd	1983	State and Private Sector	6.75	**98.74**
	Passenger Cars and Multiutility Vehicles (4)				
6.	Hindustan Motors Ltd	1942	Birla C.K.Group	8.31	
7.	Mahindra and Mahindra Ltd	1945	Mahindra and Mahindra	42.17	
8.	Maruti Udyog Ltd	1981	Private (Foreign)	36.60	
9.	Daewoo Motors India Ltd	1983	Private (Foreign)	2.68	**89.76**
	Two and Three Wheelers (9)				
10.	Bajaj Auto Ltd	1945	Bajaj Group	18.80	
11.	LML Ltd	1972	LML Group	11.58	
12.	Maharashtra Scooters Ltd	1975	Bajaj Group	7.80	
13.	TVS Motor Company Ltd	1982	T.V.S. Group	12.93	
14.	Kinetic Motor Company Ltd	1984	Firodia Group	11.75	
15.	Hero Honda Motors Ltd	1984	Hero (Munsals) Groups	10.54	
16.	Kinetic Engineering Ltd	1970	Firodia Group	9.72	
17.	Majestic Auto Ltd	1986	Hero Group	9.04	
18.	Scooters India Ltd	1972	Central Govt. Commercial Enterprise	7.65	**99.81**

The overall explanatory power of regression appears to be good. This may be inferred from the co-efficient of determination (R^2) which is the measure of extent of movement in the dependent variable that is explained by the independent variables. It is 94 per cent and the adjusted explanation is around 75 per cent.

Conclusion

It can be concluded from the above analysis that the selected variables explain 99 per cent of variation in profitability in Indian automobile industry, 94 per cent in commercial vehicles sector, 95 per cent in passenger cars and Multiutility vehicles sector and 94 per cent in two and three wheelers sector. It is evident from the results that size is the strongest determinant of profitability followed by the variables vertical integration, past profitability, growth rate of assets and inventory turnover ratio. The selected variables have both positive and negative contribution in variation of profit rate. In nutshell, it can be concluded that firms should consider all these possible determinants while considering its profitability.

References

1. Shepherd, W.G. (1972). The elements of market structure, Review of Economics and statistics, p.54.
2. Agarwal, V.K. (1978). Size, profitability and growth of some manufacturing industries, unpublished FPM thesis, IIM, Ahgmedabad.
3. Newmann, Bobel and Haid (1979). Profitability, risk and market structure in West German Industries, The Journal of Industrial Economics, Vol.27, pp.227-242.
4. Asha Jain (1981). Price–Cost margin in Indian Manufacturing Industries : An econometric analysis, Ph.D thesis, IIT, Kanpur.
5. Bothwell, J.L. et al. (1982). A new view of market structure-performance debate, The Journal of Industrial Economics and Statistics, Vol.64, pp.635-645.
6. Das, M.R. (1998). Determinants of return on equity of Indian Public sector banks : some empirical results based on cross-sectional data, Vinimaya, Vol.19, pp. 5-12.
7. Vijayakumar (2002). Determinants of corporate size, growth and profitability – The Indian Experience, in the book "Research studies in Commerce and Management", Classical Publishing Company, New Delhi, pp.66-74.

8. Samuels, J.M. and Smyth, D.J. (1968). Profits variability and Firm size, Economic and Political Weekly, Vol.35, pp.127-139.
9. Deepak Chawala (1986). An empirical analysis of the profitability of the Indian Man-made fibres industry, Decision, pp.106-115.
10. Narayanan and Barthwal (1990). Profitability and structure : A firm level study of Indian Pharmaceutical Industry, The Indian Economic Journal, No.2, Vol.38, pp.70-84.
11. Amit Mallick and Debasish Sur (1998). Working capital and Profitability: A case study, The Management Accountant, pp.805-809.
12. Sidhu, H.S. and Bhatia, G. (1993). Factors affecting profitability in Indian Textile Industry, The Indian Economic Journal, Vol.41, No.2, pp.137-143.

6

DETERMINANTS OF CORPORATE DIVIDEND IN INDIA—A STUDY OF PSU'S

Every investment is made on the expectation and assumption that it will yield some returns. Equity investment is not an exception to this. Every equity investor anticipates a good rate of return in the form of dividend to be declared by the company. So, every company pays higher attention in formulating its own dividend policy. Dividend decision is one of the most important decisions in the field of Financial Management. Dividend policy determines the relationship between a company and the capital market. Payment of dividend enhances the market price of the shares thereby increasing the wealth of the shareholders. Payment of dividend conveys to shareholders the information relating to the profitability of the firm. Economic studies generally shows that the dividends act as booster of the shareholder's confidence signaling that the company is being managed well and its future is safe.

A dividend policy must permit the distribution of regular dividend at gradually increasing pace. The desirable aim of all the companies should be the establishment of a stable dividend rate because it aids in raising additional capital, enhances reputation and increases the value of securities. Thus, deciding how much of the current earnings are to be distributed or retained is a major financial decision for a company.

Statement of the Problem

The Sugar Industry in India is one of the oldest industries but has great relevance in the context of the global economy even today. The industry has been facing an unpleasant period. The Indian Sugar Industry suffers from excessive consumer protectionism, leading to an unwarranted increase in its cost of production primarily due to political decisions leading occasionally to sharp increases in the cost of sugar, thus reducing the competitive edge.

Furthermore, Government policies hitherto have encouraged the establishment of low capacity and uneconomic sugar plants. These policies proceeded despite advice to the contrary by many experts. Under the present sugar policy, sugar factories have to surrender part of their production to the government (presently 30%) at prices about 20% below the cost of production as levy sugar for distribution to the consumers through the Public Distribution System.

Besides this, many controls and regulations on the sugar industry right from the purchase of sugarcane to the sale of sugar and by-products have had a telling impact on the economic standing of the industry. The pricing policy for sugarcane is also not free from flaws. Unfortunately, in recent years fixing of sugarcane prices has become a political issue based on the populist perceptions of the ruling and opposition parties. This is a direct consequence of the dual authority being exercised by the Central Government and State Government in case price fixing. The Central Government fixes the Statutory Minimum Price (SMP) which is used for the computation of the price of levy sugar. However, the actual cane price paid by the sugar mills is the one announced by the State Government, known as the SAP- the State Advised Price. The normal tendency on the part of the State Government is to raise the cane price beyond the economic level to appease the large number of farmers involved. Till now, no firm decision has been taken owing to its politically sensitive nature.

All the above problems have been adversely affecting the profitability of the sugar companies. For public limited companies, a fall in the level of profitability destabilizes their dividend payment schedule. Lintner (1956) observes that the financial decisions of corporations are predominantly dividend – oriented and firms pay primary importance to dividends rather than retained earnings. Is this true in the Indian Sugar Industry? To which – dividends or retained earnings-do the companies pay primary importance? Do the companies belonging to sugar industry maintain an increasing steam of dividend? What has been the trend in the dividend payment by the Sugar Industry? Further, an attempt has also been made to study the factors that influence the dividend policy of the Sugar Industry.

Review of Empirical Works

A number of studies have been carried out to examine earnings, retained earnings and dividends. The pioneering works are mostly carried out by American researchers. The nature of the studies, objectives with which they have been carried out and the results are briefly summarized in the following paragraphs. Lintmer, John (1956) conducted a study on the 'Distribution of Earnings of Corporations among Dividends, Retained Earnings and Taxes'. Twenty-eight American Corporations were chosen for the purpose of the study. He found that the corporations followed a fixed target pay out ratio. The rate of dividends was adjusted along with the increase in the level of earnings. Current year's earnings and previous year's dividend were found to be associated with current year's dividend. He also ascertained that the financial decisions of the corporations were predominantly dividend oriented.

Darling (1957)[2] proceeded on the work of Lintner. In the place of previous year's dividend, Darling introduced a substitute variable namely, previous year's profit. Two other variables were also introduced by him. They were depreciation and change in volume of sales. Depreciation was introduced because it represented undistributed cash and change in sales was introduced to represent the need for working capital. His study revealed that depreciation has a positive influence on the amount of dividend. Inverse correlation existed between dividend and growth in sales.

The impact of investment demand on the amount of dividend distribute was examined by Smith (1963).[3] He added one more variable namely 'Demand for investment' to Lintner's model and found that corporate savings and investment demand were closely associated. He came to the conclusion that dividend decision was only residual.

Purnanandam and Hanumantha Rao(1966)[4] in their study entitled "Corporate Dividends and Target Payout Ratios in the Indian Cotton Textile Industry: 1946-63" attempted to estimate the long run desired dividend payment ratios in the Indian Cotton Textile Industry using the Lintner's Dividend Model. The data were taken from several issues of 'Investor's Encyclopedia,' published by Messrs Kothari & Sons, Madras. The two variables that appeared in the study were dividends excluding the issues of bonus shares and net profits during a particular period without the intercept term 'a'. A sample of 50 textile companies was chosen for the study. The results indicated that the weights attached to profit as well as lagged dividend were high in case of homogenous equation (model without intercept term 'a') as compared to non-homogeneous equation (model with intercept term 'a'). The target payout ratios as well as the reaction coefficients were higher in the case of homogeneous equation. Their study revealed that a larger volume of dividend was paid by the Textile Industry.

Smith, Keith (1971)[5], carried out a study entitled "Increasing Stream Hypothesis of Corporate Dividend Policy. He attempted to clarify the empirical side of corporate dividend policy by postulating and testing an alternative hypothesis of it, *i.e.*, increasing Steam Hypothesis of corporate dividend policy. A large sample of 900 firms was chosen for the study. A period of 19 years from 1948-1967 was considered for the purpose of the study. The findings of the study supported the increasing stream hypothesis that firms avoid dividend cuts in favour of uninterrupted stream of non-decreasing dividend payments to common shareholders.

In India, Rao and Sarma (1971)[6], carried out a study titled "Dividends and Retained Earnings of Public and Private Limited Companies in India: 1955-56 to 1965-66-'An Econometric Analysis'. The objectives of the study were to enquire into the determinants of dividends of public and private limited companies, to estimate short-run marginal propensity to pay dividend, short-run marginal propensity to save and the long-run desired payout and savings ratios. The study covered a period of 11 years from 1955-56 to 1965-66 in respect of two categories of companies viz., (i) Non- financial and Non-Government companies with a paid-up capital of more than Rs.5 lakh and (ii) medium and large private limited companies. The Basic Lintner model was employed in the study. The results of the study indicated that there were variations in the suitability of the models employed. While the model with cash flow variable fitted well for industries like cotton textiles, iron and steel, paper products and electricity generation and supply, the model with depreciation and net profit, introduced separately, was found separately, was found to well explain the dividend behaviour of Jute and Textiles and Engineering Industries. Further it was also found that the payout ratio widely different among the selected industry groups. The study also revealed that in the case of sugar industry, the substitution of cash flow variable in place of current profits in the basic Lintner model has not improved the explanatory power of the equation as reflected in Adjusted R^2. The standard error is lower in the case of the basic Lintner model and hence this model may be preferred for the sugar industry.

Dhameja (1972)[7] in his study entitled[6] Dividend Behaviour in Indian paper industry –1950-65: A Statistical Test,' examined the statistical significance of various factors influencing dividend policy in Indian Paper Industry. The variables used were net profit, previous year dividend, weighed average of past profits, depreciation cash flow earnings (net and gross) , change in sales , accumulated reserves and provision for tax . The tools used in the study were linear multiple regression and coefficient of determination. He concluded that the increase in profit did not result in an equivalent increase in dividend and vice – versa. Dividend determination was influenced by the past year's profits and fluctuations in the earnings did not have much influence on dividend. Fluctuations in dividend determinations were influenced by current year's earnings while change in sales had a positive influence on dividend. Further it was ascertained from the study that lagged dividend was directly associated with current year dividend.

In an another study Krishnamurthy and Sastry (1975)[8] made an attempt to examine the dividend behavior of public limited companies based on the data available in the Reserve Bank of India Bulletin. The study period was from 1960 to1970 covering 11 years. They extended Lintner's model with additional variables to these companies. These variables included cash flow changed cash flow, investment expenditure and flow of debt. They found that basic Lintner's model was more appropriate in explaining the dividend behaviour.

Kumar and Khurana (1984) made an attempt to find out the factors influencing the dividend policy of selected Indian Industries. Their study entitled, 'Determinants of Corporate Dividend in India' had two main objectives. They were, (i) to find out the most important factors, which influence increase in dividend and (ii) to ascertain factors, which have a bearing in reduction of dividend. They selected 65 manufacturing companies whose shares were listed in the Bombay Stock Exchange and conducted personal interview with the managements of the selected companies. Their study period covered five years from 1979-1983 They found that whenever the companies increased dividends, they took three factors into account. The factors were (i) increase in net profit after tax, (ii) better liquidity position and (iii) better reserve position. Of these three, the first one was considered to be the most important factor. There factors, namely (i) reduction in profits after tax, (ii) poor liquidity position and (iii) expansion programmes were considered to be pertinent factors for decrease and non-payment of dividends. Of these three factors, priority was assigned to reduction in profits.

Agarwal (1986)[9], carried out a study entitled, 'Corporate Investment and Financial Behaviour- An Econometric Analysis of Indian Automobile Industry'. Their study period was 20 years from 1959-60 to 1978-79. The Basis Lintner model was used for examining the dividend behaviour of the selected seven units belonging to the Automobile Industry. To the Lintner's model, he added four more variables namely change in sales, liquidity, flow of external funds and total investment. It was found that current year's profit was the most important factor, which decided the payment of dividend. The other variables were not found to significantly influence the payment of dividend.

Mittal (1992)[10], in his study entitled 'Determinants of Corporate Retained Earnings' examined whether the decisions of retained earnings was a primary decisions variable or a residual one. The data had been collected from the Stock Exchange Official Directory, Bombay for 10 years from 1980 – 81 to 1989 – 90 regarding 23 large public limited textile companies in the private sector. Coefficient of variation had been calculated to examine whether retention of earnings was a primary or residual variable. The results of the study revealed that the retained earnings decision was a residual one since there were low variations in the dividends paid and large variations in retained earnings in textile companies.

Kevin (1992)[11] carried out a study titled 'Dividend Policy'. An analysis of some Determinants'. He examined whether private sector companies in India strive for stability in their dividend payment and how far the dividend pattern of private sector companies in India was consistent with their earnings pattern. A sample of 650 Private Sector companies was chosen and the data were collected from the 'First-ever Computerized Survey of the Top 650 Private Sector Companies' by the Commerce Research Bureau in 1986. Regression Analysis was used in the study and the variables considered were (i) dividend, (ii) net profit, (iii) operating profit, (iv) net worth, (v) net assets and (vi) net sales. The results of the study revealed that no consistent co-variation between dividend payment and earnings Pattern. The companies generally wanted to maintain stable dividend. Kevin viewed that dividend stability was the primary determinant of Dividend policy and profitability was only of secondary importance in the sense that companies strove to maintain stable dividends in spite of fluctuations in earnings. It was concluded that the dividend policy was not a passive residual but an active decision variable.

Bhat, Ramesh and Pandey (1994)[12] in their study titled'. 'Dividend Decision: A Study of 'Managers' perceptions' attempted to find out how the managers perceive the question of dividend payment and retention. A questionnaire was sent to 450 companies and was addressed to finance directors. Thirty-one questionnaires were received, of which 28 were found usable for analysis. The results of the study revealed that the ranking of determinants of Dividend was (i) current earnings, (ii) patterns of past dividends, (iii) increasing equity base and expected future earnings, (iv) liquidity and (v) preference of companies to maintain their dividend policy even if they do not have internally available cash. Moreover, analysis of manager's responses showed that they favoured the view that dividend policy influence the share price i.e., higher the dividend payout, higher would the price of equity per share. The study also revealed that investors in high tax brackets were attracted to shares having low dividend yield and investors in low tax brackets were attracted to shares having high dividend yield.

Mahesh Chand Gang, Saroj Nagpal and Verma (1996),[13] examined the factors affecting payment of dividend in the textile industry in India using ratio analysis. Their study entitled, 'Factors Determining Dividend Payments in textile Industry in India' covered a period of ten years from 1980-81 to 1989-90 and included 44 joint stock companies from the textile industry except jute textiles. Four classifications of rations had been made viz.,(i) capital structure ratios, (ii) liquidity ratios, (iii) profitability ratios and (iv) dividend practices ratios.

The results of the study revealed that capital structure; liquidity and profitability seemed to be the factors determining the dividend payments in the sample companies. With improved capital base, liquidity and profitability, dividend payments increase. Dividend payments have also been on the higher side in the diversified group. In the case of associated group, capital structure, liquidity and profitability position is better and the dividend payments are better.

In their study entitled, 'Dividend Policy of Private Sector Enterprises-A Case study of Engineering Industry', Jain and Khera (1996)[14], examined the dividend policy pursued by the corporate firms affiliated to the engineering industry and looked into its impact on the value of corporate firms. The data for the study has been collected from the "The Stock Exchange Official Directory" of the Bombay Stock Exchange pertaining to General engineering, and from the responses of the financial managers of the engineering corporate firms. The study covered a period from 1981-1991. Forty-one firms were chosen as the sample for the study. Earnings per share, dividend per share, and market price per share, total assets, equity capital, debentures, long term loans, net profit and profit retained, depreciation, net cash earnings, and dividend payout ratios were some of the variables used. It was concluded that the private sector engineering corporate firms by and large tended to practice stable dividend policy. They seemed to be following an approach akin to Lintner's model. Dividend was generally found to be an active decision variable affecting the valuation of the firm whereas decision relating to retention occupied second position. It was also observed that higher growth firms have lower dividend payout ratios as such firms had greater profitable investment opportunities needing more financial resources. Further, with announcements of bonus and right issues along with increase or no decrease in cash dividend has an appreciably favorable impact on the price of the share of the firms.

In a study entitled, 'Dividend Policy and Practices in Select Corporate Firms of India and South – East Asia: A Comparative Study', *Jain and Manoj Kumar* (1997) examined and compared dividend policies and practices of 96 corporate firms in India and three companies in South-East Asia. The study covered a period of twelve years i.e., 1994- 1995. The data had been collected from a variety of sources, viz, Bombay Stock Exchange Official Directory, Reserve Bank of India Bulletins, Kothari Economic Guide, Business Magazines like Business India etc. From the study, it was found that sample firms preferred a stable dividend policy. Retained earnings constituted an important source of funds for Indian firms. Sample corporate firms seemed to follow a policy of paying less than 45 per cent of net earnings to equity shareholders during the twelve year period (1984-1995). Corporate firms in India had a tendency to pay relatively less a dividend compared to South – East Asian companies. Majority of the companies (66 per cent) in India followed stable dividend policy. Indian Corporate firms found Retained Earning as higher significant source than their counterparts in the South-East Asian Region.

Methodology

The official stock exchange Directory, published by the Bombay Stock Exchange, Mumbai, and furnished data for all the listed companies listed amount to 67. From this, a list of companies that have provided continuous data for a period of 12 years have been shortlisted first. From this list, 16 companies have been chosen randomly. The data required for the study is secondary in nature. The main source of data for the present study is the official stock exchange Directory, published by the Bombay Stock Exchange, Mumbai. Apart from, Mumbai maintained by center for monitoring Indian Economy, Mumbai and Data provided in www.indianinfoline.com have also been used.

The data collected has been analysed through simple average, co-efficient of variation, Analysis of variance (ANOVA) and multiple regression. Determinants of dividends have been studie through multiple regression analysis. For this purpose, the following regression equation has been framed.

$$DPS_t = a + b_1 NS_t + b_2 INT_t + b_3 DEP_t + b_4 PROV_t + b_5 NPT_t + b_6 NPT_{t+1} + b_7 NPT_{t-1} + b_8 DPS_{t-1} + b_9 REPS_{t-1} + b_{10} LIQ_t + b_{11} INGB_{t+1} + e$$

Where

DPS_t = Current year's Dividend per share

a = constant

NS_t	=	current year's Sales
INT_t	=	Current year's interest
DEP_t	=	current year's Depreciation
$PROV_t$	=	current year's Provision for Tax
NPT_t	=	current year's Net Profit
NPT_{t+1}	=	subsequent year's Net Profit
NPT_{t-1}	=	previous year's Net Profit
DPS_{t-1}	=	previous year's Dividend per share
$REPS_{t-1}$	=	previous year's Retained Earnings per share
LIQ_1	=	current year's Liquidity Ratio
$INGB_{t+1}$	=	Subsequent year's increase in Gross block
e	=	Error Term

The regression eo-efficients are tested for their significance through the 't' values. The significance of R^2 has been tested through 'F' statistic. The levels of significance chosen are 1% and 5%.

Trends in Corporate Dividends

It has been found by Smith, Keith V (1971) that corporations follow a policy of increasing the level of dividend over the years. In a study titled "Increasing Stream Hypothesis of Corporate Dividend Policy", he proposes a hypothesis that corporations are oriented towards increase in the rate of dividend. Based on the methodology of Smith, Keith V, an attempt is made here to ascertain the behaviour of dividend of the companies belonging to the Indian Sugar Industry.

The average amounts of earnings dividends as well as the growth rate in dividends of all the selected companies belonging to the Sugar industry are shown in Table 6.0. It can be seen from the table that the mean amount of earnings has ranged between Rs. 1.58 and to Rs. 49.55. The mean amount of dividends has ranged between Rs. 0.08 and to Rs. 4.00. The growth rate of dividend is positive in five selected sugar industries during the study period. Among these, the highest growth rate of dividend observed in Vishnu Sugar Mills Limited, followed by Balrampur Chini Mills Limited, Ravalgaon Sugar Farm Limited, Bajaj Hindustan Limited and Bannariamman Sugars Limited. In all other selected sugar mills, the growth rate of dividend is negative during the study period. The average DPS of Sugar Industry is Rs. 2.54 during the study period. Further, the overall mean growth rate of sugar industry has been worked out as 8.20.

Table 6.0

Trends in Corporate Dividends (1989 – 2000)

Company Name	EPS Mean Value	DPS Mean Value (Rs.)	Growth Rate (%)
Revalgaon Sugar Farm Limited	49.55	4.00	6.81
Balrampur Chini Mills Limited	27.65	3.96	11.83
Vishnu Sugar Mills Limited	66.44	3.27	23.03
New India Sugar Mills Limited	20.20	3.18	-0.92
Bannariamman Sugars Limited	10.61	2.27	2.00
Andhra Sugars Limited	7.25	2.14	-6.12
Oudh Sugar Mills Limited	7.37	2.11	-1.87
Kesar Enterprises Limited	5.91	1.84	-8.81
Sakthi Sugars Limted	6.43	1.77	-7.61
Bajaj Hindusthan Limited	-1.20	1.43	5.15
Dhampur Sugar Mills Limited	19.14	1.40	-1.4
Bhopal Sugar Industries Limited	-8.34	1.08	-5.72
Ponni Sugars and Chemicals Limited	1.58	1.05	-7.70
United Provinces Sugar Company Limited	10.54	0.55	-0.51
India Sugars and Refineries Limited	-3.28	0.33	-
Belapur Industries Limited	-0.15	0.08	-
Average		**2.54**	**8.20**

EPS - Earnings Per Share

DPS - Dividend Per Share

Source: Computed

In order to ascertain whether the mean values of dividends per share have differed among the companies, Analysis of Variance

(ANOVA) test has been performed and the results are presented in Table 6.1. In this industry, the calculated F value is greater than its table value at 1% level. Hence it is inferred that there is a significant difference among the companies of this industry.

Table 6.1
Difference in Mean Dividend Per Share (ANOVA)

Source	**D.F**	**S.S**	**M.S**	**F Value**
Between Companies	15.4955	262.164.00	17.486.81	10.82*
Error	176	284.35	1.62	
Total	191	546.51		

* - Significant at 1% level

Source: Computed

Determinants of Dividends

Dividend policy has remained one of the most researched areas of study in the field of finance. Many researchers have made attempts to examine the factors that determine the dividend policy of firms. An attempt is made in this part to ascertain the factors that influence the dividend policy of the Indian Sugar Industry. Correlation analysis has been carried out to find out the factors that are correlated with dividends. Dividends are influenced by factors like net sales, net profit, previous year dividends, retained earnings etc., correlation analysis has been carried out in order to test the association between the selected eleven independent variables and dividend per share and presented in Table 6.2. If the calculated correlation value between any variable and dividend per share is greater than its table value at one per cent level then it is inferred that there exists a highly significant correlation between these two variables.

It is found that all the eleven variables namely, net sales, interest, depreciation, provision for tax, current year's net profit subsequent year's net profit, previous year's dividend per share, previous year's retained, earnings per share, liquidity, subsequent year's increase in Gross Block are significantly associated with dividend per share of the current year. All the eleven variables are positively associated with dividends and the relationship is found to be highly significant.

Table 6.2

Factors associated with Dividend

Factors	Correlation Coefficient(r)	Coefficient of Determination (R^2)
Current Year's Sales (NS_t)	0.45*	0.20
Current Year's Interest (INT_t)	0.31*	0.09
Current Year's Deprecation (DEP_t)	0.33*	0.11
Current Year's Provision for tax ($PROV_t$)	0.30*	0.09
Current Year's Net Profit (NPT_t)	0.53*	0.28
Subsequent Year's Net Profit (NPT_{t+1})	0.44*	0.19
Previous Year's Net Profit Per Share (NPT_{t-1})	0.49*	0.24
Previous Year's Dividend Per Share (DPS_{t-1})	0.79*	0.63
Previous Year's Retained Earnings Per Share ($REPS_{t-1}$)	0.46*	0.21
Current Year's Liquidity Ratio (LIQ_t)	0.33*	0.11
Subsequent Year's increase in Gross Block ($INGB_{t+1}$)	0.24*	0.06

* Signification at 1% level

Source : Computed

In order to find out the influence of the selected variables on the amount of dividends distributed, Multiple Regression has been carried out. The dividends have been regressed on the selected variables. The results of the analysis are discussed for the sugar industry, as a whole. Table 6.3 summarise the values of regression co-efficient. Only three variables, namely net profit for the current year, previous year dividend per share and liquidity ratio are found to be significantly associated with the level of dividends distributed.

Table 6.3
Factors Influencing Dividend

Variables	Regression Coefficient	Standard Error	t-Value
NS_t	0.0002	0.0005	0.472
INT_t	0.0029	0.0058	0.502
DEP_t	-0.0044	0.0110	-0.397
$PROV_t$	0.0103	0.0142	0.727
NPT_t	0.0143*	0.0039	3.631
NPT_{t+1}	0.0034	0.0037	0.914
NPT_{t-1}	0.0648	0.0971	0.667
DPS_{t-1}	0.6848*	0.1134	6.038
$REPS_{t-1}$	-0.0691	0.0972	-0.710
LIQ_t	0.2225*	0.1327	1.677
$INGB_{t+1}$	0.0005	0.0007	0.716

Constant : -0.1181
Ad; R^2 : 0.7036
R^2 : 0.7241*
F Value : 35.316*
* : Significant at 1% level
** : Significant at 5% level
Source : Computed

The regression co-efficient between dividend per share of the current year (DPS_t) and net profit of the current year (NPT_t) amounts to 0.0143 indicating that the profit is positively related with dividend per share. This indicates that an increase of one rupee in net profit will enhance the amount of dividend per share by Rs. 0.014, keeping the other variables constant. It can also be seen from the table that the influence of previous year dividend is positive and significant at one per cent level. The contribution of previous year dividend per share to current year dividend per share is 0.6848. This indicates that one per cent of increase in previous year dividend enhances the current year dividend by Rs. 0.68.

Generally, there exists an inverse relationship between dividends paid and the liquid ratio. If the dividend paid increases, the liquidity position decreases and vice versa. It can be seen from the table that the regression co-efficient between liquidity and dividend per share amounts to 0.2225 and is positively related with dividend per share which is significant at 5% level. The nature of this relationship is strange. The overall contribution of all the eleven variables is found out by calculating R^2 value. The value of R^3 amounts to 0.7241. This indicates that the contribution of all these eleven variables amounts to 72.41 per cent to dividend per share. The R^2 value is also tested for its significance through 'F' test and has been found to be highly significant.

It has been found that of the eleven variables, only two are found to have significant influence on dividend per share. In order to identify the most significant factors that influence the level of dividend per share, stepwise regression has been performed and the results were presented in Table 6.4. It is evident from the table that previous year's dividend contribution was 62.95 per cent. It can also be seen that total contribution from 62.95 per cent to 70.29 per cent. The total R^2 value inclusive of eleven independent variables between these teo reqression equations is only variables which are not included in the stepwise regression equation.

Table 6.4

Prominently Associated Variables with Dividend

Step	Constant	DPS_{t-1}	NPT_t	R^2
1	0.2083	0.9168	-	0.6265
2	0.1998	0.7991	0.0167	0.7029

Source: Computed

Conclusion

It is found that all the variables selected are significantly and positively associated with dividend per share of the current year. Three variables namely current year's net profit, previous year's dividend and liquidity have significant influence on dividend distributed. Thus, dividend payment has become almost conpulsory for every firm as the share holders are looking for short-term adn periodical returns on their investments. The present study has also revealed thta companies attach primary importance to dividends and they prefer a stable or increasing trend in dividend payments.

Reference

1. Lintner, J. (1956), 'Distribution of Income of Corporations Among Dividends, Retained Earnings and Taxes', American economic Review, pp: 97-113.

2. Darling, P.G, (1957), 'The Influence of Expectations and Liquidity on Dividend Policy', Journal of Political Economy, (June), pp: 209-224, Cited in Braj Kishore, (1980), 'Corporate Internal Finance: A Study of Overall Trends and retentions', Vikalpa, Vol. 5, No. 3. (July), p.194.
3. Smith David, C. (1963), 'Corporate Savings Behaviour', Canadian Journal of Economics and Political science, Vol. 29, No. 3, (Aug), pp: 297-130 Darling P. G, Op. cit., p.195.
4. Purananandam, J. and Hanumantha Rao, K. S. (1966), 'Corporate Dividends and Target Payout Ratios in the Indian Cotton Textile Industries 1946-63'. The journal of Industrial Economics, Vol. XV, No. 1, pp: 38-43.
5. Smith Keith, V. (1971), 'Increasing Stream Hypothesis of Corporate Dividend Policy' California Management Review, 14(Fall). pp: 56-64, in George N. Engler, Managerial Finance-Cases and Readings,(ed) .
6. Rao, G.N. and Sarma, Y.S.R. (1971), 'Dividends and Retained Earnings of Public and Private Limited Companies in India, 1955-56. An Econometric Analysis', Reserve Bank of India Bulletin, Vol. 25, No. 6, (June), pp: 860-873.
7. Dhameja, N.L. 1972), 'Dividend Behaviour in Indian Paper Industry 1950-65: A Statistical Test', Indian Economic Journal, Vol. XIX, No.3, pp:432-442.
8. Krishnamurthy, K. and Sastry, D. (1975), 'Some Aspects of Corporate Behaviour in India: A Cross Sectional Analysis of Investments. Dividends and External Finance for the Chemical industry: 1966-67', Indian Economic Review, (Oct), Cited in Braj Kishore, op.cit.,p.198.
9. Agarwal, R. N. (1987), 'Corporate Investment and Financing Behaviour-An Econometric Analysis of Indian Automobile Industry', Delhi, Commonwealth Publishers. pp: 73-90.
10. Mittal, R.K. (1992), Determinants of Corporate Retained Earnings'. Indian Management, Vol. 31, No. 3, pp. 35-38.
11. Kevin, S. (1992), Dividend Policy: An Analysis of Some Determinants', Finance India, Vol. VI, No. 2, pp. 11-20.
12. Bhat, Ramesh and I.M. Pandey, (1994), Dividend Decision: A Study of Managers Perceptions', Decision, Vol. 21, Nos. 1&2, pp: 67-86.
13. Mahesh Chand Garg, Saroj Nagpal and Verma H.L, (1996), Factors Determining Dividend Payments in Textile Industry in India', Vol. X, No.1, pp: 144-156.

14. Jain, P.K. and Khera, B.N. (1996), Dividend of policy of Private Sector Enterprises EA Case study of Engineering Industry', Journal of Accounting and Finance, Vol. X, No. 2, (Sept), pp: 221-243.
15. Jain, P.K. and Manoj Kumar, (1997), Dividend Policy and Practices in Select Corporate Firms of Indian and South-East Asia: A Comparative Study', Vision. Vol. I (2), (July-December), pp: 11-20.

PART - II

WORKING CAPITAL MANAGEMENT

7

WORKING CAPITAL MANAGEMENT IN SUGAR MILLS OF TAMIL NADU—A CASE STUDY

Working capital enables a company to make the best use of the productive capacity established by the expenditure of fixed capital. The study uses 10 sugar mills in Tamil Nadu to determine, with the help of bivariate discriminate analysis, what is the operational adequacy of working capital. Further, inflation account techniques are used, so as to distinguish the impact of inflationary conditions and of efficiency in utilization on the management of working capital.

Developing economies are confronted with the problem of inefficient utilization of the resources available to them. Capital is a limited productive resource in such economies and its proper utilization will promote growth, cut down costs and improve the efficiency of the productive system. Fixed capital and working capital are the two aspects of the total capital of any enterprise. Fixed capital investment generates productive capacity, whereas working capital makes the utilization of that capacity possible. Hence, the study of working capital occupies an important place in financial management. Working capital management which is concerned with short-term financial decisions appears to have been relatively neglected in the literature on finance.

Funds are needed in every business for carrying on day-to-day operations. Working capital funds are, therefore, the lifeblood of a business firm. A firm can work and survive without making profit, but it cannot either survive or work without working capital funds. If a firm is not earning profit it may be termed "sick", but if it does not possess working capital, it is likely to be 'dead', that is to go bankrupt and close. Working capital has acquired great significance with respect to the twin objectives of profitability and liquidity. It takes a great deal of time and effort to increase profitability and simultaneously maintain adequate liquidity at reasonable risk. Hence, the need for skilled working capital management has become greater in recent years. Viewed in this perspective, this study devoted to working capital management could be worthwhile.

Statement of the Problem

The problem of working capital management is the most critical problem in financial management. Most of the time of financial executives is devoted to managing the company's current assets and liabilities, which are the main constituents of working capital. The inefficient management of working capital can lead to loss of profits in the short-run, and ultimately to the downfall of the enterprises. An excessive investment in working capital will lower the enterprises. An excessive investment in working capital will lower the rate of return while inadequate investment will hamper the solvency position, thereby affecting the operation of business. The adequacy of working capital, together with its efficient handling virtually determines the survival or demise of an enterprises. This study attempts, to determine with the use of Bivariate Discriminate Analysis, what if the operational adequacy of working capital.

One of the important areas of working capital management is to study the short-run behaviour of the demand for working capital and its components. The demand for cash has been studied by Baumol (1952), Tobin (1956), and Friedman (1959). Our study, however, is not only limited to the study of the demand for cash but also extends to the demand for inventories, receivables, gross working capital and net working capital. In addition, the problems of working capital management, during inflation are yet to receive due attention from authors on financial management. Therefore, an attempt has been made here to use inflation accounting techniques in working capital management, so as to isolate the relative efficiency in utilization on the management of working capital.

Objectives of the Study

The specific objectives of this study are:

(*i*) To assess the operational adequacy of working capital in the selected sugar industries.

(*ii*) To estimate the demand functions of working capital and its various components; and

(*iii*) To isolate the relative impacts of inflationary conditions and of efficiency in utilization on the management of working capital.

Sampling Selection

There are 31 sugar mills operating in Tamil Nadu of which 14 are in the cooperative sector, 14 in the private sector and 3 in the public sector. Since this study aims to assess various aspects of the problem over a period of time, not all these sugar mills are taken because most of them are just a few years old and unable to provide data for the last ten years. To select the units for study a list of units established before 1975 and having a crushing capacity of 2000 metric tones per day or more was prepared. There were 13 such units, 6 in the cooperative sector and 7 in the private sector. Out of these 13 units, one in the cooperative sector and two in the private sector were excluded because financial statements for the last ten years could not be obtained from them. Thus, finally the ten units selected for the study seem to be important and representative sugar factories of Tamil Nadu. The period of study was 10 years from 1981-82 to 1991-92.

Operation Adequacy of Working Capital – A Bivariate Discriminant Analysis

There is no standard by which to measure the adequacy of working capital. However, practice suggests that the adequacy of working capital can be judged in terms of its relationship to a firm's debts. To establish such a relationship, generally the current and liquid ratios are studied. These ratios measure the technical solvency of a company, but the operational adequacy of working capital can be measured by ascertaining the magnitude of the working capital in relation to the average monthly sales turnover and monthly cost of operations. The present study attempts to apply linear discriminant analysis with only two sets of independent variables.

The sample units were classified into two categorics according to their liquidity ratios. Group A consisted of those units where the current ratio was found to be at least 2:1 while the rest of the units were put into group B. In this study, the adequacy of the quantum of net working capital is treated as dependent variable and the size of the net working capital in terms of the monthly operational requirements (X_1) and the sales requirements (X_2) is treated as an independent variable. The object is to determine the weights for X_1 and X_2 that is the value of 'a' and 'b' in the equation.

$$Z = aX_1 + bX_2$$

Where, z is the discriminant index.

After classifying the selected units into good and poor risk categories, the values of 'a' and 'b' in the discriminant functions are estimated and presented in Table 7.0. The table reveals that the size of the net working capital in terms of the monthly operational requirement appears to be stronger than the sales requirement in all the years except 1983-84 and 1989-90. The discriminant co-efficient given in Table 7.0 was multiplied by the mean value of each industry ratio to obtain the discriminant score of each unit.

Table 7.0

Discriminant Functions for the period 1982-83 to 1991-92

Year	Function	Remark
1982-83	Z =-1.490 a + 6.585 b	b > a
1983-84	Z = 0.422 a + 1.078 b	b > a
1984-85	Z = 0.706 a + 0.172 b	a > b
1985-86	Z = 1.052 a + 1.185 b	b < a
1986-87	Z = 0.091 a + 0.456 b	b > a
1987-89	Z = 1.423 a + 3.638 b	b > a
1989-90	Z = 0.489b a + 1.315b	b > a
1990-91	Z = 0.448 a + 3.291 b	b > a
1991-92	Z = 0.748 a + 4.187 b	b > a

Note: The expression a > b is to be read as "a is greater than b".

Source: Computed.

Table 7.1 presents data relating to the discriminant score of both the groups. With the help of the discriminant scores, the cut off value was calculated as follows:

Table 7.1

Discriminating Z Scores

Units	1982-83	83-84	84-85	85-86	86-87	87-89	89-90	90-91	91-92
ACS	-0.89	1.86	1.29	2.23	0.75	5.09	2.03	3.32	4.65
AMCS	-0.93	0.99	1.99	3.41	0.50	5.01	1.18	3.64	3.93
SCS	-0.65	1.80	1.27	2.62	0.63	4.90	2.51	5.12	8.75
NCS	-1.02	2.67	2.66	2.93	0.54	5.41	2.03	3.20	3.88
KCS	-1.13	1.07	0.93	2.20	0.24	3.34	1.76	5.50	5.23
ASL	0.05	3.26	2.83	6.79	1.57	9.84	2.61	4.86	8.56
SISL	-1.68	1.26	0.78	2.10	0.32	4.37	1.56	2.57	4.32
SSL	-0.17	2.41	1.86	3.98	0.86	8.22	3.52	6.52	6.92
KSL	2.15	2.24	1.50	3.05	0.72	4.63	1.93	6.01	6.80
TASL	0.12	1.25	0.88	1.73	0.52	4.02	1.67	3.27	4.77
Cut of Z Value	-0.41	1.88	1.60	3.10	0.66	5.48	2.08	4.40	5.98

Source: Computed

$$\text{Cut-off value} = \frac{n_1 N_1 + n_2 Z_2}{n_1 + n_2}$$

Where, n_1 and n_2 are the size of the samples and Z_1 and Z_2 represent the mean of the discriminant scores of group A and B respectively. The cut-off values are also presented in Table 7.2. The actual Z scores of the individual units were then compared with the discriminating Z scores. In case the Z scores were found to be more than the discriminating Z scores, it can be said that the size of the net working capital was more than needed by the operational and sales requirements. In case the Z scores were found to be more than the discriminating Z scores, it can be said that the size of the net working capital was more than needed by the operational and sales requirements.

The number of good and poor risk units with reference to the current ratio and the discriminant score are presented in Table 7.2. It is clear from the table that the misclassification does not occur in 1985-86, 1987-89 and 1989-90. Misclassification of units is noticed for the remaining years. Generally one unit in the good risk group has been misclassified under the criteria of discriminant score. Such industries are KSL in 1982-83 and 1983-84, NCS in 1986-87, ACS in 1990-91 and ACS and TASL in 1991-92. To sum up the analysis regarding the operational adequacy of working capital, it can be concluded that the size of working capital of all the selected units except AMCS and TASL was adequate in relation to the output requirements in the recent years 1990-1991 and 1991-92. In addition, NCS and SCS in the cooperative sector and ASL and SSL in the private sector maintained an adequate size of working capital in relation to sales and output requirements throughout the period under study.

Table 7.2

No. of Good and Poor risk industry

Year	As per CR and LR		As per discriminant Score	
	Good	Poor	Good	Poor
1982-83	1	9	4	6
1983-84	4	6	4	6
1984-85	2	8	4	6
1985-86	1	9	3	7
1986-87	3	7	4	6
1987-89	2	8	2	8
1989-90	1	9	3	7
1990-91	5	5	5	5
1991-92	4	6	4	6

Source: Computed

Business Demand for Working Capital

Interest in the study of the demand for working capital by sugar factories in Tamil Nadu has been stimulated by empirical works on the demand for cash. A review of these writings shows that the post-keynesian revival of interest in the demand function for cash has followed two distinct paths. Kamta Prasad (1979) and Lahiri (1981) observed economies of scale thereby supporting Baumol and Tobin, while De Allessi and Bhule LM observed diseconomies of scale thereby supporting Friedman as far as the transaction demand for cash is concerned. Similarly there are no unanimous findings in regard to the effect of capital costs on the demand for cash. Among others, De Allessi (1966) and Nadiri (1969) showed the statistically significant effect of capital costs on the demand for cash, while Friedman (1956) did not find the same in his studies on the demand for cash. It is therefore, difficult to support one view or the other in the context of selected cooperative and private sector sugar industries of Tamil Nadu. However, our investigation is not limited to a study of the demand for cash and inventories only. It is extended to test whether models similar to those explaining the demand for cash and inventories, also explain the demand for receivables, gross working capital and net working capital.

In this study, econometric models are used to describe the income and effects of the interest rate on the demand for working capital and its various components in sugar factories of Tamil Nadu. As a first approximation to the theory, the function may be written as,

$$Y^* = f(S) \ldots\ldots. \text{(i)}$$

$$Y^* = f(S, i_2) \ldots. \text{(ii)}$$

Y^* denotes YI to Y5 where Y1 is real cash, Y2 real inventories, Y3 real receivables, Y4 real gross working capital, Y5 real net working capital and S real sales. Taking the logarithm of this equation gives

$$\log Y^* = \log K + b1 \log S + b2 \log i_2 + u \ldots. \text{(iii)}$$

Where b_1 and b_2 are elasticities of Y^* with respect to the explanatory variables of the models.

The pooled regression results of the model showing the sales (S_{t-1}) effects on the demand for working capital and its components for the total industry are presented in the Table 7.3. The overall results presented in the table are encouraging. The signs of all the coefficients are as expected. The coefficients are also statistically significant and the quality of the fit of the model is also satisfactory.

With respect to the demand for cash by the sugar factories of Tamil Nadu, the results, as indicated by the Table 7.3 support the unitary or more than unitary sales elasticity (value 1.13) hypotheses of Friedman, De Allessi and Bhole L M. The finding contradicts the conclusion of Baumol, Tobin, Kamta Prasad and Lahiri. The results show that cash balances vary more than in proportion to changes in the volume of sales.

Table - 7.3

Estimated Regression Results of Estimating Demand for Working Capital

(Total Industry)

($\log Y = b + b \log S_{t-1}$)

Particulars	Constant	Sales(S_{t-1})	R^2	F
Cash	-1.74	1.13 (2.18)*	0.40	4.74
Inventory	-1.87	1.34 (4.24)*	0.72	17.97
Receivables	-5.16	2.01 (7.70)*	0.89	59.33
Gross Working	-2.08	1.44 (7.29)*	0.88	53.11
Net Working Capital	-2.92	1.57 (5.65)*	0.82	31.94

Figures in bracket show t Value

*Significant at 0.05 level

Source: Computed

Regarding the demand for inventories it may be stated that the results as indicated by Table 7.3 support the unitary or more than unitary sales elasticities (value 1.34) noticed in some of the equations of Lieberman and contradict the findings of Irvine. The results indicated by Table 7.3 show diseconomics of scale with respect to investment in working capital and its components like cash, inventories and receivables. The sales elasticity is more than unity in all cases. It varies from 1.13 for cash to 2.01 for receivables. The diseconomics of scale are thus highest for receivables (2.01) followed by net working capital (1.57), gross working capital (1.44), inventory (1.34) and cash (1.13).

Table 7.5 indicates the effect of sales and capital costs on the estimating demand function of working capital for the total industry. The overall results presented in the table are encouraging and provide an interest rate coefficient with theoretically correct signs. Previously these coefficients of capital cost measures used to be either positive or insignificant in many studies on the demand for cash.

The coefficients of sales are also highly significant and indicate that higher sales increase working capital and its components. The sales elasticity varies from 0.80 for cash to 2.20 for receivables. It is smallest for cash (0.80) followed by inventory (1.70), gross working capital (1.71) net working capital (1.96), and receivables (2.20). With respect to the demand for cash by the total industry, the result as indicated by the table shows that the sales elasticity of cash is consistently less than unity, suggesting economies of scale. This finding again seems to support the theoretical propositions of Baumol, Tobin, Frazer (1964), Nadiri, Kamata Prasad and Lahiri and contradict the propositions of Friedman, Meltzer (1963), Whalen (1965), De Allessi and Bhole (1979) but it is not statistically significant. Similarly, the results seems to support the unitary or more than unitary sales elasticity noticed in some equations of Lieberman and contradict the findings of Irvine where the demand of inventories is concerned.

Contrary to previous studies, the table also shows that fluctuations in cash and inventory levels depend in a significant manner on fluctuations in their financial carrying cost. However, the effect of capital cost in cash is not statistically significant. The effect of capital cost can also be observed for investment in receivables, gross working capital and net working capital. The sign for the interest rate coefficient is not only negative but also statistically significant in all these cases, except for receivables. The estimated elasticities of the target levels of working capital and its components with respect to capital costs indicate that the target level of net working capital is much more sensitive to capital cost fluctuations than the target level of cash, inventory, receivables and gross working capital. Among these, the target level of receivables is least sensitive to fluctuations in capital costs. All this can be seen from the interest rate elasticity of 2.91 for cash, 3.17 for inventory, 1.68 for receivables, 2.34 for gross working capital and 3.34 for net working capital (Table 7.4).

Table 7.4 reveals other facts also. Holding the sales constant, the result indicates that one percentage point increase in interest rate leads, on an average, to a 2.91 per cent decline in the cash balances. Similarly this kind of decline is noticed to be about 3.17 per cent for inventories, 1.68 per cent for gross working capital and 3.34 per cent for net working capital balance when there is one percentage point increase in interest rate. In the same way, holding the interest rate constant, one per cent point increase in sales leads on an average to about 0.80 per cent increase in the cash balance. This increase is seen to be about 1.70 per cent for inventories, 2.20 per cent of receivables, 1.71 per cent for gross working capital and 1.96 per cent for net working capital balances. The table also indicates that the fit of the model is satisfactory except in the case of cash.

Table 7.4
(Estimated for Working Capital) Estimated Regression Results of estimating Demand for working capital (Total Industry)
($\log Y = b_0 + b_1 \log S_{t-1} - b_2 \log i_2$)

Particulars	Constant	Sales(S_{t-1})	i_2	R^2	F
Cash	3.22	0.80	-2.91	0.48	2.76
		(1.25)	(0.93)		
Inventory	-7.39	1.70	-3.17	0.83	15.06
		(5.36)*	(2.03)*		
Receivables	-8.09	2.20	-1.68	0.91	31.22
		(7.08)*	(1.11)		
Gross Working	-6.14	1.71	-2.34	0.95	56.69
Capital		(10.06)	(2.81)*		
Net Working	-8.72	1.96	-3.34	0.93	37.09
Capital		(8.83)*	(2.90)*		

Figures in bracket show t Value

*Significant at 0.05 level

Source: Computed

Isolating Inflationary Effects of Working Capital

Inflation means a rise in the general level of prices or a fall in the purchasing power of money. India is today in the grip of severe inflation and prices are likely to move forward at a forward at a fast rate. The continuous upward movement in price has caused prices of industrial machinery and inputs to increase. One need not mention that the inflationary situation obtaining at present has made it necessary for financial managers to arrange larger funds for fixed and working capital requirements. However, the problems of working capital management during inflation are yet to receive due attention from authors on financial management.

Hence, in this section, an attempt is made to isolate the relative impacts of inflationary conditions and of efficiency in utilization on the management of working capital. For this purpose, it is assumed that the most significant empirical relationship displayed by working capital is with sales. Based on such an assumption, the relationship between sales and working capital changes due to inflation are studied in the sugar mills of Tamil Nadu from 1982-83 to 1991-92. Relevant figures like sales and working capital were obtained from the published accounts of the various mills. To isolate the impact of inflation, wholesale price indices of the sugar industry, with 1981-82 =100, as provided in RBI Bulletins were used.

The following simple model is used for the relationship between working capital and the price indices, using actual data.

(i) For sales (in rupees)

S_1 = S_0+ M + N, where

S_1 = actual sales in year 1

S_0 = actual sales in base year

M = Change in sales value due to the effect of inflation price.

N = real change in working capital.

(ii) For working capital (in rupees)

WC_1 = WC_0 + X + Y, where

WC_1 = actual working capital in year 1

WC_0 = actual working capital in base year

X = change in working capital due to the effect of inflation price

Y = real change in working capital.

The objective is to find out the values of M, N, X and Y for each year for the sugar mills of Tamil Nadu and the results are present in Table 7.5. These results show the segregation of inflationary effects on sales revenue and working capital. They help to obtain a clear picture of the real movements in these two variables. The ratio of the real working capital change to the real sales change, Y/N is shown in the table for each year to help in judging the effect of efficiency on working capital management. A negative Y/N ratio indicates that a real sales increase has been accompanied by a real fall in the working capital employed.

If a negative Y/N ratio is due to increased real sales and lower real working capital, this would indicate efficiency; the converse combination, although still showing a negative ratio, suggests inefficiency. A positive Y/N ratio will be produced when both Y and N move in the same direction in a given year. But if a high positive Y/N ratio is produced because the real change in working capital (Y) is more than the real change in sales, then this is indicative of reduced efficiency. Conversely if a positive Y/N ratio is due to Y having coming down more than N, then this would indicate higher efficiency. Thus, efficiency in utilisation of working capital must be related to the original direction of movement of the variables Y and N themselves.

Table 7.5
Total Industry – Sales and Working Capital Changes – Incremental
Amount Only (Base Year 1982-83=100)

Year	Inflationary S(M)	Change WC(X)	Real S(N)	Change WC/S	WC/S Y/N
1983-84	173	60	-319	-1397	-4.38
1984-85	908	316	-546	-1485	2.72
1985-86	3345	1164	819	-1053	-1.28
1986-87	3720	1295	4431	-903	-0.20
1987-89	5248	1826	9218	45	0.005
1989-90	7541	2624	10258	609	0.06
1990-91	7541	2624	6522	9401	1.44
1991-92	9819	3417	13770	10607	0.77

Source: Computed

In the sugar industry of Tamil Nadu as a whole, it is evident from the table that the Y/N ratios are –1.28 and –0.20 in 1985-86 and 1986-87 respectively. This means that for every rupee of real increase in sales, there has been a real fall of Re.1.28 and RE.0.20 respectively in working capital used during this period. This shows efficient working capital management. Among the positive Y/N ratios, the one of 1990-91 shows that the real change in working capital has been Rs.9401 lakhs more than the real change in sales (Rs.6522 lakhs). This is indicative of a reduced efficiency in working capital use. Working capital management in 1987-89, 1989-90 and 1991-92 (positive Y/N ratio) may be said to be efficient because the real change in sales is greater than the change in working capital. It is also evident from the table that in 1983-84 and 1984-85, the real decrease in working capital was more than the real decrease in sales, indicating an improved efficiency in the working capital management of the sugar factories of Tamil Nadu.

Conclusion

From this study, it is concluded that Discriminant Analysis has been a useful technique to analyse the operational adequacy of working capital of business enterprises. Further, the regression results strongly suggest that the demand for working capital and its components is a function of both sales and holding costs. It should also be pointed out that the procedure of the analysis and the logic of the interpretation have proved useful in studying the efficiency of working capital management by Tamil Nadu sugar mills during inflation.

References

1. Baumol, W. (Nov.1952), "The Transactions Demand for Cash; An Inventory theoretic approach", *Quarterly Journal of economics.*
2. Bhole, L.M. (1979), "An empirical study of liquidity Preference of Corporate Sector in India, 1951-1974", *Indian Economic Journal. Vol.27, No.1.*
3. De Allessi (August 1966), "The Demand for Money: a cross section study of British business firms", *Economica."*
4. Frazer, W.J. (April 1964),"Financial structure of Manufacturing corporations and the demand for money: some empirical findings," *Journal of Political Economy.*
5. Friedman, M. [August 1956], 'The Demand for Money: some theoretical and empirical results", *Journal of Political Economy.*
6. Irwin, F.O. (September 1981), "Retail Inventory and the cost of capital", *The American Economic Review.*
7. Kamta Prasad, & Others (July-September 1979), "Business Demand for money in India- A Temporal Cross-section Analysis", *Indian Economic Journal,* Vol. 27 No.1.
8. Lahiri, Ashok Kumar (1981), "Liquidity Behaviour on Indian Business Firms", *Indian Economic Journal*, Vol. 29, No. 11.
9. Liberman, Charles (August 1980), "Inventory Demand and cost of capital Effect", *Review of Economic and Statistics.*
10. Meltzer, Allan, H. (August 1963), 'the Demand for money: A cross-section study of Business Firms", *Quarterly Journal of Economics.*
11. Nadiri, M. I. (May 1969), "The Determinants of Real Cash Balance in the US Total Manufacturing Sector", *Quarterly Journal of Economics.*
12. Tobin, J. (August 1956), "The interest elasticity of transactions demand for cash", *Review of Economics and Statistics.*

13. Whalen, E. L. (September 1965), "A Cross-section study of Business Demand for Cash", *Journal of Finance.*

List of Sugar Mills Studied

1. Ambur Cooperative Sugars Ltd. (ACS)
2. Amaravati Cooperative Sugars Ltd. (ACSL)
3. Salem Cooperative sugars Ltd. (SCS)
4. National Cooperative Sugars Ltd. (NCS)
5. Kallakurichi Cooperative Sugars Ltd. (KCS)
6. Aruna Sugars Ltd. (ASL)
7. South India Sugars Ltd. (SIS)
8. Sakthi Sugars Ltd.(SSL)
9. Kothari Sugars Ltd. (KSL)
10. Thiru Arooran Sugars Ltd. (TASL)

8

RESPONSIVENESS OF WORKING CAPITAL MANAGEMENT—A CASE STUDY OF TAMIL NADU SUGAR CORPORATION

The Developing economies are generally faced with the problem of inefficient utilization of resources available to them. Capital is the scarcest productive resource in such economies and proper utilization of these resources promotes the rate of growth, cuts down the cost of production and above all improves the efficiency of the productive system. Fixed capital and working capital are the dominant contributors to the total capital of the developing country. Fixed capital investment generates production capacity whereas working capital makes the utilization of that capacity possible. Thus, the study of working capital behavior occupies an important place in financial management. The earlier emphasis of financial management was more on long – term financial decisions. Working capital management which is concerned with short – term financial decisions appears to have been relatively neglected in the literature of finance. Leslie R. Howard[1], rightly pointed out that a deeper understanding of the importance of working capital and its satisfactory provision can lead not only to material savings in the economical use of capital but can also assists in furthering the ultimate aim of a business, namely, that of maximizing financial returns on the minimum amount of capital which need to be employed. In addition, working capital has acquired a great significance and sound position for the twin objects of "Profitability and liquidity". All the above factors clearly indicate the crucial importance of working capital in the management of finance. Viewed in this perspective, the study devoted to working capital management may be very rewarding one.

Justification for the study

Importance of working capital management stems from the two reasons viz., (i) a substantial portion of total investment is invested in current assets and (ii) level of current assets will change quickly with the variation in sales. Hence, in this study an attempt has been made to analyze the size and composition of working capital and whether such an investment has increased or declined over a period of time. After determining the requirements of current assets, one of the important tasks of the financial manager is to select an assortment of appropriate sources of finance for the current assets. Normally, the excess of current assets over current liabilities should be financed by long – term sources. Precisely it is not possible to find out which long – term source has been used to finance current assets, but it can be examined as to what proportion of current assets has been financed by long – term funds. Therefore, an attempt has been made in this regard.

In working capital analysis, the direction of change over a period of time is of crucial importance. Not only that, analysis of working capital trends provides a base to judge whether the practice and prevailing policy of the management with regard to working capital is good enough or an improvement is to be made in managing the working capital funds. Hence in this study, an attempt is made about the trend of the working capital management of the selected enterprise. In addition, to have higher profitability, the firms may sacrifice solvency and maintained a relatively low level of current assets. When the firms do so, their profitability will improve as less funds are tied up in the idle current assets, but their solvency will be threatened. Hence, an attempt is made to study the association of profitability with the working capital ratios.

With this end in view, an effort has been made in this article to make an indepth study of a public sector sugar factory in Tamilnadu, in respect of its performance and its working capital management. The findings of this study not only throw light on technical weakness in the managerial activities of the companies, but may also help scholars and researchers to develop new ideas, techniques and methods in respect of the management of working capital.

Data and Methodology

For this study, one major public sector sugar industry namely Tamilnadu Sugar Corporation (TASCO) has been purposively selected. The period of study covers from 1985 – 86 to 1993 – 94. The study covers mainly the following aspects working capital analysis. (i) Component wise analysis (ii) Financing of working capital (iii) Trends of working capital and (iv) Working capital impacts on profitability. The data for the study was collected from the annual reports of the selected units. Statistical techniques namely co – efficient of correlation and multiple regression are used for analyzing the data.

In this study, for the purpose of establishing definite relationship between working capital ratios and profitability ratios, correlation analysis has been applied. It implies the interdependence of the set of variables. Further, in order to identify the influence of profitability, a linear multiple regression model were used.

In the analysis, working capital ratios viz., CR, LR, WTR, ITR, RTR and WC/TA are taken as the independent variables and Profit Before Tax (PBT) to total assets ratios is used as dependent variable. However, in the course of analysis, it was found that CR and RTR are highly correlated. Therefore, CR and RTR are omitted for the analysis. The model used was

$$PBT/TA = b_0 + b_1\,LR + b_2\,WTR + b_3\,ITR + b_4\,WC/TA$$

Where b_0, b_1, b_2, b_3, and b_4 are parameters to be estimated.

Results and Discussion

1.1 Working Capital Analysis

It is evident from Table 8.0 that the size of current assets have increased from Rs. 1121.6 lakhs in 1985–86 to Rs. 3849.8 lakhs in 1993–94, the increase being approximately 3.43 times. Moreover, the increase in current assets has been regular throughout the period except in 1986–87 was due to more decrease in inventory component of the selected units. The table also indicates that on an average 47.79 per cent of the total assets of the company are current assets. This signifies that during this period the major portion of the total investment of the TASCO has been made on the working capital. The share of current assets to total assets which was 42.65 per cent in 1985–86, decreased to 39.09 per cent in 1989–90 and afterwards increased to 56.12 per cent in 1993–94. The share of current assets to total assets shows increasing trend since from 1990 –91 onwards. A component – wise analysis of the working capital was also done to trace the factors responsible for the significant changes in different years. From the table it is evident that the two components namely inventory and loans and advances contributed and average of 67 per cent and 15 per cent respectively towards the gross working capital, whereas cash and bank, sundry debtors and other current assets contributed 14, 3 and 1 per cent respectively. The share of different components of current assets during the study period shows fluctuation trend in TASCO.

Table 8.0
Components of Working Capital

(Rs. in lakhs)

Particulars	1985 – 86	86 – 87	87 – 89	89-90	90 – 91	91 – 92	92 – 93	93 – 94
Cash & Bank	119.4 (10.65)	423.9 (40.52)	228.5 (12.64)	555.3 (28.85)	180.0 (6.29)	127.0 (3.84)	235.7 (6.65)	223.2 (5.80)
Inventory	812.3 (72.42)	469.4 (44.87)	1299.7 (71.88)	883.0 (45.88)	2098.8 (73.37)	2510.3 (76.0)	2641.7 (74.51)	2957.2 (76.81)
S. Debtors	5.05 (0.45)	18.65 (1.78)	32.41 (1.80)	105.6 (5.48)	138.87 (4.58)	132.96 (4.02)	102.60 (2.89)	120.27 (3.12)
Loans & Advances	182.8 (16.3)	128.6 (12.29)	240.7 (13.31)	364.1 (18.92)	424.5 (14.84)	516.31 (15.63)	542.85 (15.31)	528.68 (13.73)
Other CA	2.07 (0.18)	5.55 (0.54)	6.59 (0.37)	16.32 (0.87)	17.61 (0.65)	16.60 (0.51)	22.68 (0.64)	20.46 (0.54)
Total	1121.6 (100)	1046.1 (100)	1807.9 (100)	1924.3 (100)	2859.8 (100)	3303.2 (100)	3545.5 (100)	3849.8 (100)
Ratio of CA to TA	42.65	39.95	49.46	39.09	49.27	52.13	53.65	56.12

Figures in the bracket show the percentage to total.

Source: Computed from Annual Reports of the respective units.

1.2. Financing of Working Capital

One of the important tasks of the financial manager is to select an assortment of appropriate sources to finance the current assets. A business firm has various sources to meet its financial requirements. Normally, the current assets of a firm are supported by a combination of long–term and short–term sources of financing. In Table 8.1, an attempt has been made to explain the relative importance of long – term and short–term debt in financing working capital. It is evident from the table that the percentage of long–term funds used for financing working capital has shown fluctuating trend during the period under study. It increased from 15.70 per cent in 1985–86 to 28.78 per cent in 1987–89 and afterwards it decreased to 6.72 per cent in 1991–92. In 1992–93, it is further increased to 11.59 per cent and finally, it is decreased to 9.71 per cent in 1993 – 94. This decreasing trend shows that TASCO utilized its long – term funds more effectively by investing them in the Fixed Assets. It also depicts the fact that the capability of the TASCO to make efficient management of its current assets namely receivables and inventories.

Table 8.1

Financing of Working Capital

(Rs. in lakhs)

Particulars	1985 – 86	86 – 87	87 – 89	89 – 90	90 – 91	91 – 92	92 – 93	93 – 94
Gross Working Capital	1121.6	1046.1	1807.9	1924.3	2859.8	3303.2	3545.5	3849.8
Sources of Working Capital								
(a) L.T.	280.9	631.3	746.8	742.8	529.8	218.5	462.6	418.51
(b) S.T.	840.6	414.8	1061.0	1181.7	2330.8	3084.6	3082.9	3431.26
Total Long – Term Funds	1788.9	2203.3	2594.0	3443.4	3473.0	3251.5	3989:6	4310.03
% of L.T. Funds used for Working Capital	15.70	28.65	28.78	21.57	15.23	6.72	11.59	9.71

Source: Computed from Annual Reports.

1.3 Working Capital Trend

In working capital analysis the direction of change over a period of time is of crucial importance. Emphasizing the importance of analysis of working capital trends, Man Mohan and Goyal[2] have pointed out that it provides a base to judge whether the practice and prevailing policy of the management with regard to working capital

Table 8.2

Original and Trend Values of Working Capital

(Rs. in lakhs)

Year	Original Working Capital	Trend Value
1985 – 86	458.68	419.09
1986 – 87	713.61	697.60
1987 – 89	929.41	976.11
1989 – 90	926.45	1254.62
1990 – 91	1817.25	1533.13
1991 – 92	1988.97	1811.64
1992 – 93	2056.48	2090.15
1993 – 94	2260.30	2368.66

(Y/C = 140.58 + 278.51 X (Origin of X: 1985 – 86). X in units of years)

Source: Computed

is good enough or an improvement is to be made in managing the working capital funds. The working capital trend of TASCO is presented in Table 8.2. It is evident from the table that the working of TASCO marked an increasing trend during the period under review except in 1989–90. The net working capital of TASCO increased to Rs. 2260.30 lakhs in 1993–94 from Rs. 458.68 lakhs in 1985–86. The linear least square trend values of working capital in TASCO are also shown in Table 8.3. The yearly increase in working capital comes to Rs. 278.51 lakhs. The difference in actual and trend values were negative in the years 1987–88, 1989–90, 1992–93 and 1993–94 while they were positive in the remaining years. The calculated value of Chi – square is 167.69 while the table value of chi – square only 14.07 at 5 per cent level of significance. So it can be observed that in TASCO, the differences between the actual and trend values of working capital are significant because the calculated value of chi – square exceeds the table value of chi – square.

1.4 Impact of Working Capital on Profitability

In order to judge the liquidity position and its impact on profitability, it is necessary to analyze the different working capital ratios as exhibited in Table 8.3. It appears from the table that current ratio of TASCO has moved between 1.69 to 3.15 during the

Table 8.3

Impact of Working Capital on Profitability

Years	CR	LR	WTR	ITR	RTR	CTR	WC/TA	PBT
1985 – 86	1.69	0.47	3.76	2.12	9.19	14.45	0.17	0.05
1986 – 87	3.15	1.73	3.75	5.70	18.29	6.31	0.27	0.02
1987 – 89	2.06	0.58	3.88	2.78	13.21	15.80	0.25	0.02
1989 – 90	1.93	1.04	4.05	4.25	7.98	6.75	0.20	0.10
1990 – 91	2.74	0.73	1.40	1.21	4.50	14.09	0.31	-0.04
1991 – 92	2.51	0.60	1.95	1.54	5.97	30.54	0.31	0.00
1992 – 93	2.52	0.76	1.68	2.17	6.97	35.46	0.42	0.02
1993 – 94	2.48	0.81	2.16	2.42	5.28	18.26	0.28	0.08
Co – efficient of Correlation (r)	**-0.514**	**0.117**	**0.537**	**0.420**	**0.026**	**-0.303**	**-0.494**	

CR – Current Ratio; LR – Liquid Ratio; RTR – Receivables Turnover Ratio; CTR – Cash Turnover Ratio; WC/TA – Working Capital to Total Assets; PBT – Profit before to Total Assets

Source: Computed

period of study. On an average, it stands at 2.39 for the entire period. Conventionally, a standard of 2.1 is considered satisfactory. It is thus, discerned that the liquidity of TASCO, as measured by the current ratio is satisfactory. This signifies that the margin of safety available to short–term creditors to relatively high i.e., for every rupee of current liability the cushion available is Rs. 1.39. The co – efficient of correlation between the profitability ratio and current ratio of TASCO is 0.514. This indicates that there is a high degree of negative correlation between the two variables.

The liquid ratio of the TASCO has moved between 0.47 to 1.73 during the entire period of study which is moderately good, as compared to the standard norm of 1:1, except in the years 1985 – 86, 1987 – 89, and 1991 – 92. The co – efficient of correlation between the two variables. The correlation between profitability ratio and working capital turnover ratio indicates a moderate positive correlation of 0.537, whereas the correlation between profitability ratio and inventory turnover ratio and receivables turnover ratio indicates a moderate correlation co – efficient of 0.420 and 0.026 respectively. The correlation co – efficient between profitability ratio and cash turnover ratio and working capital to total assets indicates a negative correlation co – efficient of 0.303 and 0.494 respectively. Thus, the correlation analysis showed that LR, WTR, ITR and RTR have shown positive correlation with profitability ratio and CR, CTR and WC/TA have shown negative correlation with profitability ratio.

1.5 Multiple Regression Analysis

The pooled regression results of the model showing the impact of working capital ratios on profitability for the TASCO are presented in Table 1.5. The table indicates that the impact of liquid ratio, working capital turnover ratio, inventory turnover ratio and working capital to total assets ratio were statistically significant as seen from the value of regression co–efficient. For a unit increase in liquid ratio, profitability decreased by 0.556 unit which was statistically significant at 5 per cent level. Similarly, one unit increase in working capital turnover ratio would decrease the profitability by 0.163 units which is also significant at 5 per cent level. The co–efficient of regression between the profitability ratio and inventory turnover ratio is computed as 0.215 which implies that one unit increase in inventory turnover ratio would increase the profitability by 0.215 units and this co–efficient also statistically valid at 5 per cent level. It is also inferred from the table that one unit increase in working capital to total assets ratio would decrease the profitability by 0.857 units.

Table 8.4
Multiple Regression Analysis

Variables	Beta Co - efficient Value	t - Value	Significant/ Insignificant
Constant	0.601 (0.098)	6.09*	Significant
LR	-0.556 (0.083)	-6.74*	Significant
WTR	-0.163 (0.027)	-5.97*	Significant
ITR	0.215 (0.031)	6.87*	Significant
WC/TA	-0.857 (0.162)	-5.29*	Significant
R Squared	0.9583		
Adjusted R Squared	0.9027		
Overall F	17.23*		

* - Significant at 5% level

Source: Computed

The four independent variables contribute 96 per cent of the variations in the profitability of the TASCO. Thus, the overall results presented in the table are encouraging. The signs of all the co–efficient are as expected. The co–efficient are also statistically significant.

Comments

(*i*) The average percentage of current assets to total assets is 47.79 which indicates that the company has made investment in working capital following a moderate approach.

(*ii*) Of the components of working capital, inventory (67 per cent) and loans and advances (15 per cent) are the dominant contributory causes for the galloping increase in working capital.

(*iii*) The decreasing trend of long – term funds used for financing the working capital shows that the TASCO has to utilize its long–term funds more effectively by investing them in fixed assets.

(*iv*) The company has experienced excess of working capital in all the years under study.

(*v*) The liquidity position of the TASCO is satisfactory during the study period. The two liquidity ratios, current ratio and liquid ratio, remained equal or above the standard norms throughout the study periods.

(*vi*) The impact of working capital ratios on profitability showed both negative and positive impacts.

(*vii*) With the help of a multiple regression model, it is inferred that due to excess of current assets, the profitability of TASCO is adversely affected.

Conclusion

The above study generally indicates a moderate trend in the financial position and the utilization of working capital, variations in working capital size should be avoided. Attempts should also be made to use funds more effectively, by keeping an optimum level of working capital. Because, keeping more current assets causes a reduction in profitability. Hence efforts should be made to ensure a positive trend in the estimation and maintenance of the working capital.

References

1. Leslie R. Howard, "*Working capital – Its Management and Control*", Mac Donald & Evans Ltd., London. 1971, p.2.
2. Man Mohan and Goyal, "Principles of Management Accounting" Sahitya Prakash, Agra. 1979, p.368.
3. Keith V. Smith, "State of the Art of Working Capital Management", in issues in *Managerial Finance*, Eugene F. Brigham and Ramon E. Johnson, Eds. (Illionis; the Dryden press 1976). p. 63.
4. Panigrahi, "Working Capital Management, the Case of Large Indian Companies", *The Management Accountant*, Oct. 1990, pp. 653 – 656.
5. H.L. Verma, "*Management of Working Capital*", M/S. Deep & Deep publications, New Delhi 1989.

9

ESTIMATING DEMAND FUNCTIONS OF WORKING CAPITAL—PARTIAL ADJUSTMENT MODEL

It is well known that working capital management may be the factor that decides success or failure of business enterprises. The efficient working capital management can significantly affect the firms risk, return and share price, Management of working capital has acquired a great significance and sound position for the twin objects of 'Profitability and Liquidity'. In a period of raising capital costs and scarce funds the working capital is one of the most important areas requiring management review. It consumes a great deal of time to increase profitability as well as to maintain; proper liquidity at minimum risk.

Statement of the problem

One of the areas of working capital management is to study the nature of short – run behaviour of the demand for working capital. Interest in the study of the demand for working capital has been stimulated by the empirical works of the demand for cash. A review of the empirical works on the demand for cash showed that Frazer, Nadiri[2], and Kamta Prasad[3] observed economics of scale thereby supporting Baumol[4] and Tobin[5], while Meltzer[6], De Allessi[7] and Bhole L.M.[8] observed diseconomics of scale thereby supporting Friedman[9] as far as the transaction demand for cash is concerned. Similarly, there is no unanimous finding as regards the effect of capital costs on the demand for cash. It has therefore become difficult to support one view or another in the context of Indian Public Sector Enterprises.

Further it has been extended to test whether models similar to those explaining the demand for cash, also explain the demand for inventories, receivables, gross working capital and net working capital. The study also describe the effect of capital costs on working capital holdings. The study also takes into account a partial adjustment model of working capital behaviour. It indicates the speed with which firms adjust their actual working capital balances to the desired working capital balances.

Data and methodology

The Bureau of public enterprise brings out the official annual reports of the public enterprises in India. The necessary data on working capital and other related variables used in this study have been collected mostly from these reports. The necessary data are collected for the 15 years from 1981 – 96. The econometric models are employed in this study, which are described in the following paragraph.

Econometric models

The decision about the aggregate amount of working capital and its various components to be held may be regard as subject to wealth constraint and opportunity cost of working capital. As a first approximation to the theory, the function may be written as;

$$Y^* = f(W, i) \quad \text{........(1.1)}$$

Where Y* - Real desired cash, inventories, receivables, gross working capital and net working capital; W – Real desired wealth defined in terms of sales (S_{t-1}); i – Opportunity cost of working capital measured by the short – term interest rates of Indian Commercial Banks. In an empirical investigation, it takes the form –

$$Y^* = K\, W^{b1}\, i^{b2}\, e^{u} \quad \text{.........(1.2)}$$

Where U is assumed to be independently and normally distributed. Taking the natural logarithm,

$$\text{Ln } Y^* = K + b_1 \text{ Ln } W + b_2 \text{ Ln } i + U_1 \quad \text{...........(1.3)}$$

Where b_1 and b_2 are elasticity's of Y* with respect to the explanatory variables of the models. While estimating the above equations the figures of working capital and its components and sales have been deflated by using the National Urban Consumer Price Index.

Partial adjustment model

This model hypothesizes that each enterprise has a desired target level of working capital and that each enterprise, finding its actual working capital not equal to its optimum, attempts only a partial adjustment towards the optimum level within any one period. The models indicate the speed with which firms adjust their actual working capital balances to the desired working capital balances. The equation to be estimated is :

$$\text{Ln } Y^* = C_0 + C_1 \text{ Ln } S_{t-1} + C_2 \text{ Ln } i + (1\text{-}\emptyset) \text{ Ln } Y_{t-1} + U \text{ ....(1.4)}$$

Where, C_1 and C_2 is the short – term elasticities of working capital or its components with respect to sales and their opportunity cost, respectively and $\emptyset$ – rate of adjustment co-efficient.

Empirical Findings

Scale and capital cost effects on demand functions of working capital

The pooled regression results of the model showing the scale and capital cost effects on demand functions of working capital and its components are presented in Table 9.0. The overall results presented in the table are encouraging. The signs of all the co–efficients are as expected and the goodness of fit of the model is also satisfactory. It is evident from the table that the co–efficients of sales are highly significant except inventory and indicate that higher sales increase working capital and its components. The sales elasticity varies from 0.99 for net working capital to 3.34 for inventory. Thus, the sales elasticity is smallest for net working capital followed by gross working capital, receivables, cash and inventories. These elasticities

Table 9.0

Estimated demand for working capital in Indian public sector enterprises (1981 – 1996)

$$[\text{Ln } Y^* = \text{Ln } a + b_1 \text{ Ln } S_{t-1} - b_2 \text{ Ln } i]$$

Dependent Variables	Regression (S_{t-1})	Co – efficient (i)	R^2	Adj R^2	F value	D.W.
Cash	1.96 (9.123)*	-0.029 (0.88)	0.96	0.95	134.9	1.18
Inventory	3.34 (0.477)	-0.018 (1.51)**	0.88	0.86	41.1	0.99
Receivables	1.59 (9.40)*	-0.024 (0.81)	0.94	0.93	89.3	0.58
Gross Working Capital	1.08 (9.43)	-0.019 (0.89)	0.94	0.91	91.72	0.59
Net Working Capital	0.99 (6.22)*	-0.036 (1.14)	0.89	0.87	45.1	0.56

* Significant at 1 percent level. ** Significant at 10 percent level.

Figures in parenthesis denotes 't' value. D.W. – Durban Waston Static's

Source: Computed

are consistently more than unity in all cases except net working capital, suggesting diseconomies of scale. This finding seems to support the theoretical propositions of Friedman and contradict the propositions of Baumol and Tobin, as far as the demand for cash by the Indian public sector enterprises is concerned.

The estimated elasticities of the target levels of working capital and its components with respect to capital costs measure indicate that the target level of net working capital is much more sensitive to capital cost fluctuations as compared to the target level of cash, inventories, receivables and gross working capital. Among these, the target level of inventory is least sensitive to fluctuations in capital costs. It can be seen from the interest rate elasticity of 0.018 for inventory, 0.019 for gross working capital, 0.024 for receivables, 0.029 for cash and 0.036 for net working capital.

Holding the sales constant, Table 9.0 indicates that a one percentage point increase in interest rate leads on an average to about a 0.03 per cent decline in the cash balances. Similarly, this kind of decline is noticed to be about 0.02 per cent for inventory, 0.03 per cent for receivables, 0.02 per cent for net working capital balances when there is a one percentage point increase in interest rate. In the same way, holding the interest rate constant, a one percentage point increase in sales leads on an average to about 1.96 per cent increase in cash balances. This kind of increase is noticed to be about 3.34 per cent for inventories, 1.59 percentage for receivables, 1.08 per cent for gross working capital and 0.99 per cent for net working capital. The increase in target cash, receivables, inventories and working capital as a whole due to the increase in the capital cost may mean higher production and higher employment.

Partial adjustment model

The partial adjustment models have been widely in the studies on the demand for cash. In order to know firms adjust their actual working capital to their desired working capital and to know whether this kind of adjustment is rapid or slow in Indian Public Sector Enterprises, an attempt has been made in this section to show the nature of adjustment between desired and actual balances of cash, inventories, receivables and gross and net working capital. The estimated regression results are presented in Table 9.1.

The regression results indicated that coefficients of Y_{t-1} are significant in all cases. The coefficient of the lagged dependent variable has been observed to be 0.59 for cash, 0.57 for inventory, 0.85 for receivables, 0.82 for gross working capital and 0.88 for net working capital. Since the coefficient of lag Ln Y_t is equal to 1 minus the adjustment coefficient (1- Ø), the adjustment coefficient is equal to 0.41 for cash, 0.43 for inventory, 0.15 for receivables, 0.18 for gross working capital and 0.12 for net working capital. It seems that 41 per cent of the adjustment of actual to desired real cash balances is completed within one year. Similarly, the adjustment speed of actual to desired balance is 43 per cent for inventory, 15 per cent for receivables, 18 per cent for gross working and only 12 per cent for net working capital. The speed of adjustment is however highest for inventory followed by cash, receivables, gross working capital and net working capital.

Table 9.1
Partial adjustment model
[Ln Y* + C_0 + C_1 Ln $S_{(t-1)}$ + C_2 Ln i + (1-Ø) Ln Y_{t-1} + U]

Dependent Variables	Regression (S_{t-1})	Co - efficient (i)	(Y_{t-1})	R^2	Adj R^2	F value	D.W.
Cash	0.828	-0.002	-0.585	0.99	0.98	274.9	1.65
	(3.21)*	(0.09)	(4.76)*				
Inventory	0.095	-0.013	-0.568	0.95	0.93	61.3	1.03
	(1.17)	(1.56)**	(3.59)*				
Receivables	0.171	-0.003	0.846	0.99	0.99	493.6	0.68
	(0.98)	(0.22)	(8.74)*				
Gross Working Capital	0.117	-0.001	0.816	0.96	0.95	504.3	0.69
	(1.05)	(0.09)	(8.69)*				
Net Working Capital	0.115	-0.002	0.876	0.98	0.97	152.5	0.65
	(0.73)	(0.09)	(6.39)*				

* Significant at 1 per cent level. ** Significant at 10 per cent level.
Figures in parenthesis denotes 't' value.
D.W. – indicates that there is no auto correlation.
Source: Computed

Conclusion

To sum up, the studies concerning the demand for cash by business firms did not report unanimous findings. A lot of controversies exist with respect to the presence of economies of scale, role of capital costs and speed with which actual cash and inventory are adjusted to desired cash and inventory, respectively. This study has investigated these various issues by using the data of Indian public sector enterprises. Besides, a similar type of investigation has also been extended to receivables, gross working capital and net working capital.

The pooled regression results show the presence of diseconomics of scale with respect to the demand for working capital and its various components except inventory. The demand for inventories of Indian public sector enterprises only show economics of scale during the study period. The diseconomics of scale are highest for cash followed by receivables, gross and net working capital. The results suggest strongly that the demand for working capital and its components is a function of both sales and their holding costs. The capital cost efficients are all with theoretically correct signs but it is statistically significant only in the case of inventory. Further, the adjustment speed of actual to desired balances of working capital and its various components has been observed to be higher in the Indian public sector enterprises.

References

1. Frazer, W.J. (April 1964), "Financial Structure of Manufacturing Corporation and the demand for money; some empirical findings", The Journal of Political Economy, pp. 176 – 183.
2. Nadiri, M.I. (May, 1969), "An Empirical Study of Liquidity preference of corporate sector in India", The Indian Economic Journal, Vol. 27, No.1, pp. 65 – 80.
3. Kamta Prasad and Sampath, R.K. (July – Sept. 1979), "Business Demand for money in India – A Temporal Cross–section Analysis", The Indian Economic Journal, Vol. 27, No.1, pp. 46 – 62.
4. Baumol, W. (Nov. 1952), "The Transactions demands for Cash; An inventory theoretic approach", The Quarterly Journal of Economics, pp. 545 – 566.
5. Tobin, J. (Aug. 1956), "The interest elasticity of Transactions demand for cash", The review of economics and statistics, pp. 241 – 247.
6. Meltzer, A.H. (Aug. 1963), "The Demand for money; A cross section study of business firms", The Quarterly Journal of Economics, pp. 405 – 422.
7. De Allessi (Aug. 1966), "The Demand for money; A cross section study of British Business Firms", Economica, pp. 288 – 320.
8. Bhole, L.M. (1979), "An empirical study of liquidity preference of corporate sectors in India, 1951 – 1974", The Indian Economic Journal, Vol. 27, No. 1, pp. 65 – 80.
9. Friedman, M. (Aug. 1959), "The demand for money – some theoretical and empirical results", The Journal of Political Economy, pp. 327 – 351.

10

OPERATIONAL ADEQUACY OF WORKING CAPITAL IN SUGAR INDUSTRY OF TAMIL NADU—A BIVARIATE DISCRIMINANT ANALYSIS APPROACH

Fixed capital and working capital are the dominant contributors to the total capital of a developing country. Fixed capital investment generates production capacity whereas working capital makes the utilization of that capacity possible. Since the fifties, there has been a concerted effort to analyse the long-term corporate investment and financial decisions, but virtually no research has been conducted in an attempt to apply them to working capital decisions. It shows that earlier the emphasis in financial management was more on long-term financial decisions. Funds are needed in every business for carrying on day-to-day operations. Working capital funds are regarded as the life-blood of a business firm. A firm can exist and survive without making profit but it cannot survive without working capital funds. In addition, it has acquired great significance and sound position for the twin objects of "profitability and liquidity". It consumes a great deal of time to increase profitability as well as to maintain proper liquidity, at minimum risk. Viewed in this perspective, the study devoted to working capital, may be a very rewarding one.

1.1 Statement of the problem

The problem of working capital management is the most critical problem in financial management. Most of the time financial executives are engaged in managing the current assets and current liabilities, which are the main constituents of working capital. Inefficient management of working capital will lead to loss of profits in the short-run but it will ultimately lead to the downfall of the enterprise in the long- run. Excessive investment in working capital the solvency position and growth thereby affecting the operation of business. The adequacy of working capital together with its efficient handling, virtually determines the survival or demise of an enterprise. Hence, in this study an attempt has been made to determine the operational adequacy of working capital of the sugar industry of Tamil Nadu with the use of Bivariate Discriminant Analysis.

1.2 Sampling Design

There are about 31 sugar industries operating in Tamil Nadu, of which 14 are under co-operative sector, 14 are under private sector and 3 are under public sector. Since this study has been directed towards assessing the operational adequacy of working capital, all these sugar industries are not included because most of them are just a few years old leading to the absence of data for the last ten years. In order to select the industries for the purpose of study, first of all a list was made of those industries, which were established before 1975 and have crushing capacity of 2000 MT (per day) or more. We found 10 such industries, 5 under co-operative sector and 5 under private sector. Thus ten industries selected for the study from the important industries and seem to have represented the sugar industries of Tamil Nadu as a whole.

1.3 Adequacy of working capital

There is no standard by which to measure the adequacy of working capital. However practice suggests that the adequacy of working capital can be judged in terms of its relation with the firm's debts. In order to establish such relationship generally the current ratio and liquid ratio are studied. The current ratio and liquid ratio of the selected units are presented in Table 10.0 and Table 10.1

If the conventional liquidity of 2.1 is considered as a norm, following inferences can be drawn from Table 10.0. In industry, the working capital is observed to be excess, in private sector units it is also in excess and in the co-operative sector units only the working capital is found to be adequate. Among the co-operative sector units, in AMCS, the working capital is found to be inadequate, in ACS and KCS it has been adequate and in NCS, the working capital is found to be excess. Among the private sector units, in TASL the working capital had been inadequate and in the remaining cases, it is found to be excess.

Table 10.0
Current Ratio of the Selected Units

Year	Co-operative Sector					Private Sector					
	ACS	AMCS	SCS	NCS	KCS	ASL	SISL	SSL	KSL	TASL	X
1982-83	1.79	1.11	1.94	3.47	2.66	3.59	2.45	2.19	3.02	2.35	2.46
1983-84	1.64	1.38	1.68	1.41	1.48	4.53	1.66	2.45	2.22	2.11	2.26
1984-85	1.64	2.70	1.57	3.47	1.19	3.71	1.02	2.40	1.78	1.31	2.08
1985-86	1.79	2.86	1.62	2.12	1.80	4.71	1.51	2.72	1.90	1.27	2.23
1986-87	2.44	3.17	1.67	2.13	1.21	4.90	1.08	2.69	1.80	1.91	2.30
1987-88	2.25	1.68	1.63	2.19	1.25	3.49	1.79	3.12	1.21	1.42	2.00
1989-90	1.65	0.89	1.93	2.56	1.52	2.72	1.55	3.43	1.17	1.05	1.85
1990-91	2.19	1.44	2.39	3.32	2.80	3.51	1.85	4.19	3.65	1.94	2.73
1991-92	2.07	1.39	3.02	3.11	2.63	3.49	3.04	2.81	3.54	2.23	2.74
1992-93	2.16	1.60	2.95	3.01	2.70	3.25	2.95	2.92	3.16	1.98	2.67
1993-94	2.24	1.75	2.85	3.05	3.10	3.15	3.10	3.18	3.25	2.54	2.82
X	1.99	1.82	2.11	2.89	2.30	3.73	2.01	2.92	2.42	1.83	

Source: Computed from annual reports of the respective units

The current ratio can be used to indicate high or low level of working capital but they are unable to give an exact clue of the quality of current assets as some current assets, although classified as current, are not easily converted into cash. To offset this weakness liquid ratios are studied. If the conventional 1.1 is considered as a norm, the following inference can be drawn from Table 10.1.

Table 10.1
Liquid Ratio of the Selected Units

Year	Co-operative Sector					Private Sector					
	ACS	AMCS	SCS	NCS	KCS	ASL	SISL	SSL	KSL	TASL	X
1982-83	0.27	0.11	0.34	0.63	0.43	0.82	0.30	0.47	1.01	0.55	0.49
1983-84	1.08	0.38	1.01	1.14	0.41	1.25	0.52	1.28	1.21	0.33	0.86
1984-85	0.76	0.51	0.95	1.25	0.50	1.22	0.37	0.98	1.41	0.48	0.84
1985-86	0.29	0.34	0.77	0.59	0.26	1.55	0.43	0.94	0.89	0.33	0.64
1986-87	1.16	0.47	1.04	0.75	0.29	2.47	0.48	1.35	1.23	0.77	1.00
1887-88	0.52	0.72	0.71	0.63	0.43	1.34	0.50	1.04	0.80	0.55	0.72
1989-90	0.93	0.57	1.19	0.59	0.77	0.97	0.61	1.40	1.03	0.88	0.89
1990-91	0.71	0.91	1.23	0.52	1.29	1.00	0.52	1.41	1.33	0.73	0.99
1991-92	0.74	0.69	1.55	0.37	0.78	1.42	0.48	1.15	1.47	0.74	0.94
1992-93	0.85	0.78	1.48	0.68	0.92	1.36	0.78	1.25	1.67	0.96	1.07
1993-94	0.92	0.96	1.62	0.54	0.88	1.42	0.90	1.15	1.78	0.89	1.11
X	0.75	0.58	1.08	0.70	0.63	1.35	0.54	1.13	1.25	0.66	

Source: Computed from annual reports of the respective units

In all the co-operative sector units and the industry as a whole, the working capital is observed to be inadequate. All the co-operative sector units except SCS have inadequate working capital and in all the private sector units except SISL and TASL, the working capital is found to be excess. On the whole, it can be said that only in a few cases working capital is found to be adequate, it is either inadequate or excessively high.

1.4 Operational Adequacy of Working Capital - A Bivariate Discriminant Analysis

Current and liquid ratios measure the technical solvency working capital but the operational adequacy of working capital can be measured by ascertaining the magnitude of working capital in relation to average months sales turnover and months cost of operations. The present study attempts to apply linear discriminant analysis with only two sets of independent variables. The sample units were classified in two categories as per their liquidity ratios. Group A consisted of those units where the current ratio was found to be at least 2:1 and the rest of the units have been classified in Group B. In this study, adequacy of the size of net working capital has been treated as dependent variable and size of net working capital in terms of monthly operational requirements (X_1) and sales requirements (X_2) has been treated as in dependent variables.

The object is to determine weights for X_1 and X_2 that is the value of "a" and of "b" in

$$Z = a x_1 + b x_2$$

Where, Z is the discriminant index.

Table 10.2

Good and Poor Risk Units In Terms Of Current Ratio

(Group A Consists of Those Units Whose Current ratio is at least 2:1)

1982 -83	83-84	84-85	85-86	86-87	87-89	89-90	90-91	91-92	92-93	93-94
Group A (Good Risk)										
NCS	NCS	AMCS	AMCS	ACS	ACS	NCS	ACS	ACS	ACS	ACS
KCS	ASL	NCS	NCS	AMCS	NCS	ASL	SCS	SCS	SCS	SCS
ASL	SSL	ASL	ASL	NCS	ASL	SSL	NCS	NCS	NCS	NCS
SISL	KSL	SSL	SSL	ASL	SSL		KCS	KCS	KCS	KCS
SSL	TASL			SSL			ASL	ASL	ASL	ASL
KSL							SISL	SISL	SISL	SISL
TASL	.						SSL	SSL	SSL	SSL

							KSL	KSL	KSL	KSL
							TASL			TASL
n1=7	n1=5	n1=4	n1=4	n1=5	n1=4	n1=3	n1=7	n1=9	n1=8	n1=9
Group B (Poor risk)										
ACS	ACS	ACS	ACS	SCS	AMCS	ACS	AMCS	AMCS	AMCS	AMCS
AMCS	AMCS	SCS	SCS	KCS	SCS	AMCS	SISL		TASL	
SCS	SCS	KCS	KCS	SISL	KCS	SCS	TASL			
	KCS	SISL	SISL	KSL	SISL	KCS				
	SISL	KSL	KSL	TASL	KSL	SISL				
		TASL	TASL		TASL	KSL				
						TASL				
n2=3	n2=5	n2=6	n2=6	n2=5	n2=6	n2=7	n2=3	n2=1	n2=2	n2=1

Source: Computed

As per the rule, the selected units falling in the good and poor risk group are presented in Table 10.2. It is to be noticed that three units namely NCS, ASL and SSL appeared to be a "good" risk in all the selected years. It is also to be noticed that no units appeared to be a "poor" risk in all the selected years. After classifying the selected units into the good and poor risk class, the values of a and b in the discriminant functions are estimated and presented in Table 10.4 where the coefficient for "a" and "b" indicate the size of net working capital in terms of monthly operational requirements and sales requirement. The table reveals that the size of net working capital in terms of monthly operational requirements appeared to be stronger than sales requirements in all the years accept in 1983-84 and 1989-90.

Table 10.3
Discriminant Functions for the Period 1982-93 to 1993-94

Year	Functions	Remarks
1982-83	Z = 2.654a – 1.892b	a > b
1983-84	Z = 0.268a – 0.721b	b > a
1984-85	Z = 0.423a – 0.0054b	a > b
1985-86	Z = 5.443a – 4.196b	a > b
1986-87	Z = 0.479a – 0.304b	a > b
1987-89	Z = 0.681a – 0.317b	a > b
1989-90	Z = 1.935a + 2.235b	b > a
1990-91	Z = 0.109a + 0.062b	a > b
1991-92	Z = 0.471a – 0.169b	a > b
1992-93	Z = 0.652a – 0.156b	a > b
1993-94	Z = 0.982a – 0.169b	a > b

Note: The expression a > b is to be read as "a is stronger than b"

Source: Computed

The discriminant co-efficient given in Table 10.3 were multiplied with the mean values of each industry ratios in order to obtain the discriminant score of each unit. Table 10.4 presents the data relating to the discriminant score of both groups. With the help of the discriminant scores, the cut-off value was calculated as follows.

$$\text{Cut–off value} = \frac{n_1z_1 + n_2z_2}{n_1 + n_2}$$

Where n_1 and n_2 are the size of samples and z_1 and z_2 represents the mean of the discriminant score of Group A and Group B respectively. The cut-off values have also been presented in Table 10.4. Actual Z scores of the individual units were then compared with the discriminating Z scores. In case where the Z scores were found to be more than the discriminating Z scores, it can be said that the size of net working capital was more than the operational and sales requirements.

Table 10.4

Classification Matrix

Year	As per current Ratio		As per Discriminant Score	
	Adequate	Inadequate	Adequate	Inadequate
1982-83	7	3	6	4
1983-84	5	5	4	6
1984-85	4	6	5	5
1985-86	4	6	4	6
1986-87	5	5	4	6
1987-89	4	6	4	6
1989-90	3	7	3	7
1990-91	7	3	6	4
1991-92	9	1	7	3
1992-93	8	2	7	3
1993-94	9	1	8	2

Source: Computed

It is evident from the Table 10.4 that in the year 1982-83, the cut off Z score was 2.05. In the case of KSL and NCS, the size of working capital was found to be quite satisfactory in terms of operational and sales requirements. In the case of AMCS, SCS and ACS, the Z scores were found to be low which indicate inadequacy of the size of working capital, considering the operational and sale requirements. In rest of the cases, the size of working capital was found to be in excess in score was 1.02 Considering this as discriminant score, in the case of SCS and KSL, z scores were found to be less than 1.02 but were not top low to be inadequate. In the case ACS, AMCS, KCS and SISL, the size of working capital was found to be very low. In rest of the cases it was found that working capital was in excess as Z scores by the individual units were more than the cut off Z score.

In 1984-85, the cut-off Z scores was 1.16. In the case of ACS, the size of working capital was found to be quite satisfactory. In the case of KCS, SIS, KSL and TASL, the size of working capital was found to be very low. In rest of cases the size of working capital was found to be excess, in relation to their operational and sales requirement. In 1985-86, cut -off Z scores was found to be 2.06 . In the case AMCS, NCS, ASL and SSL the size of working capital was found to be in excess to meet their operational and sales requirement. SCS had satisfactory size of working capital as its Z score were less than 2.06 but, was not too low to be inadequate. In rest of the cases, size of the working capital was found to be inadequate in relation to operational and sales requirement.

In 1986-87, the cut off Z score was 0.55. Considering this as discriminant score, in the case of SCS and NCS, Z Scores were found to be less than 0.55 but were not too low to be inadequate. In the cease of KCS, SISL, KSL and TASI, the size of working capital was found to be very low. In rest of the cases it was found that working capital was in excess as Z score by the individual units were more than the cut was off Z score. In 1987-89, the size of working capital was found to be quite satisfactory. In the case of AMCS and TASL, working capital positions were found to be satisfactory. In the case of KCS, SISL and KSL the size of working capital was found to be too low and in rest of the cases the size of working capital was in excess to meet their respective operational and sale requirements.

In 1989-90, the cut off Z score was 0.57. Considering it as discrimination Z score, it was found that in the case of NCS, ASL, SISL and SSL, the size of working capital was found to be excess to meet their respective operational and sale requirement and in the rest of the cases the size of working capital was found to be too low.

In 1990-91, the cut off Z score was 0.97. In the case of ACS and SISL, Z scores were found to be less than 0.97 but were not too low to be inadequate. In rest of the cases it was found that working capital was in excess as Z scores by the individual units were more than the cut off Z score. In 1991-92, the cut off score was 1.65. In the case of ACS and SISL, the size of working capital was found to be quite satisfactory. In the case of AMCS and TASL, the size of working capital was found to be very low. In rest of the cases the size of working capital was found to be in excess as Z score by the individual units was more than the cut off Z score.

In 1992-93, the cut off Z score was 1.78. Considering it as discriminating Z score, it was found that in the case of ACS, NCS, KCS and SSL, Z scores were more than the cut off Z score, hence in these cases the size of working capital was observed to be quite satisfactory. In the case of AMCS, the size of working capital was found to be too low and in the rest of the cases the size of working capital was in excess to meet their respective operational and sales requirement. In 1993-94, the cut of Z score was found to be 1.08. In the case of NCS, KCS, ASL, SSL, and KSL, the working capital position was found to be satisfactory. In the cases of AMCS and TASL, the size of working capital was very low. In rest of the cases the size of working capital was found to be in excess, in relation to their operational and sale requirements.

Conclusion

To sum up the analysis regarding the operational adequacy of working capital, it can be concluded that all the selected units except ANCS and TASL maintained adequate size of working capital in relation to sales and output requirements in the recent years 1990-91 and 1991-92. In addition NCS and SCS in the co-operative sector and ASL and SSL in private sector maintained adequate size of working capital in relation to sales and output requirements throughout the period under study.

The number of good and poor risk units as per the current ratio as per the discriminant score presented in Table 10.5. It is clear from the table that the mis-classification does not occur in the year 1985-86, 1987-89 and 1989-90. Mis-classification of units were noticed for the remaining years. Generally one unit in the good risk group has been mis-classified under the criteria of discriminant score. Such industries are KSL in the years 1982-83 and 1983-84, NCS in 1986-87, ACS in 1990-91 and ACS and TASL in the year 1991-92, SISL in industries appeared to be good risk under the criteria of descriminant score. Such a unit is SCS in the year 1984-85. From this study, it is concluded that Discriminant Analysis is a very useful technique to analyse the adequacy of working capital of the business enterprises.

References

1. A.K. Mukherjee, *Management of working capital in public Enterprises.* Allah a bad: Vohra publishers & Distributors, 1988.
2. S.K. Bhattacharya, M. Raghavachari, "Determinants of effective working capital Management – A discriminant Analysis Approach", working paper No. 151, Indian Institute of Management, Ahmedabad, March 1977.
3. ACS- Ambur Co-operative Sugar Ltd.
   AMCS – Amaravathi Co-operative Sugars Ltd.
   SCS – Salem Co-operative Sugars Ltd.
   NCS – National Co-operative Sugars Ltd.
   KCS – Kallakurichi Co-operative Sugars Ltd.
   ASL - Aruna Sugars Ltd.
   SISL – South India Sugars Ltd.
   SSL - Sakthi Sugars Ltd.
   KSL – Kothari Sugars Ltd.
   TASL – Thiru Arooran Sugars Ltd.

11

TRANSACTIONS DEMAND FOR WORKING CAPITAL IN INDIAN PUBLIC SECTOR ENTERPRISES: SOME THEORETICAL AND PRACTICAL RESULTS

Fixed capital and working capital are the dominant contributors to the total capital of a developing country. Fixed capital investments generate production capacity whereas working capital makes the utilisation of that capacity possible. Especially in small firms, working capital management may be the factor that decides success or failure; in larger firms, efficient working capital management can significantly affect the firms' risk, return and share price. A firm can exist and survive without profitability but cannot survive without working capital. Management of working capital has acquired a great significance and sound position for the twin objects of profitability and liquidity. In a period of rising capital costs and scarce funds, the working capital is one of the most important areas requiring management review. It consumes a great deal of time to increase profitability as well as to maintain proper liquidity at minimum risk. Viewed in this perspective, the study devoted to working capital management may be very rewarding one.

Statement of the Problem

One of the areas of working capital management is to study the nature of short-run behaviour of the demand for working capital and its components. Interest in the study of the demand for working capital by Indian public sector enterprises has been stimulated by the empirical works on the demand for cash showed two distinct paths. Frazer (1964), Nadiri (1969), Kamata and Sampath (1979) and Lahiri (1981) observed economics of scale, thereby supporting Baumol (1952) and Tobin (1956), while Meltzer (1963), Whalen (1965), De Allessi (1966) and Bhole (1979) observed diseconomics of scale, thereby supporting Friedman (1959) as far as the transaction demand for cash in concerned. Similarly, there is no unanimous finding as regards the effects of capital costs on the demand for cash. Among others, De Allessi and Nadiri showed the statistically significant effect of capital costs on the demand for cash, while Friedman did not find the same.

Like studies on the demand for cash, the earlier studies on the demand for inventories also did not present unanimous findings. Liu (1963), Kuznets (1964), Liberman (1980), Irvine (1981) and Akhtar (1983) observed significant effects of capital costs on the demand for inventories, while Robinson (1959), Lovell (1964), Joyce (1973) did not observe the same. Similarly, some reported economics of scale with respect to holding inventories, while others did not report the same. It has therefore become difficult to support one view or another in the context of Indian public sector enterprises.

However, investigation in this section is not limited to the study of the demand for cash and inventories only. It has been extended to test whether models are similar to those explaining the demand for receivables, gross working capital, and net working capital. The analysis of this study determines empirically whether transactions working capital balances, including cash and inventories, vary proportionately or less than in proportion to changes in the volume of sales (S_1) or one year lagged sales (S_{t-1}). It also describes the effect of capital costs on working capital holdings of the Indian public sector enterprises. The study also takes into account a partial adjustment model of working capital behaviour. It indicates the speed with which firms adjust their actual working capital balances to the desired working capital balances.

Data Source and Methodology

The Bureau of Public Enterprise brings out the official annual reports, which contain the balance sheets, and profit and loss accounts of public enterprises in India. The necessary data on working capital and other related variables used in this study have been collected mostly from these reports. Besides, the information has also been supplemented from the Economic Survey published by the Ministry of Finance. The necessary data are collected for the 15-year period from 1979/80 to 1993/94. The econometric models employed in this study are described in the following paragraph.

Econometric Models

In this study, econometric models are used to describe the transactions demand for working capital and its various components of Indian public sector enterprises. The demand for working capital has been viewed in a way similar to the demand for cash and inventories. The decisions about the aggregate amount of working capital and its various components to be held may be regarded as subject to wealth constraint. As a first approximation to the theory, the function may be written as

$$Y^* = f(W) \tag{1}$$

where Y^* means real desired cash, inventories, receivables, gross working capital and net working capital and W is real desired wealth defined in terms of sales (S). In an empirical investigation, it takes the form

$$Y^* = KW^b e^u \tag{2}$$

where u is assumed to be independently and normally distributed. Taking the natural logarithm of this equation (2) gives

$$\ln Y^* = \ln K + b \ln W + u \tag{3}$$

So far the opportunity cost of working capital has been ignored. A review of the empirical works on the demand for cash and inventories suggests that the opportunity cost of capital should be included as an explanatory variable in the models. Hence, the opportunity cost of working capital and its various components measured by the short-term interest rates of Indian commercial bank (i_2) has been included in the models. Equation (1) is now stated as

$$Y^* = f(W, i_2) \tag{4}$$

Similarly, equation [2] takes the form

$$Y^* = KW^b\ i_2\ be^{\ u} \tag{5}$$

taking the natural logarithm

$$\ln Y^* = K + b_1 \ln W + b_2 \ln i_2 + u \tag{6}$$

where b_1 and b_2 are the elasticities of Y^* with respect to the explanatory variables of the models.

While estimating the above equations, the figures of working capital and its components and sales have been deflated by using the national urban consumer price index. In addition, the study also takes into account a partial adjustment model of working capital behaviour. The models indicate the speed with which firms adjust their actual working capital balances to the desired working capital balances. The equation to be estimated is

$$\ln Y^* = c_o + c_1 \ln W + c_2 \ln i_2 + (1\text{-}0) \ln Y_{t-1} + u \tag{7}$$

where c_1 and c_2 are the short-term elasticities of working capital and its components with respect to sales and their opportunity cost and 0 is the rate of adjustment coefficient.

Empirical Findings

Scale and Capital Cost Effects on Demand Functions of Working Capital

The demand function of working capital and its various components has been simplified to assert that $Y^* = g(W)$, where $g>0$. Let $g(W) = AW^{a}$. Then the statistical hypothesis may be expressed in logarithmic form as $\ln Y^* = a_0 + a_1 \ln W + u$, where a_0 is the intercept, a is the elasticity of Y^* with respect to either S_t or S_{t-1} and u is the error term. The pooled regression results of the model showing the sales (S_{t-1}) effects on transactions demand for working capital and its components are presented in Table 11.0.

Table 11.0

Estimated Demand for Working Capital in Indian Public Sector Enterprises (1981/82 to 1993/94)

($\ln Y^* = \ln\ a + b \ln S_{t-1}$)

Independent Variables	Regression Coefficient (S_{t-1})	t Value	R^2	F Value	D.W.
Cash	2.064 (0.123)	16.56*	0.96	274.20	1.07
Inventory	0.406 (0.477)	8.50*	0.86	72.19	0.98
Receivables	1.078 (0.123)	13.60*	0.94	185.00	0.56
Gross Working Capital	1.145 (0.084)	13.63*	0.94	185.80	0.55
Net Working Capital	1.121 (0.120)	9.31*	0.88	86.61	0.58

Source: Computed.

Notes:

S_{t-1} – sales of the period 't-1'.

* Significant at 1% level.

Figures in parentheses denote standard error of the estimate.

D.W. indicates that there is no autocorrelation.

It is to be noted that the values marked with the asterisk sign (*) shows that the results are significant at the 1 per cent level of significance. The dependent variables are the deflated average value of cash, inventories, receivables, gross working capital and net working capital. Similarly, the independent variables, namely S_t or S_{t-1} and i_2 denote deflated sales and short-term interest rates of commercial banks. The overall results presented in Table 11.0 are encouraging. The signs of all the coefficients are as expected. The coefficients are also statistically significant and the goodness of fit of the model is also satisfactory.

With respect to the demand for cash by Indian public sector enterprises, the result as indicated by Table 11.0 contradicts less than unitary sales elasticity hypotheses of Baumol, Tobin, Frazer and Nadiri. The finding is to some extent consistent with the conclusion of Friedman, Meltzer, Whalen, De Allessi and Bhole. The results show that transactions cash balances vary more than in proportion to changes in the volume of sales (S_{t-1}). Regarding the demand for inventories, it may be stated that the results as indicated in Table 11.0 support the findings of Akhtar and Irvine and contradict unitary or more than unitary sales elasticites noticed in some of the equations in Liberman.

The results indicated by Table 11.0 do not show economics of scale with respect to investment in working capital or its components except inventory. The signs of all the coefficients are as expected. The sale elasticity coefficients are statistically significant and the goodness of fit to the model is also satisfactory. The sales elasticity is less than unity only in the case of inventory. It varies from 1.121 for net working capital to 2.064 for cash. Thus, the diseconomies of scale are highest for cash (2.06), followed by receivables (1.68), gross working capital (1.15), and net working capital (1.12).

Table 11.1
Estimated Demand for Working Capital in Indian Public Sector Enterprises (1981/82 to 1993/94)
($\ln Y^* = \ln a + b \ln S_t$)

Independent Variables	Regression Coefficient (S_t)	t Value	R^2	F Value	D.W.
Cash	2.560 (0.144)	17.73*	0.96	314.40	1.46
Inventory	0.488 (0.068)	7.16*	0.81	51.24	0.89
Receivables	2.056 (0.174)	11.84*	0.92	139.50	0.59
Gross Working Capital	1.399 (0.121)	11.54*	0.92	133.10	0.60
Net Working Capital	1.368 (0.163)	8.40*	0.85	70.60	0.61

Source: Computed.
Notes:
S_t – sales of the period 't'.
* Significant at 1% level.
Figures in parentheses denote standard error of the estimate.
D.W. indicates that there is no autocorrelation.

The above estimated results are based on S_{t-1} as a proxy for W. These results may not be directly comparable to the results of these earlier studies, which used S_t as a proxy for W. This applies mainly to the studies on the demand for cash and inventories. Hence it is felt necessary to use S_t as a proxy for W in order to see whether the functions using S_t produce results similar to the functions using S_{t-1}. The results are presented in Table 11.1 When Table 11.0 is compared with Table 11.1 it may be seen that the use of S_{t-1} or S_t produced similar results. Most of the equations with S_{t-1} have slightly better values of 't' and 'R^2,. Thus there is basically no difference between the equations with S_t and S_{t-1}. Due to this, only the equations with S_{t-1} are presented in the following aspects.

So far the opportunity cost of funds has been ignored. In the absence of changes in opportunity cost of capital, a firm's balance of working capital and its components should increase in relation to sales. Theoretically, the levels of working capital and its components of an enterprise desires to hold depend not only on sales but also on holding costs. It is however surprising that there has been repeated failure of many of the earlier empirical studies to find any significant influence of holding cost as a determinant of the demand for cash and inventories is thus a controversial issue. The controversy seems to cater on signs and magnitude of the interest elasticity of cash and inventory balances. In order to test it in the context of Indian public sector enterprises, the short term interest rate of commercial banks is included in the explanatory variable together with sales and the pooled results are presented in Table 11.2.

It is evident from the Table 11.2 that all the equations are strong and provide interest rate coefficients with the theoretically correct signs. The coefficients of sales are also highly significant and indicate that higher sales increase working capital and its components. The sales elasticity is smallest for inventories followed by net working capital, gross working capital, receivables and cash. These elasticities are consistently more than unity in all cases except inventory, suggesting economics of scale. Further, the coefficients are also statistically significant except inventory.

This finding again seems to support the theoretical propositions of Baumol and Tobin as far as demand for cash is concerned. Similarly, the results seem to support the findings of Akhtar and Irvine, and contradict unitary or more than unitary sales elasticity noticed in some of the equations of Liberman showing the demand for inventories. The results also show that fluctuations in inventory levels depend in a statistically significant manner on fluctuations in their financial carrying costs.

Table 11.2
Estimated Demand for Working Capital in Indian Public Sector Enterprises (1981/82 To 1993/94)
($\ln Y^* = \ln a + b_1 \ln S_{t-1} - b_2 \ln i$)

Independent Variables	Regression (S_{t-1})	Coef. (i)	R^2	Adj R^2	F Value	D.W.
Cash	1.96	-0.029	0.96	0.95	134.90	1.18
	(0.123)*	(0.088)				
Inventory	3.344	–0.018	0.88	0.86	41.08	0.99
	(0.477)	(1.51)**				
Receivables	1.595	–0.024	0.94	0.93	89.31	0.58
	(9.40)*					
Gross Working	1.078	–0.019	0.94	0.93	91.72	0.59
Capital	(9.43)*	(0.89)				
Net Working	0.999	–0.036	0.89	0.88	45.07	0.56
Capital	(6.22)*	(1.14)				

Source: Computed.
Notes: S_{t-1} – sales of the period '*t-1*'.
* Significant at 1% level.
** Significant at 10% level.
Figures in parentheses denote 't' value.
D.W. indicates that there is no autocorrelation.

The effect of capital costs can also be observed for investment and receivables, gross working capital and net working capital. The sign of interest rate coefficient is negative but it is not statistically significant in all these cases. Thus the results indicate that the target level of inventories is much more sensitive to capital cost fluctuations as compared to the target level of cash, receivables, and gross and net working capital. Among these, the target level of inventory is least sensitive to fluctuations in capital costs. In all can be seen from interest rate elasticity of 0.029 for cash, 0.018 for inventory, 0.024 for receivables, 0.019 for gross working capital, and 0.036 for net working capital.

Partial Adjustment Model

A partial adjustment model of cash, inventories, receivables and working capital as a whole has still not been tested. The partial adjustment models have been widely used in studies on the demand for cash and inventories. Among others, Nadiri reported that firms adjust their actual cash balance rapidly to their desired cash balances. Similarly, Irvine observed rapid adjustment while Lovell observed slow adjustment of actual inventory levels to the desired inventory levels. In order to know whether this kind of adjustment is rapid or slow in Indian public sector enterprises, an attempt has been made in this section to show the nature of adjustment between desired and actual balances of cash, inventories, receivables and gross and net working capital. The estimated regression results are presented in Table 11.3.

Table 11.3

Partial Adjustment Model

$$\text{In } Y^* = \text{In } a + b_1 \text{ In } S_{t-1} - b_2 \text{ In}^i + b_3 \text{ In } Y_{t-1}$$

Independent Variables	Regression Coefficient			R^2	Adj R^2	F Value
	(S_{t-1})	(i)	(Y_{t-1})			
Cash	0.828	-0.002	0.585	0.99	0.98	274.90
	(3.21)*	(0.09)	(4.76)*			
Inventory	0.095	-0.013	0.568	0.95	0.93	61.26
	(1.17)	(1.56)	(3.59)			
Receivables	0.170	0.003	0.846	0.99	0.99	493.60
	(0.98)*	(0.22)	(8.74)*			
Gross Working Capital	0.117	-0.0008	0.846	0.99	0.99	504.30
	(1.05)	(0.09)	(8.74)*			
Net Working Capital	0.115	-0.001	0.876	0.98	0.97	152.50
	(0.73)	(0.09)	(6.39)			

Source: Computed.

Notes: * Significant at 1% level

** Significant 10% level

Figures in parentheses denote 't' value.

The regression results indicated that coefficients of Y_{t-1} are significant in all cases. The coefficient of the lagged dependent variable has been observed to be 0.59 for cash, 0.57 for inventory, 0.85 for receivables and gross working capital, and 0.88 for net working capital. Since the coefficient of lag ln Y_t is equal to 1 minus the adjustment coefficient (1-0), the adjustment coefficient is equal to 0.41 for cash, 0.43 for inventory, 0.15 for receivables and gross working capital, and 0.12 for net working capital. It seems that 41% of the adjustment of actual to desired real cash balances is completed within one year. Similarly, the adjustment speed of actual to desired balances is 43% for inventory, 15% for receivables and gross working capital, and only 12% for net working capital. The speed of adjustment is however highest for inventory, followed by cash, receivables and gross working capital, and net working capital.

Conclusion

To sum up, the pooled regression results show the presence of diseconomies of scale with respect to the demand for working capital and its various components except inventory. The demand for inventories of Indian public sector enterprises only shows economics of scale during the study period. The diseconomies of scale are highest for cash followed by receivables, gross and net working capital. The results suggest strongly that the demand for working capital and its components is a function of both sales and their holding costs. The capital cost coefficients are all with theoretically correct signs but it is statistically significant only in the case of inventory. Further, the adjustment speed of actual to desired balances of working capital and its various components has been observed to be higher in the Indian public sector enterprises.

References

1. Agarwal, J.D. (1988). A Goal Programming Model for Working Capital Management. *Finance India,* Vol. II, No.2, June: 139 – 149.
2. Akhtar, M.A. (1983). Effects of Interest Rates and Inflation on Aggregate Inventory Investment in US. *The American Economic Review,* June: 319 – 328.
3. Baumol, W. (1952). The Transaction Demands for Cash: An Inventory Theoretic Approach. *The Quarterly Journal of Economics,* November: 545 – 566.
4. Bhole, L.M. (1979). An Empirical Study of Liquidity Preference of Corporate Sectors in India, 1951 – 1974. *The Indian Economic Journal,* Vol. 27, No.1 : 65 – 80.
5. De Allessi (1966). The Demand for Money: A Cross-Section Study of British Business Firms. *Economics,* August: 228 – 320.
6. Frazer, W.J. (1964). Financial Structure of Manufacturing Corporation and the Demand for Money; Some Empirical Findings. *The Journal of Political Economy,* April: 176 – 183.

7. Friedman, M. (1959). The Demand for Money: Some Theoretical and Empirical Results. *The Journal of Political Economy,* August: 327 – 351.
8. Irvine, P. (1981). Retail Inventory Investment and the Cost of Capital. *The American Economic Review,* September: 633.
9. Joyce, J.M. (1973). Cost of Capital and Inventory Investments, Further Evidence. *The Southern Economic Journal,* October: 323 – 329.
10. Kamata, P. and Sampath, R.K. (1979). Business Demand for Money in India: A Temporal Cross-Section Analysis. *The Indian Economic Journal,* Vol. 27, No.1, July-September: 46 – 62.
11. Kuznets, P.W. (1964). Financial Determinants of Manufacturing Inventory Behaviour: A Quarterly Study Based on US Estimates. *Yale Economic Essays,* Fall: 331 – 369.
12. Lahiri, A.K. (1981). Liquidity Behaviour of Indian Business Firms. *The Indian Economic Journal,* Vol. 29, No.1: 1 – 9.
13. Liberman, C. (1980). Inventory Demand and Cost of Capital Effects. *The Review of Economics and Statistics,* August: 348 – 356.
14. Liu, T.C. (1963). An Exploratory Quarterly Model of Effective Demand in the Postwar US Economy. *The Econometrica,* July: 301 – 308.
15. Lovell, M. C. (1964). Determinants of Inventory Behaviour. In *Models of Income Behaviour, edited by* Edward F. Denson and Lawrence R, Klein. New York.
16. Meltzer, A.H. (1963). The Demand for Money: A Cross-Section Study of Business Firms. *The Quarterly Journal of Economics,* August: 405 – 422.
17. Nadiri, M.I. (1969). An Empirical Study of Liquidity Preference of Corporate Sector in India. *The Indian Economic Journal,* Vol. 27, No. 1, May: 65 – 80.
18. Robinson, N. Y. (1959). The Acceleration Principles; Departmental Store Inventories, 1920–1956. *The American Economic Review,* June: 348 – 358.
19. Sampath, P. S. (1988). Managing Working Capital by Strategic Choice. *Vikalpa,* Vol. 13, No. 1, January – March: 72 – 81.
20. Saran, S. and Singh, P. N. (1995). Quantitative Tools in Management of Working Capital. In *Working Capital Management,* edited by J.D. Agarwal: 130 – 138.

21. Tobin, J. (1956). The Interest Elasticity of Transactions Demand for Cash. *The Review of Economics and Statistics,* August: 241 – 247.
22. Vijayakumar, A. (1994). Working Finance in National Cooperative Sugar Mills Ltd., Tamil Nadu – A Case Study. *Management & Labour Studies*, Vol. 19, No.2, April: 91 – 97.
23. Whalen, E. L. (1965). A Cross-Section Study of Business Demand for Cash. *The Journal of Finance,* September: 423 – 443.

PART - III

LIQUIDITY ANALYSIS

12

ASSESSMENT OF CORPORATE LIQUIDITY—A DISCRIMINANT ANALYSIS APPROACH

Liquidity is defined as the ability to realise value in money, the most liquid of assets. It refers to the ability to pay in cash, the obligations that are due. The corporate liquidity has two dimensions viz., quantitative and qualitative concepts. The quantitative concept includes the quantum, structure and utilization of liquid assets and in the qualitative concept, it is the ability to meet all present and potential demands on cash from any source in manner that minimizes cost and maximizes the value of the firm. Thus, corporate liquidity is a vital factor in business. Excess liquidity, though a guarantor of solvency would reflect lower profitability, deterioration in managerial efficiency, increased speculation and unjustified expansion, extension of too liberal credit and dividend policies. Too little liquidity then may lead to frustration of business objections, reduced rare of return, business opportunity missed and weakening of morale.

Statement of the Problem

Lack of liquidity implies lack of freedom of choice as well as constraints on management's freedom of movement. If sufficient liquidity is not maintained, the enterprise is technically insolvent and at least faces the financial embracement of renegotiating its obligations to creditors. The control of liquidity requires active working capital management. Thus, in this paper an attempt has been made to determine the short-term liquidity position in the context of the selected sugar factories of Tamil Nadu during the period 1984-85 to 1993-94.

Sampling Design

There are 28 firms in the sugar industry operating in Tamil Nadu of which 14 are under co-operative sector and 14 under private sector. Most of them are just a few years old for which data for the last ten years are not available. In order to select the units for the purpose of the study, only those units which were established before 1984 and were having a crushing capacity of 2000 MT (per day) or more have been considered. There were 10 such units of which 5 are under co-operative sector and 5 are under the private sector. Thus, the ten units are available for the study and to represent the sugar industry of Tamil Nadu as a whole. The necessary data have been collected mostly from the annual reports of the selected units for the relevant periods.

Liquidity assessment and discriminant analysis

The use of ratio analysis to judge the liquidity position of the enterprises is not free from limitations. The limitations arise from the fact that the methodology is basically univariate; that is, each ratio is examined in isolation. Due to this, the financial analyst has to use his own judgement to assess the combined effects of two or more ratios. The application of discriminant analysis to two category classification problems in empirical financial research has substantially increased in recent years. The need for use of the discriminant analysis is felt in this study due to the fact that if the selected enterprises approach a bank for loan or credit, the bank may determine their risks with the help of it. Here, the risks refer to good and poor risks indicating good and poor liquidity position respectively.

It is no doubt; the bank manager may evaluate their liquidity or risk on the basis of current and quick ratios. It is difficult particularly when some enterprises have high current ratios but low quick ratios and other enterprises have low current ratios but high quick ratios. In such cases, it is difficult to state which of these enterprises are good risks. A discriminant analysis is useful here because it takes into account the effect of both of the ratios in order to distinguish good risks from the poor ones. In this study, the current ratio (X_1) and liquid ratio (X_2) as reliable indicators of liquidity behaviour have been considered for the selected units. The object now is to determine weights for X_1 and X_2, that is the values of 'a' and 'b' in

$$Z = a X_1 + b X_2$$

Where, Z is the discriminant index.

Empirical Findings

1.1 Analysis of liquidity

There are several measures with the help of which the short term liquidity of an enterprise may be assessed. Among them, networking capital itself provides the one, which indicates a 'margin of safety' of protection provided to creditors. Table 12.0 indicates that almost all the selected units have positive net working capital. The average networking capital is comparatively high in private sector units than the cooperative sector units. The average net working capital is largest to SCS, followed by KCS, NCS, ACS and AMCS in the co-operative sector, whereas in the private sector, it is the highest for SSL followed by ASL, KSL, SISL and TASL. The measure of networking capital does not indicate true ability to pay the current debts when they become due. The networking capital (CA-CL) comprised illiquid inventories; these inventories cannot be easily converted into cash. Therefore, while dealing with liquidity, the measure of quick networking capital has been assumed as more relevant then the measure of networking capital. It is evident from the Table 12.0 that the average quick networking capital has been positive only in SCS among co-operative sector and ASL, SSL, and

Table 12.0
Mean Values of Traditional Liquidity Indicators (1984-85 to 1993-94)

Company	NWC (Rs. in lakhs)	QNWC (Rs. in lakhs)	CR	LR	Cash to Current Liabilities
Co-operative Sector					
ACS	526.03	-152.7	1.94	0.72	31.67
AMCS	273.90	-192.6	1.85	0.52	9.08
SCS	880.40	18.4	1.94	0.98	36.90
NCS	527.05	-110.0	2.86	0.72	10.09
KCS	535.05	-215.6	1.84	0.57	9.65
Private sector					
ASL	1663.98	177.5	3.85	1.34	60.80
SISL	509.00	-306.7	1.78	0.47	5.08
SSL	2404.76	169.3	2.89	1.11	31.70
KSL	544.08	72.6	2.25	1.15	37.40
TASL	504.42	-134.7	1.73	0.06	8.21
Total Industry	**836.99**	**-67.49**	**2.25**	**0.82**	**19.08**

NWC–Networking capital, QNWC–Quick Networking capital CR- Current Ratio; LR-Liquid Ratio

Source: Computed

KSL among private sector, Thus, the ability to pay current debts out of quick assets by the selected industries goes much lower.

However, nothing concrete can be concluded depending solely upon the networking capital or quick networking capital. While assessing the liquidity position, the problem is that they do not show the extent of margin of safety provided to the current creditors. Due to this, the current ratio (CR) and liquid ratio (LR) are regarded as better measures of liquidity. The current ratio and liquid ratio in the selected sugar industries of Tamil Nadu are presented in Table 12.0. A relatively high value of the recurrent ratio is considered as an indication that the firm is liquid and has the ability to pay its bills. On the other hand, a relatively low value of the current ratio is considered as an indication that the firm will find difficulty in paying its bills. As a conventional rule, a current ratio of 1: 1 or more is considered to be satisfactory. But the size of current ratio depends upon many factors; a standard of common current ratio cannot be designated as appropriated for all types of business. Therefore, as regards the industrial firms with larger investment in fixed assets and slower operating cycle, the standard of this ratio may fall around 1:5:1. It is evident from the table that all the selected sugar industries have average current ratios of greater than 1.5 during the study period.

Though the current ratio of 1: 1 is generally acceptable, the acceptability of a current ratio is highly dependent on the predictability of the firms cash flows. The more predictable the cash flows, the lower the current ratio required. The high current ratio need not indicate higher liquidity, because current assets comprise of inventories, which can't be converted into cash easily. Viewed in this way liquid ratios are considered more relevant than current ratios. If the standard liquid ratios are to be taken as 1:1, the majority of the selected sugar industries (7 out of 10) have average liquid ratios of less than 1. It is also evident from the table that the average liquid ratios are less than one for all the selected sugar industries under co-operative sector. But the average liquid ratios are greater than one in ASL, SSL and KSL in the private sector.

While dealing with liquidity, an additional ratio, which measures cash adequacy, should be mentioned. The ratio is to compute the proportion of cash to current liabilities, which shows how much cash is available to pay current obligations. These ratios computed for the selected sugar industries are presented in Table

12.0. It is evident from the table that the average cash to current liabilities ratio has been excessively high for certain industries particularly SCS and ACS in the co-operative sector and ASL, KSL and SSL in the private sector. It reveals that the level of cash maintained by these industries is higher than the current liabilities on most of the occasions. In a nutshell, it can thus be concluded that comparatively private sector sugar industries has maintained sound liquidity position than the co-operative sector sugar industries during the study period.

Estimation of discriminant function

First of all, the selected sugar industries have been classified into two groups. The industries which have current and liquid ratios of 2:1 and 1:1 or more respectively have been classified as good risks and the remaining industries as poor risks. As per this rule, the

Table 12.1

Discriminant Functions for the period 1984-85 to 1993-94

Year	Function	Remark
1984-85	Z = -1.490 a + 6.585 b	b > a
1985-86	Z = -0.422 a + 1.078 b	b > a
1986-87	Z = -0.706 a + 0.172 b	a > b
1987-89	Z = 1.052 a + 1.185 b	b > a
1989-90	Z = 0.091 a + 0.456 b	b > a
1990-91	Z = 1.423 a + 3.638 b	b > a
1991-92	Z = 0.489 a + 1.315b	b > a
1992-93	Z = 0.448 a + 3.291 b	b > a
1993-94	Z = 0.748 a + 4.187 b	b > a

Note: The expression a>b is to be read as 'a' is greater than 'b'

Source: Computed

number of industries falling in the good and poor risk groups are presented in Table 12.3. After classifying the selected sugar industries into the good and poor risk classes, the values of 'a' and 'b' in the indiscriminant functions are estimated. The discriminant functions of the selected years are presented in Table 12.1 where the co-efficient for 'a' and 'b' indicate values for current and liquid ratios respectively. It is evident from the table that liquid ratios appeared to be stronger than current ratios from 1984-85 to 1993-94 except in the year 1986-87. In 1986-87, current ratios have turned out to be stronger than liquid ratio.

Estimation of discriminant scores

The discriminant function given in Table 12.1 was multiplied with the mean values of each industry ratios in order to obtain the discriminant score of each industry. Table 12.2 presents the data relating to the discriminant score of both groups. Similarly, those industries, which have higher 'Z' values, are said to be in a good liquidity position. It is evident from the table that among the selected industries, the first three industries with good liquidity position may be indicated as KSL, TASL and ALS in 1984-85; ASL., NCS and SSL in 1985-86; ASL, NCS and AMCS in 1986-87; ASL, SSL, and AMCS in 1987-89; ASL, SSL and ACS in 1989-90; ASL, SSL and NCS in 1990-91; SSL, ASL and SCS in 1991-92; SSL,KSL and KCS in 1992-93; and KSL, SCS and ASL in 1993-94.

Table 12.2

Discriminating Z Scores

Units	1984-85	85-86	86-87	87-89	89-90	90-91	91-92	92-93	93-94
ACS	-0.89	1.86	1.29	2.23	0.75	5.09	2.03	3.32	4.65
AMCS	-0.93	0.99	1.99	3.41	0.05	5.01	1.18	3.64	3.93
SCS	-0.65	1.80	1.27	2.62	0.63	4.90	2.51	5.12	8.75
NCS	-1.02	2.67	2.66	2.93	0.54	5.41	2.03	3.20	3.88
KCS	-1.13	1.07	0.93	2.20	0.24	3.34	1.76	5.50	5.23
ASL	0.05	3.26	2.83	6.79	1.57	9.84	2.61	4.86	8.56
SISL	-1.68	1.26	0.78	2.10	0.32	4.37	1.56	2.57	4.32
SSL	-0.17	2.41	1.86	3.98	0.86	8.22	3.52	6.52	6.92
KSL	2.15	2.24	1.50	3.05	0.72	4.63	1.93	6.01	8.80
TASL	0.12	1.25	0.88	1.73	0.52	4.02	1.67	3.27	4.77
Cut off Z Value	-0.41	1.88	1.60	3.10	0.66	5.48	2.08	4.40	5.98

Source: Computed

With the help of the discriminant scores given in Table 12.2, the cut off values was calculated as follows.

$$\text{Cut off value } \frac{n_1 z_1 + n_2 z_2}{n_1 + n_2}$$

Where n_1 and n_2 are the size of sample and z_1 and z_2 are mean of the discriminant score of Group A and Group B respectively. These cut off values have also been presented in Table 12.2. Actual z scores of the individual industries were then compared with the discriminating z scores. If the z scores, it can be said that such industries have good liquidity position.

Assessment of corporate liquidity - a discriminant analysis approach

The good risk industries as indicated by z values are ASL, SSL, KSL, and TASL in 1984-85; NCS, ASL, SSL and KSL in 1985-86; AMCS, NCS, ASL and SSL in 1986-87; AMCS, ASL and SSL in 1987-89; ACS, ASL, SSL and KSL in 1989-90 ASL and SSL in 1990-91; SCS, ASL and SSL in 1991-92, SCS, KCS, ASL, SSL and KSL in 1992-93 and SCS, ASL, SSL and KSL in 1993-94. It is also inferred from the table that AMCS in co-operative sector classified as poor risk in all the selected years as per CR and LR, have become good risk in the year 1986-87 and 1987-89 as per discriminating Z score.

Classification matrix

The number of good and poor risk industries as per the criteria of current and liquid ratios and as per the discriminant score are presented in Table 12.3. It is clear from the table that the misclassification does not occur in years 1985-86, 1990-91, 1992-93 and 1993-94 respectively. It means that there is no difference between the criteria of current and liquid ratios and the criteria of discriminant score in these four years. Misclassification of industries is noticed for the remaining years. Generally, the industries with lower current and liquid ratios in the good risk group and the industries with higher current and liquid ratios in the poor risk group have been misclassified under the criteria of discriminant score. It is to be noticed that the number of good risk industries as per the criteria of discriminant score is more than the number of good risk enterprises as per the criteria of current and liquid ratios. It is also inferred that the poor risk industries under criteria of current and liquid ratios appeared to be good risks under the criteria of discriminant score. Such industries are ASL, SSL and TASL in 1984-85; AMCS and SSL in 1986-87; AMCS and SSL in 1987-89; KSL in 1989-90; and SCS and ASL in 1991-92.

Table 12.3
Classifications Matrix

Year	As per CR and LR		As per Discriminant Score	
	Good	Poor	Good	Poor
1984-85	1	9	4	6
1985-86	4	6	4	6
1986-87	2	8	4	6
1987-89	1	9	3	7
1989-90	3	7	4	6
1990-91	2	8	2	8
1991-92	1	9	3	7
1992-93	5	5	5	5
1993-94	4	6	4	6

Source: Computed

Conclusion

The discriminant analysis discussed above may be of great value to all those who are interested in evaluating liquidity position or credit worthiness. The advantage of discriminant analysis is that it is simple and can be performed even by the junior executives of the enterprise. However, the limitation of the discriminant analysis is that it is still based on the traditional current and liquid ratios. Despite of the above limitations, the way discrimination analysis has been employed is a useful exercise to determine the combined effects of two ratios. This is more so at a time when some enterprises have high current ratios but low liquid ratios and other enterprise have low current ratios but high liquid ratios, making it difficult to determine which of these enterprises are good risks.

References

1. Horold Bierman, Jr. and Jerome E. Hass, (1975). An Introduction to Managerial Finance, London; Pitman Publishing Ltd.
2. Maurice Joy, D. and John D. Tollefson, on the Financial Applications of Discriminant Analysis, The Journal of Financial and Quantitative Analysis, pp.723-739.
3. Walter, J.E (1959), A Discriminant Function for earnings price ratios of Large Industrial Corporation, Review of Economics and Statistics, pp. 44-52.

4. Altman, E.l., Financial Ratios, Discriminant Analysis and Prediction of Corporate Bankruptcy, The Journal of Finance, Vol. XXIII, No. 4, pp. 589-609.
5. R.S. Pradhan; Management of Working Capital, National Book Organisation, New Delhi, 1986.
6. ACS – Ambur Co-operative Sugar Mills Ltd.

   AMCS – Amaravathi Co-operative Sugar Mills Ltd.

   SCS – Salem C-operative Sugar Mills Ltd.

   NCS – National Co–operative Sugar Mills Ltd.

   KCS – Kallakurichi Co–operative Sugar Mills Ltd.

   ASL – Aruna Sugars Ltd.

   SISL – South India Sugar Ltd.

   SSL – Sakthi Sugars Ltd.

   KSL – Kothari Sugars Ltd.

   TASL – Thiru Arooran Sugars Ltd.

PART - IV

PRODUCTIVITY ANALYSIS

13

TOTAL FACTOR PRODUCTIVITY IN INDIA: EVIDENCE FROM INDIAN PAINT INDUSTRIES

For the growth of the economy it is necessary that industries should be productive. The measurement of productivity is pre-eminently a quantitative and technical problem. The concept of factor productivity gives the contribution which one or all used factors make to production. This concept is reflected in a ratio between product (output) and the factor or factors used (input). The study of factor productivity is an important aspect of the analysis of development since it quantifies the contribution of the different factors of production. Higher levels of growth can be attained through better utilization of available resources i.e., capital and labour. It is the most useful measurement of the variations of productivity in time. It is the best means of evaluating the contribution of the various factors. Therefore, the study of factor productivity has particular significance in the formulation of policies at the state as well as national level.

In India major economic reforms have been undertaken since July 1991 with the objective of increasing the productivity and competition among the companies. The new policies have liberalized many government controls on production capacity, imported capital goods, and intermediate inputs making them cheaper and more accessible to both domestic and international competition. These reforms have altered the economic environment in which the companies operate. Therefore, an attempt has been made in this part to analyze the impact of these reforms on productivity of Indian paints Industry.

The study is done for the Paints Sector of Indian Chemical industries. The period chosen for this study is 1991-2002.The purpose of this study is to measure total factor productivities, as well as partial factor productivities for the selected sector of chemical industry overtime. Further an attempt has also been made to explain annual variations in factor productivities with the help of multiple regression frameworks. The basic data source for this study is the PROWESS Database of CMIE.

SECTION - I

Concept of productivity

The study of productivity of the factors of production is important in view of the limited availability of the factors of production, particularly capital. Depending upon the nature of the product and the process of production, different industries employ different combinations of the factor inputs. In the labour intensive industries using unskilled and or semi- skilled workers with a relatively low wage rate, the emphasis is on increasing the productivity of capital. On the other hand, in the capital- intensive industries, the prime concern is to increase labour productivity. As such, there are considerable variations in the factor intensities across different industries as well as different states. Therefore, when the objective is to examine variations in the levels of productivities, the concept of total productivity rather than partial productivity becomes more relevant.

In this part an attempt has been made to measure and analyse the productivity performance of the Indian Paints Industry after liberalization(1991-2002) in terms of such aspects as labour productivity, capital productivity and total productivity. Further, an attempt has also been made to explain annual variations in factor productivities with the help of a multiple regression framework.

Concept and Methods of Measurement of TFP

The concept of Total Factor Productivity (TFP) defined as the ratio of output to a weighted combination of input has been used. Three methods of measuring TFP, namely, Kendrick Index, Solow Index and Divisia Index which differ from one another with regard to the weighting scheme, have been used.

$$\text{Total Factor Productivity (TFP)} = \frac{\text{Output Index}}{\text{Factor Input Index}}$$

The method of measuring Total Factor Productivity under Kendrick Index, Solow Index and Divisia Index methods are explained in the following paragraph. The above three methods of measuring TFP are based on the assumption of constant returns to scale, perfect competition and payment to factors according to their marginal product.

Methods of Measurement of Total Factor Productivity (TFP)

The trends in Total Factor Productivity (TFP) in this study have been measured by using the following three different methods of productivity Kendrick Index, Solow Index and Divisia Index.

Kendrick Index

The Kendrick Index is the ratio of the actual output to change in output, which would have resulted from the use of increased inputs in the absence of technological changes. It is defined as

$$TFP(K) = \frac{V_t}{W_0 L_t + R_0 K_t}$$

Where V stands for indices of real value added, L for indices of Labour, K for indices of Capital, W_0 and R_0 being the share of labour and capital in value added in the base year.

Solow Index

Solow Index of TFP is based on the rate of productivity change and is obtained as follows:

$$\frac{\Delta A_t}{A_t} = \frac{\Delta V_t}{V_t} \left\{ W_t \frac{\Delta K_t}{L_t} + R_t \frac{\Delta K_t}{K_t} \right\}$$

Where $\frac{\Delta V_t}{V_t}$, $\frac{\Delta L_t}{L_t}$ and $\frac{\Delta K_t}{K_t}$ are the rates of change in the real value added, labour and capital and W_t or R_t is the share of labour and capital in value added in year t. The total factor productivity is

$$A_{t+1} = A_t \left[1 + \frac{\Delta A_t}{A_t} \right] \text{ for base } A_{t=1}$$

Divisia Index

Divisia index of TFP is also based on the rate of productivity change and is obtained as follows

$$\frac{\Delta P_t}{P_t} = \frac{\Delta V_t}{V_t} - \left[W_t \frac{-\Delta L_t}{L_t} + R_t \frac{-\Delta K_t}{K_t} \right]$$

Where

$\frac{\Delta V_t}{V_t}$, $\frac{\Delta L_t}{L_t}$ and $\frac{\Delta K_t}{K_t}$ are approximated by corresponding logs of ratios of variables over successive year respectively and

$\overline{W}_t = 1/2\,(W_{t+1} + W_t)$ and

$\overline{R}_t = -\,(R_{r+1} + R_t)$

Where W_t and R_t are the shares of capital and labour in value added. The Divisia Index is then derived as

$$P_{t+1} = P_t \left[1 + \frac{\Delta P_t}{P_t} \right], \text{ Where base year } P(0) = 1$$

The above methods of measuring TFP are based on the assumption of constant returns to scale, perfect competition and payment to factors according to their marginal product.

Production function Method of Estimating Growth Rate of TFP

In the production function approach to measure TFP, we relax the constant return to scale.

Cobb-Douglas (CD) Production Function

The CD production function including the technological progress variable can be stated as follows

$$V = Ae^{\lambda t} L^{\propto} K^{\beta}$$

Where V is value added, L is Labour, K is Capital and t is time. Further elasticity's of Labour and Capital are given by $\propto$ and β respectively and exponential growth rate of TFP is given by λ. This function implies unitary elasticity of substitution. The log form of CD production function is given by

$$\text{Log } V = \text{Log } A + \beta \text{ Log } K + \propto \text{Log } L + \lambda t$$

It can also be reformulated as

$$\text{Log } (V/L) = a + b_1 \log (K/L) + b_2 \log L + \lambda t$$

$$\text{Where } b_1 = \beta,\ b_2 = \propto + \beta - 1$$

If a return to scale is unity, then the co-efficient of log L should be significant.

Constant Elasticity of Substitution (CES) production Function

CES production function including exponential technological progress variable can be stated as follows:

$$V = Ae^{\lambda t} [\ \delta L^{-P} + (1-\delta) K^{-P}]^{-V/p}$$

Where V is value added, L is Labour, K is capital, t is time and δ is distribution parameter. V gives returns to scale. P is related to elasticity of substitution by the following formula:

$$\sigma = 1/(1 + p)$$

and λ is exponential growth rate of TFP. For estimating CES production function we consider equation based on equality of marginal productivity of labour to wages (w). Under the assumption of perfect competition and profit maximization:

$$\text{Log } V/L = a + b_1 \log w + b_2 t + b_3 \log L$$

Where $b_1 = V / (V+P)$

$b_2 = \lambda p / (V+P)$

$b_3 = P(V-1) / (V+P)$

Solving these three equations, we get

$$V = (b_3 - b_1 + 1)/(1 - b_1)$$

$$P = (b_3 - b_1 + 1)/b_1$$

$$\lambda = b_2/(1 - b_1) \text{ and}$$

$$\sigma = b_1 / (1 + b_3)$$

If a return to scale is constant, then co-efficient b_3 is significant. If co-efficient b_3 is insignificant implying returns to scale to be unity, then co-efficient b_1 gives elasticity of substitution. σ. In such cases σ is tested for the hypothesis that is unity. However, where a return to scale is not unity, a has not been tested against unity because of problems involved in estimation of its standard error.

Functions for Annual Variations in Factor Productivity

It is postulated that factor productivity depends on scale of production and institutional framework such as labour-management relations. Growth in scale of production permits adoption of technologies, which improve productivity. Expansion of scale also provides division of labour, which in turn improves the productivity. Labour management relations affect motivation of workers, which in turn affects their will to work.

Based on the above hypothesis function for TFP is specified as below:

$$P = f(V, t)$$

where P = Productivity index

V = real value added as proxy for scale of production

t = time variable as proxy for management and labour relations.

For P, all measures of total factor productivity (TFPK, TFPS, TFPD) and partial productivity of labour are taken separately. The functions are estimated in log form.

SECTION -II

Indian Paint Industry-Profile

The Indian paint industry has come a long way from the days when paints where considered a luxury item. Today the awareness level on preventing corrosion through paints is relatively high, a development that should be a huge boost to the paint industry. The Indian paint industry is a Rs. 49 billion sector. The demand for paints is relatively price-elastic but is linked to the industrial and economical growth. The paint industry was divided into two consumer segments : Industrial (such as automotive) and Decorative (such as housing). The organized sector of India paint industry was divided as follows :

Nerolac Paints Ltd. (GNPL), Berger Paints, Jenson & Nicholson Ltd (J&N) and ICI (India) Ltd. Asian Paints is the industry leader with an overall market share of 33 per cent in the organized paint market. The Berger Group and ICI share the second slot in the industry with market.

Organized Sectors of Indian Paint Industry

Company	Decorative	Industrial	Overall	Estimated Point Revenue
Asian Paints	38%	14%-16%	32.5%	Rs. 6,980 MM
Goodlass Nerolac	7.8%	40%	14%	Rs. 3,007 MM
ICI India Ltd	8%-9%	12%	10.5%	Rs. 2,254 MM
Jenson and Nicholson	6.9%	6.9%	6.9%	Rs. 1,482 MM
Growth Rate	8.9%	18%	11%	
Total (Rs.)	15,033 MM	6,442 MM	21,476 MM	

In India the organized sector controls 70 per cent of the total market with the remaining 30 per cent being in the hands of nearly 2000 small-scale units. In India the industrial paint segment accounts for 30 percent of the paint market while the decorative paint segment accounts for 70 per cent of paints sold in India. In most developed countries, the ratio of decorative paints vis-a-vis industrial paints in around 50:50. Similarly, the per capita consumption of paints in India is very low at 0.5 kg per annum if compared with 4 Kgs in the South East Asian nations and 22 Kgs in developed countries. The global average per capita consumption is 15 kg.

The leaders in the organized paint industry are Asian Paints (India) Ltd (APIL), Goodlass shares of 17 per cent each. GNPL has a market share of 15 per cent in the organized sector. APIL dominates the decorative segment with a 38 per cent market share.

The Indian paint industry did not fall under the protected 'Priority' sectors as established by the Indian Government. Therefore, this industry was open to foreign players. All the paint majors have tie-ups with global paint leaders for technical know-how. The Indian Paints Industry is in a consolidation phase and only those Indian paint companies with a strong technical alliance, better distribution net-work and an ability to compete in the global markets would emerge victorious in the paint war.

SECTION - III

Review of Empirical Studies on Productivity Analysis

Anita Kumari (1993)[1] studied the productivity in the public sector- Analysis at Industrial Group Level. In this study an attempt has been made to analyse productivity trends at the group level of public sector enterprises for 11 groups of manufacturing industries- steel, minerals and metals, coal, chemicals, Power, petroleum, heavy engineering goods, transportation equipment, consumer goods and textiles. The period chosen for the study is 1971-72 to 1987-88. The purpose of this study is to measure total factor productivity as well as partial factor productivity for various public sector groups over time. Further an attempt has also been made to explain the annual variations in factor productivity with the help of multiple regression frameworks. Finally, inter-group variations in productivity have also been discussed. Analysis of productivity trends at the group level reveals marked inter-industrial differences in productivity growth. Estimates of total factor productivity for steel group and consumer goods group show a falling trend in all the three measures of total factor productivity. Labour and capital productivity for these groups also show a falling trend. But in the remaining groups' estimates of total factor productivity show a rising trend in all the three measures.

Tarlok Singh and D. Ajit (1993)[2] studied the production function in the manufacturing industries in India: 1974-1990. This study examines the sources of growth in various industries in the manufacturing sector in India using conventional production function (Cobb Douglas, C.E.S and Tanslog) as well as a new production function recently introduced by Burman production function. The study period is 1973-74 to 1989-90 i.e., 17 years. The study finds that Cobb Douglas and Burman production function perform better than other production functions and the results of the study confirms the validity of decreasing returns to scales for most of the industries in the manufacturing sector.

Balakrishnan and Pushpakandan (1994)[3] raised the question on the validity of TFPG estimates obtained on the basis of single deflation method of measurement of real value added. They argued that the single deflation method of real value added yields bias in the estimates of TFPG especially in the presence of non-consistency of index of relative price of raw materials. In order to construct an index of materials input, a series of weighted average of whole sale prices of 19 major inputs has been constructed, the weights have been calculated from the matrix of input-output transactions published by the Central Statistical Organization (CSO). They rejected the presence of the phenomenon of "turnaround" in the TFPG in the early eighties as forwarded by Aluwalia (1991). Their estimates of TFPG for aggregate Indian manufacturing sector for the period 1970-71 to 1988-89, which were based on the double deflation method of measurement of real value added indicated that, contrary to what is believed, productivity growth in the 1980s may, actually, have been slower than in the earlier period.

Singh and Ajit (1995)[4] estimated different parameters of production function for Indian industries by using ASI data for the period 1974-90. They used both conventional production function specifications, a namely, Cobb-Douglas, CES and Translog as well as new production function introduced by Bairam (1989). The results showed that the Agro-based industries have lost their shares not only in manufacturing output, fixed capital and employment during 1974-90. Similar trends were evident in engineering industries. However, the shares of chemical industries in manufacturing output, fixed capital and employment have shown improvements. There has been an increase in use of capital relative to that of labour in most of the manufacturing industries. Capital productivity recorded marginal improvements in 70s followed by gradual decline in 80s. The labour productivity has shown steady improvements during 1974-90, with the signs of significant improvements in the eighties. Among the production functions, Cobb-Douglas and Bairam production functions performed better than CES and Translog production function. The poor performance of the latter two production functions (CES and Translog) can be attributed to the obvious problem of multi collinearity accentuated by the appearance of quadratic and cross- product terms.

Srivastava (1996)[5] has estimated production function for aggregate Indian manufacturing and various two-digit industries using panel data for public limited companies for the period 1980 to 1989. The data have been extracted from the balance sheets of companies available with Reserve Bank of India (RBI). A three-input (Cobb-Douglas and Translog) model has been used taking capital, labour and materials as the three inputs. The production function has been so specified as to allow a Hicks-neutral productivity factor vary across firm and over time. He has paid particular attention to the estimation problems associated with the panel data and emphasized the need for choosing an appropriate estimator. The author applied a number of alternative estimators including the "dummy variable " or "within" estimator, the "between" estimators, the first and higher order difference estimators and the generalized method of moments, instruments variable estimators. The study reported a decline in productivity in the liberalization policy regime since 1980s.

Ramaswamy, K.V. (1996)[6] pooled the data for 18 industry groups for the period 1975 to 1990 and estimated a multiple regression model with a time dummy to capture the effects of two periods, 1974-75 to 1979-80 and 1980-81 to 1989-90. He regressed the labour productivity growth on output growth rates, net entry and capital intensity. He founded that output growth has a positive effect on productivity growth. His estimates supported the hypothesis that entry in the period of industrial deregulation had a positive impact on productivity growth.

Beghel and Pendse (1997)[7] made an attempt to analyse productivity trends and statistical estimation of production function and technical change in the aggregate manufacturing sector in India. The ASI data for the period 1973-74 have utilized for computing Solow and Kendrick indices of TFP growth along with partial factor productivity indices of labour, capital and raw material and econometric estimation of Cobb-Douglas, CES and VES production functions. The analysis revealed that the Indian manufacturing sector have not experienced technological change which was evident from the growth rates of TFP growth indices as well as parameters of time variable in the production functions. The excessive doses of capital have not resulted in technological progress in Indian Manufacturing sector as the capital intensity is found to be increasing all time. The study suggested that there is a need to promote R & D efforts in the manufacturing sector of India so that it may survive in the newly emerging era of globalization and liberalization.

Keya Sengupta (1998)[8] have made a study of an empirical exploration of the performance of fertilizers industry in India: An econometric analysis. The controversy relating to the provision of fertilizers subsidy and the recent debate over its withdrawal has necessitated the present study to examine the performance of the fertilizers industry in India. Analysis of cost functions and Cobb-Douglas production function have been made to study the performance of the industry, the results of which reveal that the industry is subject to the law of increasing costs. The findings get further support from the examination of the production function, which reveals that the average productivity of labour exceeds its marginal productivity. Analysis of shifting cost functions further highlight that the firms belonging to this industry expand capacities, even before fully exploiting the existing capacity conforming to the oligopolistic behavioral tendency of the firms belonging to the fertilizers industry.

Ghosh and Neogi (1998)[9] tried to see the impact of liberalization on the performance of four selected industry groups, namely, (i) chemicals, (ii) textiles (iii) non-metallic mineral products, and (iv) electrical machinery, by using firm level data for the period 1989-94. The performance indicators chosen to verify the impact of economic reform on the firms were growth of value added capital intensity, labour productivity and total factor productivity. The estimates of technical efficiencies of selected industrial groups have obtained by using frontier production model with the help of Correlated Ordinary Least Square (COLS) method. The results indicated that productivity growth and efficiency levels have not improved as per expectation during the post–reform period and the distribution of efficiency is skewed. The TFP growth has fallen very sharply during the period of reforms with the exception of chemical industry. The relationship between labour and productivity and capital intensity indicated a general downfall of efficiency of firms during the study period. The level of technical efficiency for all the industries was found to be very low and no significant improvement has been observed in this level during the post-reform period.

Pradhan and Brik (1999)[10] captured the total factor productivity growth (TFPG) during the period 1963-93 for aggregate manufacturing sector and eight selected industries by estimating the Translog cost function. The scale factor for aggregate Indian manufacturing sector was found to be less than unity and a declaration in scale factor during the 1980s has been noticed. Except pulp and paper, a declaration in scale factor has been found in all selected industries in 1980s. For aggregate manufacturing sector and most of the individual industries, a declining trend in technical change has been noticed in recent years. On the whole, a decline trend of TFPG in Indian manufacturing sector-both at aggregate and dis-aggregate levels- has been noticed. They observed that a decline in both scale economies and technical change seems to have produced the present character of TFPG, although decline in the latter does not appear to be as sharp as the former.

R.N. Agarwal (2001)[11] studied the Technical Efficiency and Productivity Growth in the Central Public Sector Enterprises in India during 1990s. The study is based on the data for 58 large Central Public Sector Enterprises (CPSE) manufacturing / producing goods as well as data on industry groups provided by the Department of Public Enterprises, Ministry of Industries, Government of India for the period 1990-91 to 1998-99. The objective of the study is to analyse the technical change, technical efficiency and total productivity growth of CPSE, industry group-wise and firm-wise. Partial productivities and the Solow index of total factor productivity growth have been used for estimating productivity growth at the industry group level while panel data estimation method using the Random Effects Model and a modified form of the composite Error Term Frontier production Function Model as developed by Cornwell, has been used for estimating the technological change during the growth of technical efficiency at the firm level. The results show that the public sector enterprises have not experienced a significant technological change during the 1990s. Further, the result point to a decreasing returns to scale in production. Results also suggest that a majority of the firms have low levels of technical efficiency and that the efficiency has not improved significantly over time. However, the growth of technical efficiency is observed in some firms in the engineering sector and many firms in the petroleum producing / selling sector.

SECTION - IV

Measurement of Variables

Estimate of Value Added

The data for arriving at the partial factor productivity and total factor productivity are obtained from the summary results of Prowess database. Data relating to value added and value of gross fixed capital are taken from this database. The Prowess database provides value added at current prices has been deflated by indices of wholesale prices given in Index number of Wholesale Prices (Base 1981-82 = 100) in India. For the chemical industry, the index numbers of drug, base industry chemicals, fertilizers, paints and pesticides are applied.

Estimate of Gross Fixed Capital

The value of gross fixed capital stock at constant (1981-82) prices has been taken as the measure of capital input. The value of gross fixed capital stock is obtained by adding gross block, unallocated expenditure during construction and capital work in progress. To estimate time series of the real fixed capital stock, perpetual inventory method is employed. Once the estimate of real gross fixed capital for the bench year is obtained, the real gross investment of the next year is added to this to obtain real gross fixed capital for the entire period, the same procedure has been followed throughout. To get the deflator for gross fixed capital, the Wholesale

Price Index of Machinery and Machine tools at 1981-82 prices have been applied.

Estimate of Factor Share

Labour share has been calculated as the percentage of share of salaries and wages, in gross value added at current prices. The capital share then obtained as a residual subtracting the labour share from the corresponding value added at current prices.

Estimate of Wage Rate

The estimate of wage rate was obtained by dividing the salaries and wages and other benefits including bonus by total number of employees. The total number of employees can be obtained from the ASI data. Further wage rates were deflated by the corresponding wholesale price indices at 1981-82 prices, which are same as those used for deflating gross value added at current prices. Time (t) has been taken as proxy for technical change and residual effects and inserted in the regression equation as 1,2,3...n i.e., for 1991-92, 1992-93 and so on up to 2001-02.

SECTION - V

Empirical Findings

Estimates of factor productivities, production functions and regression functions for annual variations in factor productivities are presented in Table 13.0 to Table 13.2. The total factor productivity and partial factor productivity are also shown in the Figure 1 and Figure 2.

Estimates of Factor Productivities

Factor productivity indices for this industry are given in Table 13.0. Kendrick index, from base of 100 in 1991-92, it rises to 121 in 1992-93. But afterwards it falls to a level of 96 only in 1993-94. Again it starts increasing, except the year 1999-00 and 2000-01, and reaches a peak of 199 in 2001-02. Solow index shows an increasing trend till 1997-98 with an index of 197 except in the years 1993-94 and 1995-96. The index starts falling thereafter and shows a decreasing trend till 2000-01 where the index is 115 only. Thereafter, this index rises and reaches to 173 in 2001-02. Divisia index shows increasing trend till 1998-99 with a peak index of 198 except in the year 1993-94. It suddenly falls down to 125 in 2000-01. Then it starts improving and reaches to 175 in 2001-02. Kendrick index, Solow index and Divisia index increases at an annual rate of 1.15 per cent, 1.41 per cent and 1.15 per cent respectively over the entire period.

Table 13.0
Indices of Total Factor Productivities of the Indian Paint Industry (1991-92 to 2001-02)

Year	Total Factor Productivities			Partial Productivity	
	Kendrick Method	Solow Method	Divisia Method	Labour	Capital
1991-92	100	100	100	100	100
1992-93	121	151	110	89	96
1993-94	96	145	103	116	134
1994-95	108	169	134	121	114
1995-96	114	156	150	197	112
1996-97	178	181	151	164	125
1997-98	184	197	193	114	123
1998-99	181	191	198	116	169
1999-00	141	120	130	117	131
2000-01	100	115	125	195	102
2001-02	199	173	175	114	124
CAGR	**1.15**	**1.41**	**1.15**	**1.10**	**1.08**

Source: Computed

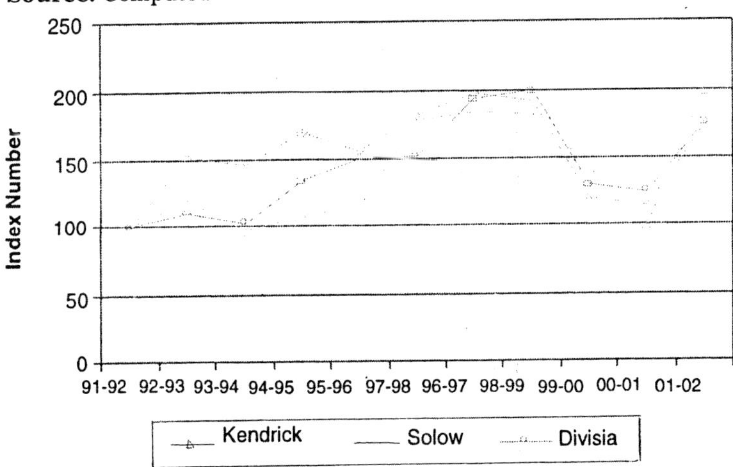

Figure 1. Total Factor Productivity Index of Paint Industry (1991-92 to 2001-02)

Labour productivity shows an upward trend with an annual growth rate of 1.10 per cent. Over the entire period, it moves up and down with a lowest index of 89 in 1992-93 and highest index of 197 in 1995-96. Capital productivity shows fluctuating trend with an increasing rate of 1.08 per cent per annum. Over the entire period, it moves up and down with a lowest index of 96 in 1992-93 and highest index of 169 in 1998-99. Over the entire period, labour productivity increases at an annual rate of 1.10 per cent whereas capital productivity increases at an annual rate of 1.08 per cent.

Productivity Estimates based on Production Function

Production function estimates for paint industry is given in Table 13.1 In the equation for CD function, co-efficient of log L is significant. This indicates that return to scale is not constant for paint industry. The sign of this co-efficient is, however, negative. The co-efficient of log K/L is also significant. Co-efficient of t is significant. Growth rate of TFP given by the co-efficient of t is 6.43 per cent. The value of R^2 indicates that 64 per cent of variations in the value of value added to labour could be accounted for by the variations in proportion of capital to labour, labour and technical change. As the calculated value of "F" is grater than the critical table

Table 13.1
Estimates of Production Functions: Paint Industry (1991-92 to 2001-02)

Eq. No	Dependent Variable	Co-efficient of					R^2	Adj R^2	F	DW
		Constant	Log (K/L)	Log (W)	Log (L)	t				
1	Log (V/L)	-23.381 (-.798)	0.389* (9.025)		-0.870* (3.441)	0.0643* (3.131)	0.64	0.54	19.39	1.684
2	Log (V/L)	-43.225 (-1.632)		-2.848* (2.951)	-5.459* (5.542)	0.053 (1.566)	0.57	0.31	10.5	1.788

Notes:
1. Equation (1) refers to CD function.
2. Equation (2) refers to CES function.
3. Figures in parenthesis denote 't' values.
4. * indicates significance at 5 per cent level.
5. V-Value added; L-Labour; K- Capital; W- Wage rate; t- time; DW- Durbin -Waston

Source: Computed

value the whole model fits perfectly. The value of "F" is significant at 5% level. In case of CES production function, co-efficient of log L is significant. Hence, return to scale is not constant. But the sign of this co-efficient is negative. Co-efficient of W implies that elasticity of substitution is less than unity. Co-efficient of t is insignificant. It gives a TFP growth rate of 5.3 per cent. The value of R^2 indicater that 57 per cent of variations in the value of value added to labour could be accounted for by variations in wage rate, labour and technical change. As the calculated value of "F" is greater than the critical table value, the while model fits perfectly.

Functions for Annual Variations in Factor Productivities

Regression functions for this industry are presented in Table 13.2. In the functions for TFP, co-efficient of real value added turns out to be significant with a positive sign and that of time turns out to be significant with a positive sign. Thus, total factor productivity is generated by scale economies and labour management relations. In the functions for labour productivity also, co-efficient of real value added is positively significant and the co-efficeint of time is positive but insignificant. Labour productivity is, thus, generated by significant scale economies and labour management relations for the paint industry during the study period.

Table 13.2

Regression functions for Total Factor Productivity and Labour Productivity: Paint Industry (1991-92 to 2001-02)

Eq. No	Dependent Variable	Co-efficient of			R^2	Adj R^2	F	DW
		Constant	Log (V)	t				
1	Log(TFPK)	5.101	2.124*	5.665*	0.65	0.42	2.89	2.261
		(10.921)	(6.134)	(2.361)				
2	Log (TFPS)	5.432	3.112*	1.637	0.37	0.038	16.40	1.503
		(11.97)	(7.55)	(0.702)				
3	Log (TFPD)	5.187	1.120*	4.880*	0.72	0.52	4.33	1.716
		(15.569)	(14.538)	(2.581)				
4	Log (LP)	4.267	1.100*	2.244				
		(8.502)	(3.853)	(0.870)	0.49	0.39	1.056	1.759

Notes:

1. Figures in parenthesis denote 't' values.
2. * indicates significance at 5 per cent level.

3. TFPK- Kendrick Method; TFPS- Solow Method; TFPD-Divisia Method; LP- Labour Productivity ; DW- Durbin Waston.

Source: Computed

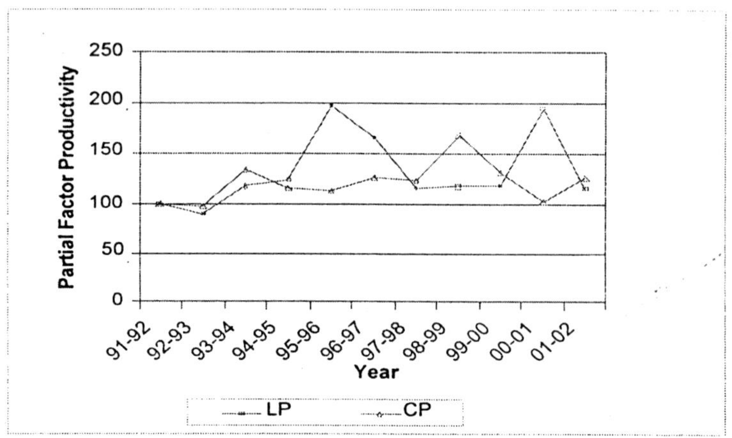

Figure 2. Partial Factor Productivity of Labour and Capital of Paint Industry (1991-92 to 2001-02)

Conclusion

It is concluded that estimates of TFP for paint industry shows a rising trends in all the three direct measures of TFP. Labour Productivity and Capital Productivity of Drug Industry also show a rising trend during the study period. Estimates of the Cobb-Douglas production function reveals that returns to scale is not constant for Paint Industry during the study period. Estimates of the CES production function also shows that returns to scale is not constant for Paint Industry. Further, elasticity of substitution is less than unity for Paint Industry during the study period. Annual Variations in factor productivities shows that a significant positive relationship is observed with value of added for this industry. This shows that expansion in scale of production has been generating growth in total factor productivity. Further, there is a positive significant relationship with time is observed for Paints Industry. This indicates that total factor productivity is generated by labour management relations in this sector during the study period.

References

1. Anita Kumari (1993). "Productivity in the public sector- Analysis at Industrial Group Level", *Economic Political Weekly*, pp. M145-M162.
2. Tarlok Singh and D. Ajit (1993). "Production function in the manufacturing industries in India: 1974-1990", pp- 125-155.
3. Balakrishnan, P. and K. Pushpangadan (1994). "Total Factor Productivity Growth in Manufacturing Industry: A fresh Look". *Economic and Political* Weekly. pp 2028-35.
4. Singh, T. and D. Ajit (1995). Production function in the manufacturing industries in India: 1974-90. Reserve Bank of India Occasional papers. Vol.16, No.2, June, pp.241-66.
5. Srivastava (1996). "Productivity growth and technical efficiency in manufacturing firms in India". Deep and Deep Publications, New Delhi.
6. Ramaswamy, K.V. (1996). "Productivity of the Indian Manufacturing Industries. M/s Print Well Publishers, Jaipur.
7. Beghel, L.M.S. and Pendse (1997). An Econometric Analysis of Productivity Growth and Technical Change in Total Manufacturing Sector of India". *The Indian Economic Journal.* Vol.44, No.2, pp.39-58.
8. Keya Sengupta (1998). "An empirical exploration of the performance of fertilizers industry in India: An econometric analysis". *Artha Vijnana.* Vol.XL, No.3, pp.252-262.
9. Ghosh, B. and C. Neogi, (1998). "Impact of Liberalization on Performance of Indian Industries. Firm Level Study". *Economic and Political Weekly.* pp. M16-M24.
10. Paradhan G. and K. Barik (1999). "Total Factor Productivity Growth in Developing Economies: A Study of Selected Industries in India". *Economic and Political Weekly*, July, pp. M92-M97.
11. R.N. Agarwal (2001). "Technical Efficiency and Productivity Growth in the Central Public Sector Enterprises in India during 1990s". *Economic and Political Weekly.* pp.1-24.

14

AN ECONOMETRIC ANALYSIS OF PRODUCTIVITY GROWTH IN INDIAN DRUG INDUSTRIES : A FIRM LEVEL STUDY

For the growth of the economy it is necessary that industries should be productive. The measurement of productivity is pre-eminently a quantitative and technical problem. The concept of factor productivity gives the contribution which one or all used factors make to production. This concept is reflected in a ratio between product (output) and the factor or factors used (input). The study of factor productivity is an important aspect of the analysis of development since it quantities the contribution of the different factors of production. Higher levels of growth can be attained through better utilization of available resources i.e., capital and labour. It is the most useful measurement of the variations of productivity in time. It is the best means of evaluating the contribution of the various factors. Therefore, the study of factor productivity has particular significance in the formulation of policies at the state as well as national level.

In India major economic reforms have been undertaken since July 1991 with the objective of increasing the productivity and competitions of the companies. The new policies have liberalized many government controls on production capacity, imported capital goods, and intermediate inputs cheaper and more accessible to both domestic and international competition. These reforms have altered the economic environment in which the companies operate. Therefore, an attempt has been made in this part to analyze the impact of these reforms on productivity of Indian chemical Industry.

The study is done for the Drug Sector of Indian Chemical Industries. The period chosen for this study is 1991-2002.The purpose of this study is to measure total factor productivities, as well as partial factor productivities for the selected sector of chemical industry overtime. Further an attempt has also been made to explain annual variations in factor productivities with the help of multiple regression frameworks. The basic data source for this study is the PROWESS Database of CMIE.

Empirical Findings

Estimates of factor productivities, production functions and regression functions for annual variations in factor productivities are presented in Table 14.0 to Table 14.2. The total factor productivity and partial factor productivity are also shown in the graph.

Estimates of Factor Productivities

To examine movements in TFP over the time period of 1991-92 to 2001-02 in Indian drug industry, the three measures of TFP i.e., Kendrick, Solow and Divisia indices are calculated and presented in Table 14.0.

Table 14.0
Indices of Total Factor Productivities of the Indian Drug Industry (1991-92 to 2001-02)

Year	Total Factor Productivities			Partial Productivity	
	Kendrick Method	Solow Method	Divisia Method	Labour	Capital
1991-92	100	100	100	100	100
1992-93	103	102	109	102	108
1993-94	106	116	126	124	114
1994-95	137	154	146	183	169
1995-96	181	194	192	184	168
1996-97	196	192	196	188	172
1997-98	112	121	105	111	104
1998-99	199	189	184	164	194
1999-00	154	165	148	188	161
2000-01	197	194	190	189	163
2001-02	185	194	192	191	172
CAGR	**1.05**	**1.11**	**1.17**	**1.07**	**1.08**

Source: Computed

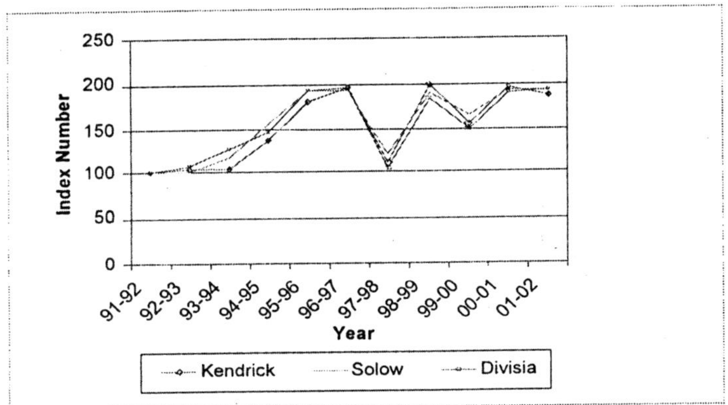

Figure 1
Total Factor Productivity Index of Drug Industry (1991-92 to 2001-02)

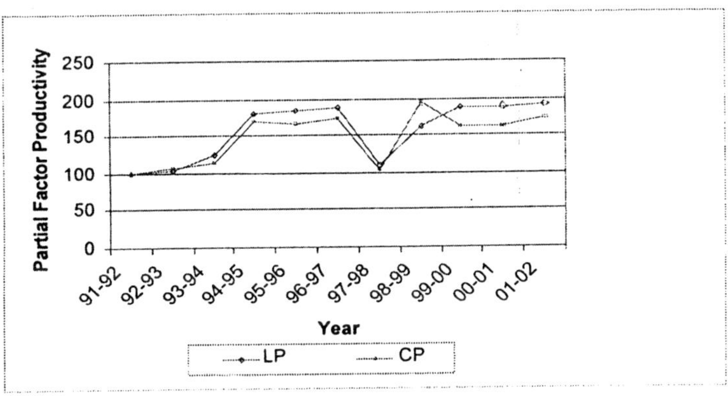

Figure 2
Partial Factor Productivity of Labour and Capital of Drug Industry (1991-92 to 2001-02)

Kendrick indices are marked by mixed variations. From a base of 100 in 1991-92, it raises to 199 in 1998-99. But in the year 1997-98, it goes down to 112 from 196 in 1996-97. Again it starts falling and reaches a level of 154 in 1999-00. Further, it starts rising and reaches a level of 197 in 2000-01. Solow and Divisia indices also reveal fluctuations. Solow index also shows an increasing trend till 2000-01 except in the years 1997-98 and 1999-00. Divisia index also reveals the same patterns. It reaches 196 in 1996-97 but it is 105 only in 1997-98. Further, index reaches a level of 192 in 2001-02. On the whole, all the indices show an increasing trend till 1996-97 recording a peak of 199 in Kendrick index in the year 1998-99, 194 in Solow index in the year 2001-02 and 196 in Divisia index in the year 1996-97. After 1996-97, all the indices shown fluctuating trend till 2001-02. Over the entire period, TFP for the Indian drug industry increases at an annual rate of 1.05 per cent according to Kendrick Method, 1.11 per cent according to Solow method and 1.17 per cent according to Divisia method.

Partial factor productivity indices of labour and capital have also been computed and also shown in Table 14.0. Labour productivity shows an upward trend up to 1996-97 and reaches 188 in 1996-97. Afterwards its starts falling and in 1997-98, the index is only 111. Labour productivity again picks up and reaches a maximum of 191 in 2001-02. Capital productivity after rising to 172 in 1996-97 comes down to 104 in 1997-98. And then again it moves up and reaches 194 by 1998-99. This pattern is not smooth but accompanied by fluctuations. Over the entire period, labour productivity increases at an annual rate of 1.07 per cent whereas capital productivity increases at an annual rate of 1.08 per cent.

Productivity Estimates based on Production Function

Estimates of the Cobb-Douglas (CD) production function and Constant Elasticity Substitution (CES) production function for the Indian drug industry are presented in Table 14.1. In the CD function, the co-efficient of log L is insignificant implying thereby that return to scale is constant. The sign of this co-efficient is, however, negative. The co-efficient of log (K/L) is also insignificant with a negative sign. Co-efficient of time is significant. Annual growth rate in TFP given by this co-efficient is being 9.68 per cent.

Table 14.1

Estimates of Production Functions: Drug Industry (1991-92 to 2001-02)

Eq. No	Dependent Variable	Co-efficient of					R^2	Adj R^2	F	DW
		Constant	Log (K/L)	Log (W)	Log (L)	t				
1	Log (V/L)	-82.120 (-1.799)	-15.723 (-0.681)		-0.497 (-0.055)	0.968* (2.409)	0.79	0.62	3.95	2.18
2	Log (V/L)	-0. 353 (-0.325)		-0.4849 (-0. 302)	-4.098 (-0.283)	0.098 (0.740)	0.55	0.31	1.03	2.43

Notes:

1. **Equation (1) refers to CD function.**
2. **Equation (2) refers to CES function.**
3. **Figures in parenthesis denote 't' values.**
4. *** indicates significance at 5 per cent level.**
5. **V-Value added; L-Labour; K- Capital; W- Wage rate; t- time; DW- Durbin - Waston**

Source: Computed

In the equation of CES production function, co-efficient of log L is insignificant. Thus return to scale is constant. The sign of this co-efficient is negative. The co-efficient of W is not significant. Co-efficient of W implies that elasticity of substitution is less than unity. The co-efficient of time is insignificant. This shows increase in TFP at an annual rate of 9.8 per cent. It may be noted that the co-efficient in the production function may be affected by multi-collinearity.

Functions for Annual Variations in Factor Productivities

Regression functions for annual variations in factor productivities for this industry are shown in Table 14.2. As formulated, explanatory variables are real value added, indicative of scale of production and time as proxy for institutional factors like management labour relations. It is observed from Table 5.3 that in functions for TFP, co-efficient of real value added is positive for all the three methods of TFP. Thus, expansion in scale of production has been generating growth in total factor productivity. However, this is not significant. Further, the co-efficient of time is negative and significant in Solow method. This indicates that deteriorating institutional environment as reflected in labour management relations have been adversely affecting total factor productivity. In function for partial factor productivity of labour, co-efficient of real value added turns out to be significant with a positive sign and co-efficient of time turns out to be significant with a negative sign. Thus, labour productivity is also generated by scale economies but deteriorated by adverse labour management relations in the drug industry.

Table 14.2
Regression functions for Total Factor Productivity and Labour Productivity: Drug Industry (1991-92 to 2001-02)

Eq. No	Dependent Variable	Co-efficient of			R^2	Adj R^2	F	DW
		Constant	Log (V)	T				
1	Log (TFPK)	5.11 (2.702)	1.41 (0.275)	-7.521 (1.79)	0.75	0.56	5.10	2.37
2	Log (TFPS)	5.466 (3.164)	0.223 (0.477)	-7.873** (2.05)	0.77	0.59	5.74	1.793
3	Log (TFPD)	6.012 (3.111)	0.350 (0.667)	-6.054 (1.41)	0.54	0.29	1.67	2.353
4	Log (LP)	7.705 (6.73)	0.842 (2.71)	-0.119* (4.70)	0.89	0.79	15.15	1.532

Notes:

1. Figures in parenthesis denote 't' values.
2. * indicates significance at 5 per cent level.
3. ** indicates significance at 10 per cent level.
4. TFPK- Kendrick Method; TFPS- Solow Method; TFPD- Divisia Method; LP- Labour Productivity ; DW- Durbin - Waston.

Source: Computed

Conclusion:

It is concluded that estimates of TFP for drug industry shows a rising trends in all the three direct measures of TFP. Labour Productivity and Capital Productivity of Drug Industry also show a rising trend during the study period. Estimates of the Cobb-Douglas production function reveal constant returns to scale for Drug Industry during the study period. Estimates of the CES production function also shows that returns to scale is constant for Drug Industry. Further, elasticity of substitution is less than unity for Drug Industry during the study period. Annual Variations in factor productivities shows that a significant positive relationship is observed with value of added for this industry. This shows that expansion in scale of production has been generating growth in total factor productivity. On the other hand with time a significant negative relationship is observed for drug industry but significant only in respect of Solow index. This indicates that deteriorating institutional environment as reflected in labour management relations have been adversely affecting total factor productivity. Thus, it is concluded that growth in factor productivities of drug industry would have been much higher if labour-management relations would have been better.

15

PRODUCTIVITY AND PROFITABILITY OF THE PAPER INDUSTRY—A CASE STUDY OF SESHASAYEE PAPER AND BOARDS LIMITED, TAMIL NADU

Paper plays a vital role in the cultural development of human beings. Paper constitutes one of the most important segments of India's Industrial Economy and is treated as a basic sector. Its performance is crucial to the economy as much as to the growth of service sectors like education, communication, trade and commerce, banking and insurance, public administration, journalism, all of which greatly depend on supplies of printing and writing paper and newsprint. The industrial sector also requires paper and newsprint, both for packaging and for its service sector. One index for measuring a nation's development and progress is the level of per capita consumption of paper. This is lagging far behind in India. The importance of paper and paper products in modern life is so obvious because no other manufactured product possesses such a diversity of uses. Time importance of the growth of this industry in a developing economy like that of India where the literacy rates are to be considerably improved, school enrolments are increasing, newspaper subscriptions are rising and the printing and publishing industry has to make further headway cannot be over emphasised.

In India, the tradition of making paper by hand can be traced to the 8th century A.D. The first paper mill was successfully started in 1870 and the second in the 1930's in West Bengal. Today there are about 350 paper mills spread over the country. The industry is providing employment to nearly 300,000 persons. It also provides indirect employment to large numbers. The Indian paper industry at present is beset with various problems like raw materials shortage, rising cost of production, and downward trend in capacity utilisation. Moreover, the paper industry is a highly capital intensive industry and has a long gestation period and so suffer in regard to profitability. However, there are a few paper mills which run at full capacity and with comfortable profit margins.

Statement of the Problem

Government interventions in an industry through policy measures aim to influence the structure, the running and the performance of firms so as to achieve specific goals. Since there have been substantial changes in the regulatory framework of the paper industry, one would expect that such policy measures would have impact on the firms operating in this industry. Therefore, the objective of this study was to examine the determinants of productivity and profitability in the paper industry.

Productivity involves a comparison between the quantity of goods or services produced and the quantity of resources employed in turning out these goods and services. When the same resources that were employed in the past now produce more than they did before, we say that productivity has increased. Productivity acts as a barometer to measure the efficiency of an industry. Productivity studies help to estimate the measure of protection to be granted to an industry. They also assist in evaluating the influence of production on employment. In this study, an attempt has been made to measure productivity, by using the Cobb-Douglas production function.

Profitability is determined by structural as well as behavioural variables. The structural factors which have a bearing on profitability are size, growth, barriers to entry of new units degree of vertical integration, diversification and cost conditions. Corporate policies relating to various organizational functions will obviously affect profitability. Some policies are relevant in the short-run while others have an impact in the long run. One has to identify certain specific variables considering the purpose of the study and the relevance of different factors in explaining profitability in this industry during the period of study. Financial ratios are used to measure the variables. Hence, in this study, an attempt has been made to identify the factors influencing profitability by using Multiple Regression Analysis.

The Present Study

The Cobb-Douglas production function is a type of linearly homogeneous production function which has proved particularly useful for empirical work. The general formula for this function is

$$Y = A K^{\alpha} L^{\beta}$$

Where $0 < \alpha < 1$, K is Productive capital and L is Labour. In order to arrive at the estimator of the function, the model parameters are linearised by a log transformation.

$$\text{Log } Y = \text{Log } A + \alpha\text{Log } K + \beta\text{Log } L$$

Where Y is Gross output; K is capital; L is Labour; A is constant term; α is co-efficient of capital; and β is coefficient of labour. This function characterises the returns to scale as below:

$\alpha + \beta > 1$: Increasing returns to scale

$\alpha + \beta = 1$: Constant returns to scale

$\alpha + \beta < 1$: Decreasing returns to scale

As, there are a number of factors which explain profitability and the measurement of the variables employed can also be different, it is important to mention the variables and explain how they are measured.

Return on assets and return on sales are widely used measures of profitability. It is assumed that the management is concerned with the effective utilisation of all resources. These two measures would then be proper. The profit rates measured by sales will give a short-term perspective of profitability because sales are annual flows. On the other hand, the return on assets will give us a long term perspective of profitability. In this sense, return on assets has been used as a dependent variable.

The size of the firm affects its profit. The increase in money capital not only increases the absolute profits of the firm but also increases its earning power per unit of investment. However, this will be true only if large firms are efficient and innovative. Though the positive relationship between size and profitability has been found to be significant, after a certain point, profitability increases at a rate proportional to the increase in size. The size of the firm is sought to be measured in this study by the total sales revenue.

The other variables considered here are Capacity Integration (CI) and Capacity Utilisation (CU). High profitability may be the result of adjustments in capacity which were lagging behind changes in demand and/or improvements in efficiency of operation. Firm-specific vertical integration, motivated by considerations such as avoidance of the costs incurred in using the market to organize production, government policies and also considerations of market power, is an important determinant of profitability. In this study, the degree of vertical integration is sought to be measured by the value-dded to the sales ratio.

Another variable which can influence the profitability is the leverage ratio. A firm with high leverage ratio represents a greater financial risk than a firm with relatively lower leverage ratio. If competition equalises earnings, then, high debt should result in higher return on net worth. Another variable which can influence the profitability is the inventory turnover ratio. A low inventory ratio will adversely affect the ability of a firm to meet customer demand and in return will affect its profitability. In inter-firm comparisons, the firm with a higher current ratio has better liquidity. A low inventory ratio may be indicative of slack management practices which affect the profitability.

Apart from the factors discussed above, operating expenses are included as an explanatory variable in this study. The implication of a low operating expenses ratio is that it improves the profitability of the concern.

The model specified for estimating profitability is as follows:

$$PP = b_o + b_1 S + b_2\, CI + b_3\, CU + b_4\, VI + b_5\, DTA + b_6\, ITR + b_7\, CR + b_8\, OPES$$

Where PP is Measure of Profitability; S is Sales; CI is Capacity Integration; CU is Capacity Utilisation; VI is Vertical Integration; DTA is Debt/Total Assets; ITR is Inventory Turnover Ratio; CR is Current Ratio; and OPES is Operating Expenses to Sales Ratio.

Objectives of the Study

The main objectives of the study were:

i) to analyse the growth in production, employment, sales and profit of Seshasayee Paper and Boards Limited;

ii) to identify the determinant factors of profitability in the company.

Methodology

The productivity analyses are done using the Cobb-Douglas production function. Determinants of profitability are analysed using the technique of multiple regressions analysis. Based on the existing theories and on relevant econometric empirical works, variables are selected. While using regression technique, efforts are made to reduce the problem of multicollinearity and auto correlation. Moreover, by using cross-section data in combination with time series data, one can avoid the high intercorrelation between the explanatory variables. Though, in practice, multicollinearity cannot be completely avoided, it can be reduced by using appropriate explanatory variables. The Durbin-Watson test is used to arrive at an idea of the existence of autocorrelation. The Durbin-Watson statistics are reported in regressions results. The period of study was from 1981-1982 to 1993-1994. The recent data available and the relevance of the period were considered in selecting the study period.

Empirical Findings

Growth of Production, Labour and Productive Capital. Production is one of the most basic economic relationships, and ideally it expresses the technical relationship between the physical quantity of inputs into the production process and the physical quantity of output produced; this description should be applied at the macro economic level, for a single firm or a single homogeneous product and a few homogeneous inputs. Actual production has been examined by economists to measure the relationship between changes in physical inputs and physical outputs and is naturally given a technical consideration. Therefore, the efficiency of technology, technologically determined economics of scale, the capital intensity of technology and the ease with which factors can be substituted for each other can be expressed in terms of the quantum of production.

The production of paper and boards in Seshasayee Paper and Boards Limited for the period 1981-1982 to 1993-1994 is presented in Table 15.0. It is evident from the table that the production of SPB Ltd fluctuated during the period of study. However, on the whole it increased from Rs.4,174.55 lakhs in 1981-82 to Rs.11,603.38 lakhs in 1993-94. The percentage of increase in production over the previous year ranged from 0.74 in 1987-89 to 37.91 in 1993-94. The highest increase in production was noticed in 1983-84, 1984-85, 1985-86, 1989-90, 1991-92 and 1993-94. The table also depicts loss in production ranging from – 15.98 per cent in 1982-83 to – 2.08 per cent in 1988-89 through – 9.05 per cent in 1986-87.

Labour cost depends upon the number of workers employed. The labour employed in SPB Ltd are both skilled and unskilled. The total number of labourers employed in SPB Ltd during the study period is presented in Table 15.0. The table indicates that the total number of labourers employed showed a generally decreasing trend during the study period. The number of workers decreased from 2617 in 1981-82 to 2224 in 1993-94, even though the production had nearly trebled.

The capital structure of a paper industry includes both fixed and working capital. The sum of fixed and working capital is termed productive capital. The productive capital of SPB Ltd during the study period is presented in Table 15.0. The table shows that the total productive capital was increasing over the years. It increased from Rs.5,034.25 lakhs in 81-82 to Rs.10,492.29 lakhs in 1993-94. But the percentage increase over the previous year shows ups and downs over the period.

Thus, it is inferred from this analysis that the production growth and productive capital of SPB Ltd show an increasing trend whereas the total number of labourers registered a decreasing trend during the study period.

Table 15.0

Growth of Production, Capital and Labour of SPB Ltd.

Years	Production (Value in Rs. in Lakhs)	Productive Capital (Rs. in Lakhs)	No. of Labourers
1981-82	4174.55	5034.25	2617
1982-83	3507.80 (-15.98)	4945.76 (-1.76)	2567 (-1.92)
1983-84	4837.62 (37.91)	5584.26 (12.91)	2580 (0.50)
1984-85	4425.05 (-8.53)	5989.74 (7.26)	2604 (0.93)
1985-86	5766.25 (30.31)	7572.78 (26.43)	2664 (2.30)
1986-87	5244.59 (-9.05)	7550.69 (-0.29)	2569 (-3.57)
1987-88	5283.16 (0.74)	6951.63 (-7.93)	2527 (-1.64)
1988-89	5172.90 (-2.08)	6787.82 (-2.36)	2195 (-13.14)
1989-90	6054.50 (17.04)	7539.65 (11:08)	2373 (8.11)
1991-91	7426.56 (22.66)	8211.79 (8.91)	2335 (-1.61)
1991-92	8547.10 (15.09)	8337.58 (1.53)	2299 (-1.54)
1992-93	9125.18 (6.76)	9439.32 (13.21)	2261 (-1.66)
1993-94	116063.38 (27.16)	10492.29 (11.16)	2224 (-1.64)

Note: Figures in parantheses indicates the percentage change from the previous year.

Source: Computed

Productivity of SPB Ltd.

A production process can be studied empirically in terms of either the production function or the cost function. Estimates of the parameters of these functions provide valuable insights into the technology of firms and industries. Many actual production functions have been examined by economists to measure the relationship between changes in the physical inputs and the output. The important questions relating to technology are (i) whether the production-process display decreasing, increasing or constant returns to scale, (ii) how technological progress affects the parameters of the production process and (iii) at what rate technological progress has occurred. The Cobb-Douglas production function gives an explicit measurement of returns to scale and output elasticities for different factors of production. In the analysis, the Cobb-Douglas production function is used to test the hypothesis that "constant returns to scale" operate in SPB Ltd.

Table 15.1 shows the estimates of the Cobb-Douglas production function fitted for SPB Ltd from 1981-82 to 1993-94. The value of R^2 indicates that 90 per cent of the variations in the value of the output could be accounted for by variations in capital (K) and labour (L). As the calculated value of 'F' is greater than the critical table value, the whole model fits perfectly. The value of 'F' is greater than the critical table value, the whole model fits perfectly. The value of 'F' is significant at 5% level. The coefficient of capital reveals that one unit increase in output could be brought in by a 1.28 units increase in the capital of SPB Ltd. The statistical validity of this coefficients is significant at 1% level. The coefficient of labour (β) is not significant and it explains that 0.67 unit decrease in labour would bring about one unit increase in the value of output. This model shows that SPB Ltd experienced a condition of increased return to scale. This is supported by the estimated values of (1.28) and (-0.67). The sum of

Table 15.1
Regression Estimates of Cobb-Douglas Production Function of SPB Ltd. (1981-82 to 1993-94)
(Log Q = Log A + Log K + Log L)

Name of the Unit	Constant term (A)	Co-efficient of Capital (K)	Co-efficient of Labour (L)	R^2	Adj R^2	F Ratio	D.W.
SPB LTD	1.138	1.277 (0.198) t=6.44*	-0.675 (0.701) t=0.96	0.9019	0.8823	45.98*	1.31

Note: Figures given in brackets show the standard errors of the parameter.

* Significant at 1% level. Where Q – output; K – Capital; and L–Labour

Source: Computed

these values is more than one; therefore the hypothesis is not acceptable. Thus, it is concluded that the law of constant returns to scale is not in operation.

Profitability of SPB Ltd

The profitability function was estimated using the least-square method. While estimating, checks were made for model violations such as multicollinearity and auto correlation with the help of the Correction Matrix and the Durbon-Watson Statistics. It is evident from Table 15.2 that none of the selected variables is highly correlated. This shows there is no multicollinearity between the variables selected for the study. The results of the model are presented in Table 15.3.

Table 15.2

Pairwise Correlation Matrix of Independent Variables in SPB Ltd.

Variables	S	CI	CU	VI	DTA	ITR	CR
Sales (S)	1.000						
Capacity Integration (CI)	-0.6578	1.000					
Capacity Utilisation (CU)	-0.1553	0.5458	1.000				
Vertical Integration (VI)	0.3630	0.2936	0.3984	1.000			
Debt./Total Assets (DTA)	-0.5165	0.0288	-0.4727	-0.2819	1.000		
ITR	0.4937	-0.0362	0.0898	0.4149	-0.5290	1.000	
Current Ratio (CR)	0.4798	-0.5413	-0.5809	-0.5923	0.3655	0.0920	1.000
Operating Expenses Sales (OPES)	0.3560	-0.3327	-0.4434	-0.9943	0.3177	-0.4478	0.6090

Source: Computed

The estimated equations are found to be statistically fit and with reasonably high explanatory power. The measure of profitability used was return on assets (net profit/total assets). In the estimated equation for the period 1981-94 all the independent variables such as sales, capacity integration, capacity utilisation, vertical integration, debt to total assets ratio, inventory turnover ratio, current ratio and operating expenses to sales ratio are found to be statistically significant in explaining the profitability of SPB Ltd. The significance of an operating expenses ratio with a negative coefficient is that firms which are operationally efficient are able to earn more than inefficient firms.

Table 15.3

Determinations of Profitability of SPB Ltd.

	Variables	Beta Co-efficients	t-Value	
	Constant	-612.42	4.28	
1.	Sales (S)	0.068	2.05	Significant ***
2.	Capacity Integration (CI)	-66.17	2.98	Significant **
3.	Capacity Utilisation (CU)	1.069	3.78	Significant **
4.	Vertical Integration (VI)	515.55	4.91	Significant **
5.	Debt./Total Assets (DTA)	-64.23	5.73	Significant *
6.	ITR	3.76	1.88	Significant ***
7.	Current Ratio (CR)	7.20	3.33	Significant **
8.	Operating Expenses/Sales (OPES)	-5.58	3.93	Significant **
	R^2	0.9918		
	Ad j R^2	0.9700		
	F Value	45.49		
	DW Stat	2.03		

Note: * - Significant at 1 per cent level

** - Significant at 5 per cent level

*** - Significant at 10 per cent level

Source: Computed

The results presented in the table also indicate that the coefficient of sales, capacity utilisation, vertical utilisation, inventory turnover ratio and current ratio are positive while that of capacity integration, debt to total assets ratio, and operating expenses to sales are generally negative. The coefficient of size (sales) is significant at the 0.10 level. Seen in quantitative terms however the size effect is not very strong. It is evident from the coefficient of sales that one unit increase in size would result in an increase of 0.07 percentage points in profitability. The strongest structural determinant of profitability appears to be vertical integration. Its coefficient is significant at 0.01 level of significance. The coefficient also shows that an increase of 515.55 percentage points in the degree of vertical integration can result in a one percentage point increase in profitability.

The inventory turnover ratio is also statistically significant in explaining profitability. The coefficient is positive which indicates that SPB Ltd had good inventory management during the period of study. It is quite possible that firms in the paper industry went in for expansion and modernisation. Regarding, leverage, the negative coefficient explains that the companies which had lower debts were able to produce higher return compared to others. The other structural variable, capacity utilisation is seen to have little effect on profitability. The overall explanatory power of the regressions appears to be high. This may be inferred from the F statistic which is significant at 0.01 level.

Conclusion

The study demonstrates that the law of constant return to scale was not in operation in SPB Ltd during the period of study. The regression analysis further shows that capacity integration, vertical integration, the debt to total assets ratio, inventory turnover ratio, current ratio and operating expenses ratio are permanent variables in determining the profitability of SPB Ltd. The significance of the operating expenses rations with a negative coefficient is that SPB Ltd is operationally efficient and earned more profit. The analysis also demonstrates that under the condition of government price controls the most significant determinant of the profitability of firms like SPB Ltd is vertical integration. Size and capacity utilisation do not appear to be major determinants. In conclusion, there is a strong indication that all the selected variables had a very significant role to play in determining profitability in the Seshasayee Paper and Boards Limited, during the period of study.

References

1. Agarwal, R.N. (1991) "Profitability and Growth in Indian Automobile Manufacturing Industry", *Indian Economic Review,* Vol.26, No.1, p.81.
2. Datta, Kamal Kumar, Dan, S. S. & Datta, Amal Kumar. (1989) "Productivity, Profitability and Income Distribution in Capture Fishery: A study of the Orissa Coast", *Economic & Politial Weekly,* Vol.24, No.51, p.A-181.
3. Ekpenyong, D. B. (1993) "Operational Performance of Newly Privatised Public Companies in Nigeria: A Financial Appraisal of Selected Companies", *Journal of Financial Management & Analysis,* Vol.6, No.1, p.13.

4. Nagarajan, Mohan, Barthwal, R.R. (1989), "Profitability and Size of Firms in the Indian Pharmaceutical Industry", *Indian Journal of Economics,* Vol.69, No.275, p.405.
5. Narayanaswamy, N. and Banu, V. (1993) "Size, Cost and Profitability: An Empirical Study of Pandyan Grama Bank in Tamil Nadu", *Finance India,* Vol.7, No.1, p.97.
6. Pathak, S. "Production, Productivity & Profitability of Jute in India", *Productivity,* Vol.30, No.2, 1989, P.150.
7. Porwal, K. Hamendra and Parwal, Sangeetha (1991) "Risk and Profitability on New Issues – An Empirical Study", *The Chartered Accountant,* Vol.40, No.1, p.20.

16

TOTAL FACTOR PRODUCTIVITY AND PRODUCTION FUNCTION ANALYSIS FOR ORGANIC AND INORGANIC CHEMICAL INDUSTRY IN INDIA

For the growth of the economy it is necessary that industries should be productive. The measurement of productivity is pre-eminently a quantitative and technical problem. The concept of factor productivity gives the contribution which one or all used factors make to production. This concept is reflected in a ratio between product (output) and the factor or factors used (input). The study of factor productivity is an important aspect of the analysis of development since it quantities the contribution of the different factors of production. Higher levels of growth can be attained through better utilization of available resources i.e., capital and labour. It is the most useful measurement of the variations of productivity in time. It is the best means of evaluating the contribution of the various factors. Therefore, the study of factor productivity has particular significance in the formulation of policies at the state as well as national level.

In India major economic reforms have been undertaken since July 1991 with the objective of increasing the productivity and competitions of the companies. The new policies have liberalized many government controls on production capacity, imported capital goods, and intermediate inputs cheaper and more accessible to both domestic and international competition. These reforms have altered the economic environment in which the companies operate. Therefore, an attempt has been made in this part to analyze the impact of these reforms on productivity of Indian paints Industry.

The study is done for the organic and inorganic chemical industries. The period chosen for this study is 1991-2002.The purpose of this study is to measure total factor productivities, as well as partial factor productivities for the selected sector of chemical industry overtime. Further an attempt has also been made to explain annual variations in factor productivities with help of multiple regression frameworks. The basic data source for this study is the PROWESS Database of CMIE.

Empirical Findings

Estimates of factor productivities, production functions and regression functions for annual variations in factor productivities are presented in Table 16.0 to Table 16.5. The total factor productivity and partial factor productivity are also shown in the graph.

ORGANIC INDUSTRY

Estimates of Factor Productivities

To examine movements in TFP over the time period of 1991-92 to 2001-02 in Indian Organic Industry, the three measures of TFP i.e., Kendrick, Solow and Divisia Indices are calculated and presented in Table 16.0.

Table 16.0
Indices of Total Factor Productivities of the Indian Organic Industry (1991-92 to 2001-02)

Year	Total Factor Productivities			Partial Productivity	
	Kendrick Method	Solow Method	Divisia Method	Labour	Capital
1991-92	100	100	100	100	100
1992-93	93	94	92	109	85
1993-94	98	102	105	185	106
1994-95	101	103	101	103	190
1995-96	129	128	124	117	131
1996-97	158	145	185	177	168
1997-98	185	180	186	172	179
1998-99	153	138	187	136	120
1999-00	196	117	120	178	162
2000-01	158	185	165	190	188
2001-02	143	196	190	105	114
CAGR	**0.94**	**0.96**	**0.96**	**1.19**	**1.10**

Source: Computed

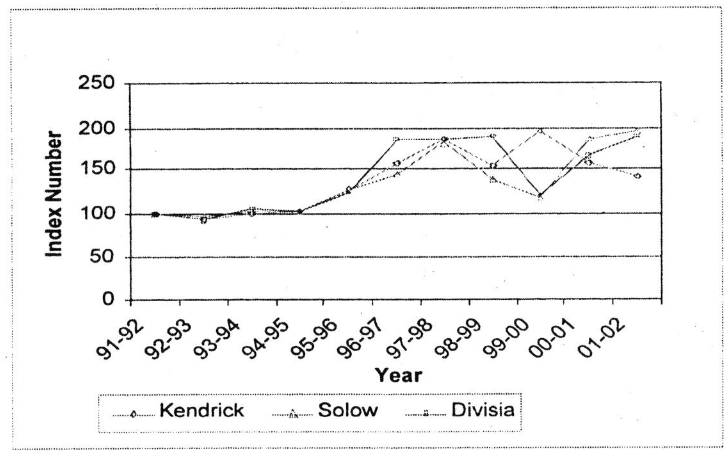

Figure 1
Total Factor Productivity Index of Organic Industry
(1991-92 to 2001-02)

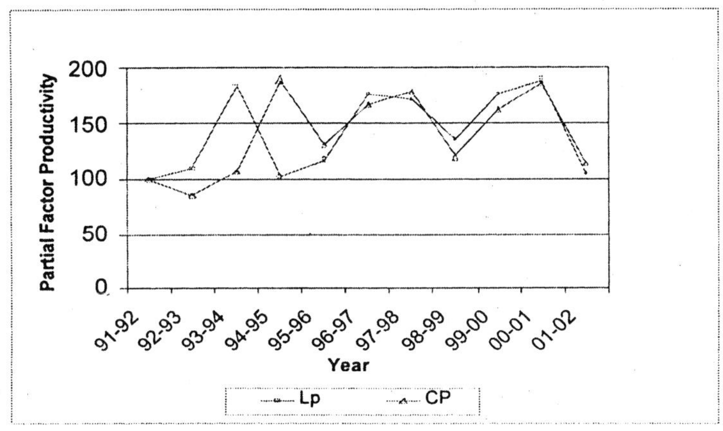

Figure 2
Partial Factor Productivity of Labour and Capital of Organic Industry
(1991-92 to 2001-02)

Kendrick index is marked by frequent fluctuations. From a base of 100 in 1991-92, it first raises and reaches a peak of 196 in 1999-00. But in the year 1998-99, it goes down to 153. Afterwards it starts falling and shows index of 143 in 2001-02. Solow index and Divisia index also reveal fluctuations. Solow index first starts increasing and reaches 180 in 1997-98. Then it starts falling down and shows an index of 117 only in 1999-00. Then again the index goes on increasing till 2001-02 where the index is 196. Divisia index with a peak of 187 in 1998-99 falls down to 120 in 1999-00. The index starts rising again and reaches a level of 190 in 2001-02. On the whole all the indices show an increasing trend till 1997-98 recording a peak of 196 in Kendrick index in the year 1999-00, 196 in Solow index and 190 in Divisia index in the year 2001-02. Annual growth rates of TFP over the entire period are being 0.94 per cent, 0.96 per cent and 0.96 per cent respectively due to Kendrick, Solow and Divisia method.

Labour productivity and capital productivity indices for the organic industry are also shown in Table 16.0. Labour productivity is marked by fluctuations during the study period. From an index of 100 in 1991-92, it first rises and reaches 185 in 1993-94. Then it starts falling and comes down to 103 in 1994-95. Labour productivity again picks up and reaches a maximum of 190 in 2000-01. Capital productivity shows fluctuating trend over the entire period. It first start rising and reaches a peak of 190 in 1994-95. Then it starts falling and comes down to 114 in 2001-02 with ups and downs in between. Over the entire period labour productivity increase at an annual rate of 1.19 per cent whereas capital productivity increases at an annual rate of 1.10 per cent.

Productivity Estimates based on Production Function

Production function estimates for this industry are given in Table 16.1. In the CD function, the co-efficient of log L is significant. This indicates that a return to scale is not constant. The co-efficient of log (K/L) is also significant with a positive sign. Co-efficient of time is insignificant. Annul growth rate in TFP given by this co-efficient is 15.9 per cent. In CES production function, co-efficient of log L is significant. Returns to scale is, thus, not constant. The co-efficient of W implies that elasticity of substitution is less than unity. The co-efficient of time is significant. The growth rate of TFP is 29.9 per cent.

Table 16.1
Estimates of Production Functions: Organic Industry (1991-92 to 2001-02)

Eq. No	Dependent Variable	Co-efficient of					R^2	Adj R^2	F	DW
		Constant	Log (K/L)	Log (W)	Log (L)	T				
1	Log (V/L)	16.091	0.448*		0.658*	0.1592	0.73	0.6 9	11.14	1.713
		(-1.823)	(4.070)		(4.556)	(1.660)				
2	Log (V/L)	14.916		0.875*	8.042*	0.299*	0.58	0.33	1.16	2.163
		(-1.909)		(4.098)	(3.262)	(4.368)				

Notes:

1. Equation (1) refers to CD function.
2. Equation (2) refers to CES function.
3. Figures in parenthesis denote 't' values.
4. * indicates significance at 5 per cent level.
5. V-Value added; L-Labour; K- Capital; W- Wage rate; t- time; DW- Durbin - Waston.

Source: Computed

Functions for Annual Variations in Factor Productivities

Table 16.2 gives regression functions for annual variations in factor productivities for organic industry. In all the functions for TFP, co-efficient of real value added is positive and highly significant and that of time is negative and significant only in Kendrick method. Growth in scale of production has been generating in total factor productivity but labour management relations have been deteriorating the total factor productivity in the organic industry. In function for partial factor productivity of labour, co-efficient of real value added turns out to be positively significant. Thus growth in scale of production has been generating labour productivity. Co-efficient of time turns out to be negatively significant. Labour management relations have been adversely affecting labour productivity in the organic industry.

Table 16.2
Regression functions for Total Factor Productivity and Labour Productivity: Organic Industry (1991-92 to 2001-02)

Eq. No	Dependent Variable	Co-efficient of			R^2	Adj R^2	F	DW
		Constant	Log (V)	t				
1	Log(TFPK)	2.176	1.621*	-4.456*	0.91	0.83	18.91	2.194
		(3.755)	(14.158)	(3.720)				
2	Log (TFPS)	3.619	2.282*	-2.940	0.48	0.23	1.18	1.221
		(2.820)	(12.852)	(1.109)				
3	Log (TFPD)	3.831	0.4225*	-3.835	0.49	0.24	1.27	1.170
		(2.744)	(16.626)	(1.329)				
4	Log (LP)	5.112	7.126*	-6.181*	0.73	0.53	4.43	2.661
		(5.088)	(6.488)	(2.977)				

Notes:

1. Figures in parenthesis denote 't' values.
2. * indicates significance at 5 per cent level.
3. TFPK- Kendrick Method; TFPS- Solow Method; TFPD- Divisia Method; LP- Labour Productivity; DW- Durbin Waston.

Source: Computed

Inorganic Industry Estimates of Factor Productivities

Factor productivity indices for the inorganic industry over a period of 1991-92 to 2001-02 are presented in Table 16.3. A Kendrick index is marked by frequent fluctuations. From a base of 100 in 1991-92, it first raises to 113 in 1992-93. Then it starts falling down to 104 in 1994-95. After that again it moves up and down and falls down to a low level of 102 in 1999-00. Then it starts gaining and reaches a level of 193 in 2000-01. Solow index, on the other hand, after showing an increase in 1992-93, falls down to 102 in 1994-95. Then again it starts increasing and records a peak of 181 in 1999-00 with fluctuations in between. Divisia index follows the pattern of Solow index. After rising to 182 in 1992-93, it falls down to 105 in 1994-95. It starts increasing again and records a peak of 197 in 2000-01 with ups and downs in between. Kendrick index increases at an annual rate of 1.05 per cent over the entire period. Solow index and Divisia index increases at an annual rate of 1.02 per cent and 1.33 per cent respectively over the entire period.

Table 16.3
Indices of Total Factor Productivities of the Indian Inorganic Industry (1991-92 to 2001-02)

Year	Total Factor Productivities			Partial Productivity	
	Kendrick Method	Solow Method	Divisia Method	Labour	Capital
1991-92	100	100	100	100	100
1992-93	113	105	182	82	112
1993-94	106	106	102	95	169
1994-95	104	102	105	91	118
1995-96	119	136	132	135	123
1996-97	179	155	193	196	181
1997-98	143	142	142	160	107
1998-99	177	116	181	172	101
1999-00	102	181	127	122	121
2000-01	193	141	197	177	165
2001-02	107	179	179	144	164
CAGR	**1.05**	**1.02**	**1.33**	**0.91**	**1.15**

Source : Computed

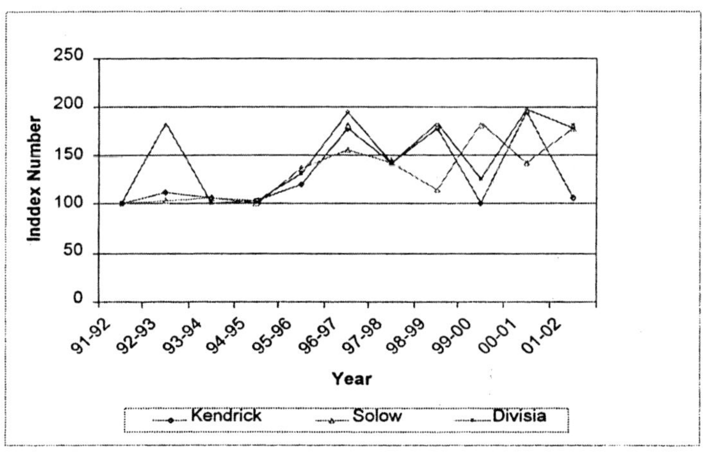

Figure 3
Total Factor Productivity Index of Inorganic Industry (1991-92 to 2001-02)

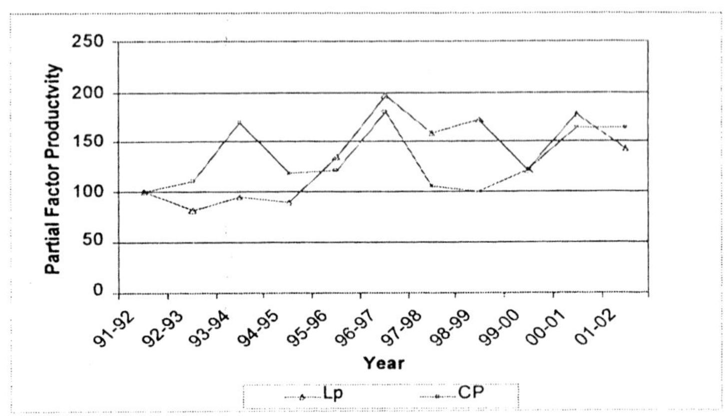

Figure 4
Partial Factor Productivity of Labour and Capital of Inorganic Industry (1991-92 to 2001-02)

Labour productivity shows the fluctuating trend with an annual growth rate of 0.91 per cent. Over the entire period, it moves up and down with a lowest index of 82 in 1992-93 and highest index of 196 in 1996-97. Capital productivity after rising to 169 in 1993-94 declines to 101 by 1998-99. But in the year 1996-97, it reaches a peak of 181. Annual growth rate of partial productivity of capital is 1.15 per cent over the entire period.

Productivity Estimates based on Production Function

Production function estimates for the inorganic industry is given in Table 16.4. In case of CD production function, co-efficient of log L is significant. This indicates that a return to scale is not constant. But the sign of this co-efficient is negative. The co-efficient of log K/L is also significant. Co-efficient of time is significant. Annual growth rate in TFP given by this co-efficient is 9.6 per cent. In the equation of CES production function, co-efficient of log L is significant. Thus returns to scale is not constant. The sign of this co-efficient is negative. Co-efficient of W implies that elasticity of substitution is less than unity. The co-efficient of time is insignificant. Growth rate of TFP is 11.2 per cent.

Table 16.4
Estimates of Production Functions: Inorganic Industry (1991-92 to 2001-02)

Eq. No	Dependent Variable	Co-efficient of					R^2	Adj R^2	F	DW
		Constant	Log (K/L)	Log (W)	Log (L)	t				
1	Log (V/L)	12.470	0.723*		-0.422**	0..096*	0.88	0.74	13.59	1.483
		(-1.735)	(3.739)		(-1.948)	(3.491)				
2	Log (V/L)	-16.228		0.304**	-0.498*	0.112	0.66	0.44	6.80	1.890
		(-4.058)		(2.044)	(-2.891)	(0.823)				

Notes:

1. Equation (1) refers to CD function.
2. Equation (2) refers to CES function.
3. Figures in parenthesis denote 't' values.
4. * indicates significance at 5 per cent level.
5. ** indicates significance at 10 percent level
6. V-Value added; L-Labour; K- Capital; W- Wage rate; t- time; DW- Durbin - Waston.

Source: Computed

Functions for Annual Variations in Factor Productivities

Regression functions for annual variations in factor productivities for inorganic industry is given in Table 16.5. In functions for TFP, co-efficient of real value added turns out to be insignificant with a positive sign. Thus growth in scale of production has been tending to generate total factor productivity. Co-efficient of time, on the other hand, turns out to be significant in Kendrick and Divisia methods, with a negative sign. This indicates that deteriorating institutional environment reflected in labour-management relations have been adversely affecting total factor productivity. In the function for partial factor productivity of labour also, co-efficient of real value added is positively insignificant and that of time is negatively significant. Thus, labour productivity is generated by significant scale economies but deteriorated by adverse labour management relations in the inorganic industry.

Table 16.5

Regression functions for Total Factor Productivity and Labour Productivity: Inorganic Industry (1991-92 to 2001-02)

Eq. No	Dependent Variable	Co-efficient of			R^2	Adj R^2	F	DW
		Constant	Log (V)	T				
1	Log(TFPK)	7.750	1.980	-7.798**	0.59	0.35	12.18	1.985
		(3.598)	(1.443)	(2.047)				
2	Log (TFPS)	3.095	1.464	-3.060	0.84	0.70	19.52	1.441
		(2.518)	(1.197)	(1.410)				
3	Log (TFPD)	7.533	1.857	-7.411**	0.57	0.32	3.90	2.516
		(3.352)	(1.209)	(1.865)				
4	Log (LP)	5.871	1.443	-8.489**	0.73	0.53	8.49	1.634
		(2.688)	(0.643)	(2.198)				

Notes:

1. Figures in parenthesis denote 't' values.
2. ** indicates significance at 10 per cent level.
3. TFPK- Kendrick Method; TFPS- Solow Method; TFPD- Divisia Method; LP- Labour Productivity ; DW- Durbin - Waston.

Source: Computed

Conclusion:

Analysis of productivity trends at the group level marked inter-industrial differences in productivity growth. Estimates of TFP for Organic and Inorganic sectors of Chemical industry shows a rising trend in all the three direct measures of TFP. Labour Productivity and Capital Productivity also show a rising trend in these sectors during the study period. Estimates of the Cobb-Douglas production function reveals that returns to scale is not constant for organic and inorganic sectors of chemical industry during the study period. Further, elasticity of substitution is less than unity for organic and inorganic sectors of Indian chemical industry during the study period.

Annual variations in factor productivities have been explained with the help of regression functions. A significant positive relationship is observed with value added for organic and inorganic sectors of Indian chemical industry. This shows that expansion in scale of production has been generating growth in total factor productivity. On the other hand with time a significant negative relationship is observed for organic and inorganic sectors. Again in case of organic sector though the relationship with time is negative but significant only in Kendrick index. For inorganic industry also, the relationship with time is negative but significant only in respect of Kendrick and Divisia index. This indicates that deteriorating institutional environment as reflected in labour management relations have been adversely affecting total factor productivity. It is concluded that growth in factor productivities would have been much higher if labour-management relations would have been better in organic and inorganic sectors of Indian Chemical Industry.

PART - V

PERFORMANCE APPRAISAL

17

GROWTH PERFORMANCE OF TAMIL NADU SUGAR INDUSTRY IN 2000 AD

The Sugar Industry being the second largest organised industry next in importance to textile industry plays eminent role in economic life of India. The Sugar Industry has a great significance, which cannot be devalued in its relation to agricultural and industrial economy of the rural region of India. It is an industry, which affects agriculture fundamentally. Therefore, the expansion of sugar industry in India is an indispensable factor for the uplift of socio-economic life of India. Sugar is an agro-based industry. The most outstanding feature of the industry is the vital link between the factory and cultivators whose interest and well-being are inter-dependent. No other agro-based industry can compete with it in having great impact and close contact between the agriculturists and factory owners. Located in rural areas sugar industry has provided the most effective instrument for carrying progressive trends into the country side.

Importance of Sugar Industry to National Economy

Sugar Industry is the largest among the processing industries next to cotton textiles. Located in rural areas they have an intrinsic symbiotic relationship with the rural masses and serve as a nerve center for rural development. There were 400 sugar factories out of which 385 were in operation during 1990-91 season. On an average sugar factory receives cane supplies, from 35,000 to 40,000 cane growers per annum.

The total number of sugar cane suppliers in the country including their dependents is over 35 million. Sugar Mills paid over Rs.5000 crores millions to the cultivators by way of cane price in 1990-91. This apart, the Sugar Mills distribute cane seeds, fertilizers and agricultural inputs of the order of Rs.200 crores annually.

Sugar Industry is the largest single employer in the rural areas. It provides employment to over 3.5 lakh workers. The annual wage bill of the industry is of the order of Rs.525 crores. The contribution of the industry to the central exchequer by way of central excise duty is Rs.700 crores. Besides, the state also collect about Rs.350 crores per annum as purchase tax and cane cess and societies commission on sugarcane. The total exports in 1983 were of the order of 7.24 lakh tonnes and foreign exchange earnings were of the order of about Rs.180.96 crores. This is an industry best suited to promote rural transformation. Each industry deals with 100 to 400 villages for its cane supplies or an average 200 villages.

Indian Sugar Industry –A Retrospect

India has been known as the original home of sugar and sugarcane. The growth of the sugar industry is full of tales of adventure and conquest. It received attention of the builders of different empires from time to time. It was between the fourth and sixth centuries that the art of making sugar was discovered in India. The cane was cut into pieces and crushed by a heavy weight and the juice thus obtained was boiled and stirred until solids formed. These solids being of uneven shapes and sizes were called "Sarkara", the Sanskrit term for gravel. The modern word "Sugar" is a derivate of the word Sarkara. Historically it is said that the modern process of sugar manufacturers was introduced in the west as early as in 1953 but the same process came to India as late as in about 1903 when the first sugar factory with vacuum pan process and modern milling method was commissioned in Saran at Marhowrah in Bihar in 1904.

Progress of the Industry

The history of Sugar Industry in India begins in 1903 when a sugar factory was set up in Bihar and U.P. each. Before 1932, there were only 32 factories operating in the country. In that year tariff protection was granted to the industry and as a result, the number of factories shot up to 137 by 1937 and India became self-sufficient in sugar. The performance of the industry during the various plans has been remarkable as brought out by the fact that the number of sugar mills in the Country increased from 139 in 1950-51 to 385 in 1990-91 (220 in the Co-operative Sector and 165 in the Private Sector and Public Sector). A notable feature of the development of the sugar industry after Independence is its remarkable expansion in the Co-operative Sector, out of 385 factories working in 1990-91, 220 were in the Co-operative Sector which accounted for about 57 per cent of the total sugar production in the country. This is a welcome feature because it enables the farmers to derive all benefits of co-operation.

Sugar Industry in Tamil Nadu

Tamil Nadu is one of the leading producers of sugar in the Country. The production of sugar by the Tamil Nadu is about 10 per cent of the Country's production. Income generated from cane sale proceeds in Tamil Nadu exceeds Rs.400 crores a year. During 1990-91, 31 sugar mills were functioning in the State. Of these 14 are in co-operative sector, 3 in public sector and 14 in private sector.

Agricultural Economics of Sugarcane in Tamil Nadu

It would be seen that the average area under sugarcane in Tamil Nadu during the period 1973-74 to 1992-93 was 187 thousand hectare. The annual growth rate of sugarcane area in Tamil Nadu is 2.44 per cent which is more than all India growth rate (1.37 per cent) and also significant at 1 per cent level of significance. The average annual sugarcane production in Tamil Nadu during the same period was 18,930 thousand tonnes which accounts nearly 10 per cent of the country's sugarcane production. The annual growth rate of production of sugarcane in Tamil Nadu (3.05 per cent) was also higher than the all India sugarcane production (2.91 per cent) and also significant at 1 per cent level of significance.

Technical performance

The total installed crushing capacity of sugar mills in Tamil Nadu was increased from 5.74 lakh tonnes to 10.04 lakh tonnes from the year 1981-82 to 1990-91. The capacity utilization by the Tamil Nadu Sugar Mills always exceeds 100 per cent except in the year 1983-84 and also it was higher than all India average. It is evident that the average duration of crushing season by Tamil Nadu mills was 171 days, which was higher than the all India average. This shows annual growth rate of 1.27 per cent, which is not significant. The average annual cane crushed by the Tamil Nadu Sugar Mills was 7,178 thousand tonnes which accounts nearly 10 per cent of the Country's total sugarcane crushed. The annual growth rate of sugarcane crushed was 6.93 per cent, which was higher than the all India average and significant at 1 per cent level of significance.

The average sugar production of Tamil Nadu Sugar Mills was 659 thousand tonnes which accounts nearly 8.9 per cent of Country's total sugar production. The annual growth rate of sugar production by Tamil Nadu Sugar Mills was 7.22 percent which was higher than the all India growth rate and significant at 1 per cent level of significance. The average recovery of sugar by Tamil Nadu Sugar Mills was 9.08 per cent with the annual growth rate of 0.65 per cent which is significant at 1 per cent level of significance. The per capita consumption sugar in Tamil Nadu is on par with the all India consumption.

Forecast about the Industry

The total area under sugarcane in Tamil Nadu in 2000 AD will be estimated as 263 thousand hectare with the annual increase of 5 thousand hectare. Similarly, the total estimated sugarcane production of Tamil Nadu in 2000 AD will be 28,361 thousand tonnes which accounts nearly 10.5 per cent of Country's total Sugarcane production. The annual increase of sugarcane production of Tamil Nadu will be 572 thousand tonnes. The yield of cane per hectare in 2000 AD by Tamil Nadu will be 109.90 tonnes per hectare, which is higher than the all India level.

For the next seven years, the production of sugar by Tamil Nadu Sugar Mills will be increased at the rate of 45 thousand tonnes per annum. On this basis, total sugar production by the Tamil Nadu sugar mills in the year 2000 AD will be 1,399 thousand tonnes which accounts nearly 9.8 per cent of Country's total sugar production. Similarly, the consumption of sugar in Tamil Nadu will also increase at the rate of about 27 thousand tonnes per annum. On this basis, the total sugar consumption in Tamil Nadu in the year 2000 AD will be 829 thousand tonnes reflecting the surplus of 570 thousand tonnes.

Conclusion

Despite all handicaps and difficulties, no other industry in the State of Tamil Nadu has developed as fast as the Sugar Industry. The Industry has indeed very bright prospects, as there is abundant supply of raw materials, cheap labour and huge local market. The Government is bound to continue on a long-term basis partial control and dual pricing system so that the interests of consumers on the one hand and that of industry on the other hand are protected and reconciled.

18

ASSESSMENT OF FINANCIAL HEALTH OF INDIAN PUBLIC SECTOR MANUFACTURING ENTERPRISES-BEFORE AND AFTER LIBERALISATION

Financial analysts have traditionally used ratio derived from the balance sheet and the statement to measure financial strength. The ratios can be grouped into four categories: liquidity, leverage, activity, and ability. Each measures a different aspect of financial condition. Liquidity ratios gauge the ability of a firm to pay its obligations as they come due, while leverage ratios measure the extent to which a firm uses debt in its capital structure. Activity ratios, sometimes called turnover, measure the productive use of assets and profitability ratios indicate a firm's rate of profit on some basis (such as sales, assets or net worth).

Many of the individual accounting ratios used frequently to predict the financial performance of an enterprise may only provide warnings when it is too late to take a corrective action. Further, a single ratio does not convey much of the sense. There is no internationally accepted standard for financial ratio against which the results can be compared. Statistical techniques, such as Multiple Discriminant Analysis (MDA), have been used to weight the different ratio types into a multiple regression model that produces an index, or credit score. By combining ratios into a model, it is hoped that the predictive abilities of these ratios can be enhanced. One such example of MDA applied to ratio analysis is the Altman (1968)[1] Z score model, which combined a number of accounting ratios (liquidity, leverage, activity and profitability) to form an index of the profitability, which are effective indicators of corporate performance in predicting bankruptcy well over the years.

In this direction, a variety of studies have been conducted, over the period, by applying Multiple Discriminant Analysis (MDA) to predict the corporate failure, as for instance, Bevar (1966)[2], Argenti John (1976)[3], Gupta (1979)[4], Ohlson (1980)[5], Etebari (1987)[6], Makridakis (1991)[7] and Sastry[8] (1994) while the Altman model is most often associated with bankruptcy forecasting, it can be useful in several other important ways: (i) It can be utilized to assess the overall relative financial strength of companies and (ii) it can identify the key variables behind the financial strength or weakness. It is for this purpose that the model is employed on selected Indian Public Sector Manufacturing Enterprises before and after liberalization periods.

Methodology

The objective of this study is to predict the financial health and viability of the selected Indian public sector manufacturing enterprises before and after liberalization period with an objective to improve their operational efficiency and effectiveness, productivity and profitability. The study is mainly based on secondary data. The required accounting information about Indian public sector manufacturing enterprises for the Z scores analysis was obtained from the PROWESS Corporate Data Base of CMIE. The data collected are first analysed with the help of five accounting ratios. These different ratios are combined into a single measure – Altman Z score analysis. The model is as follows.

$$\mathbf{Z = 0.012\, X_1 + 0.014\, X_2 + 0.033\, X_3 + 0.006\, X_4 + 0.999\, X_5}$$

Where

X_1 = (WC / TA) x 100, (or) Working Capital to Total Assets; a liquidity measure. The higher this ratio, the more liquid and thus the stronger, is the firm, and vice-versa. Very low ratios are indicative of financial stress.

X_2 = (NOP / S) x 100 (or) Net operating profit to Sales; a profitability measure. Obviously, the higher this ratio, the stronger the firm.

X_3 = (EBIT / TA) x 100 (or) Operating profit to Total Assets; a measure of current profitability on the firm's assets base. The higher this ratio, the stronger the firm.

X_4 = (MVE / BVD) x 100, (or) the ratio of the Marker Value of a firm's Equity to the Book Value of its Debt. This is a leverage measure. The higher this ratio, the stronger the firm's financial structure. Very low ratios can be signs of severe financial distress.

X_5 = (S / TA) x 100, (or) Sales to Total Assets, an activity or turnover measure. Higher ratios indicate more efficiency in using assets, and low ratios can indicate problems with management's operating strategies.

The intercept terms in the equation are those weights derived by the MDA process. The critical value of the Z score in studies is 1.81 and 2.99. Firms with scores less than 1.81 are stressed. They tend to either fail or be reorganized. Firms with indices of 2.99 or higher are strong, while values in between these extremes form the grey area.

Selection of enterprises for the Study

The study has selected three leading Indian central public sector enterprises to analyze the operational adequacy before and after liberalization period due to the following three reasons. Firstly, the comparative study of the operational adequacy of central public sector manufacturing enterprises before and after liberalization has remained untouched. Therefore, this study encompasses a group of three central public sector manufacturing enterprises, which are predominant in terms of capital outlay [viz., Steel (n=9), Power (n=4) and Petroleum (n=12)] among all the Indian central public sector manufacturing enterprises. Secondly for any country's economic development, manufacturing enterprises should be given a priority. Thirdly, to meet the needs of growing population of India, production of central public sector manufacturing enterprises should be increased. To increase the production of manufacturing enterprises a clear and elaborate study for assessing their financial health is to be made to encourage entrepreneurship.

Table 18.0

Altman Guidelines for Healthy Zone

Situation	Z Scores	Zone
I	Below 1.8	Bankruptcy zone – certain to fall
II	1.8 – 3	Healthy zone – uncertain to predict
III	3 and above	Too Healthy zone – not to fall

Results and discussion

Steel Sector

The 'Z' scores with respect to steel sector before and after liberalisation period have been computed and presented in Tables

18.1 and 18.2. Further using the data points, the scores obtained over the period have been represented graphically in Figures 18.1 and 18.2. It is seen from the analysis that the 'Z' scores for the steel sector are less than 1.8 during the entire periods of pre-liberalisation. It is also revealed that the financial health of the sector is never in healthy zone during the pre-liberalisation periods. This may be due to under trading owing to the excess working capital, negative operating profit, poor ratio of turnover, etc. It is also found from the tables that the 'Z' scores for the steel sector are more than 1.8 from 1995-96 to 1998-99 in post-liberalisation period. The 'Z' scores during this period increased from 0.60 in 1991-92 to 1.93 in 1998-99. Then the score registers a decrease from 1.58 in 1999-2000 to 1.47 in 2000-01. It is also revealed that its financial health is never in too healthy zone in post-liberalisation period.

Table 18.1

'Z' Score of Steel Sector (Before Liberalisation)

Year	X_1	X_2	X_3	X_4	X_5	'Z' SCORE
1981-1982	13.97	- 0.05	1.87	1.19	0.44	0.68
1982-1983	14.47	- 4.99	0.78	1.66	0.45	0.59
1983-1984	9.84	- 6.94	-0.81	3.19	0.45	0.46
1984-1985	7.77	- 1.95	0.95	1.30	0.49	0.59
1985-1986	10.74	1.92	3.22	13.63	0.53	0.87
1986-1987	11.17	- 0.57	1.80	1.08	0.48	0.67
1987-1988	12.31	0.93	1.40	1.02	0.53	0.74
1988-1989	16.41	2.60	4.41	1.12	0.90	1.28
1989-1990	19.04	0.60	2.08	0.89	0.87	1.18
1990-1991	8.48	- 3.98	0.97	0.82	0.52	0.60

X_1 : Working capital to total assets

X_2 : Net operating profit to net assets

X_3 : Earning before interest and taxes to total assets

X_4 : Market value of equity to book value of debt

X_5 : Sales to total assets

Source: Computed

Power Sector

The 'Z' scores with respect to power sector before and after liberalisation period has been computed and presented in Tables

18.3 and 18.4. Further, using the data points, the scores obtained over the period have been plotted through a graph in Figures 18.3 and 18.4. It is seen from the analysis that the 'Z' scores for the power sector are less than 1.8 during the entire period of pre-liberalisation. It has also disclosed that the financial health of the power sector is never in the too healthy zone in pre-liberalisation era. This is attributable to under trading owing to the excess working capital, failure to achieve adequate sales, under utilisation of capacity, etc. It is also witnessed from the tables that the 'Z' scores for power sector are more than 1.8 from 1996-97 to 1999-2000. The 'Z' scores for the same period range from 0.70 in 1991-92 to 2.28 in 1999-2000. In post-liberalisation period also the power sector's financial health is never in too healthy zone.

Table 18.2

'Z' Score of Steel Sector (After Liberalisation)

Year	X_1	X_2	X_3	X_4	X_5	'Z' SCORE
1991-1992	6.86	- 5.93	1.09	0.63	0.56	0.60
1992-1993	15.23	- 1.73	2.26	0.77	0.52	0.76
1993-1994	16.12	- 0.84	3.81	0.71	1.10	1.41
1994-1995	16.31	4.50	4.78	0.78	1.33	1.75
1995-1996	19.45	6.01	5.17	0.59	1.31	1.80
1996-1997	19.31	4.23	4.90	0.50	1.36	1.81
1997-1998	19.20	4.05	3.76	0.47	1.41	1.82
1998-1999	19.19	0.00	3.17	0.44	1.59	1.93
1999-2000	19.22	0.00	2.75	0.71	1.26	1.58
2000-2001	21.50	- 5.69	5.15	0.72	1.12	1.47

X_1 : Working capital to total assets

X_2 : Net operating profit to net assets

X_3 : Earning before interest and taxes to total assets

X_4 : Market value of equity to book value of debt

X_5 : Sales to total assets

Source: Computed

Petroleum Sector

The 'Z' scores with respect to petroleum sector before and after liberalisation period have been computed and presented in Tables 18.5 and 18.6. Further using the data points, the scores obtained over the period have been represented graphically in Figures 18.5 and 18.6. It is clear from the table that in pre-liberalisation period, petroleum sector touches the too healthy zone in 1981-82 and 1982-83. In the remaining years in pre-liberalisation period the petroleum sector is in the healthy zone (1.8 and above) in almost all the years except 1990-91 during, which it shows as 1.78. This is due to improved productivity, modernisation and diversification of the petroleum sector. It is also found from the tables that the 'Z' scores for the petroleum sector are more than 1.8 in almost all the years in

Table 18.3

'Z' Score of Power Sector (Before Liberalisation)

Year	X_1	X_2	X_3	X_4	X_5	'Z' SCORE
1981-1982	- 4.19	0.00	0.00	3.42	0.04	0.01
1982-1983	- 0.44	20.64	1.39	2.73	0.03	0.38
1983-1984	2.06	22.49	2.60	2.49	0.06	0.50
1984-1985	9.66	29.02	4.35	1.92	0.09	0.77
1985-1986	10.58	0.35	4.61	1.61	0.10	0.39
1986-1987	19.20	33.64	4.15	1.24	0.09	0.94
1987-1988	5.59	33.41	4.20	1.15	0.09	0.77
1988-1989	7.81	28.15	4.58	1.36	0.11	0.76
1989-1990	11.61	26.38	5.03	0.93	0.12	0.80
1990-1991	10.95	28.99	5.45	1.02	0.12	0.84

X_1 : Working capital to total assets

X_2 : Net operating profit to net assets

X_3 : Earning before interest and taxes to total assets

X_4 : Market value of equity to book value of debt

X_5 : Sales to total assets

Source: Computed

post-liberalisation period except 2000-01 when it shows poor performance. Apart from 1993-94 and 1994-95 it is nearby to the healthy zone. The 'Z' scores during the period range from 0.91 in 2000-01 to 3.09 in 1999-2000. It can be interpreted from the graph that the petroleum sector's performance reflects almost the same trend both in the pre and post-liberalisation period.

Table 18.4

'Z' Score of Power Sector (After Liberalisation)

Year	X_1	X_2	X_3	X_4	X_5	'Z' SCORE
1991-1992	0.89	24.86	5.74	0.80	0.15	0.70
1992-1993	21.01	20.02	4.91	0.80	0.15	0.85
1993-1994	21.05	15.58	4.39	0.78	0.17	0.79
1994-1995	13.51	15.61	4.45	0.75	0.19	0.72
1995-1996	14.68	16.38	6.55	0.73	1.12	1.74
1996-1997	16.06	17.58	6.68	0.78	1.23	1.89
1997-1998	19.05	17.88	7.77	0.74	1.26	2.00
1998-1999	21.98	20.26	12.29	0.83	1.29	2.25
1999-2000	23.63	19.73	11.67	0.84	1.33	2.28
2000-2001	21.91	21.18	11.69	0.86	0.79	1.74

X_1 : Working capital to total assets

X_2 : Net operating profit to net assets

X_3 : Earning before interest and taxes to total assets

X_4 : Market value of equity to book value of debt

X_5 : Sales to total assets

Source: *Computed*

Reasons for the Poor Financial Health

The following are the important reasons for poor financial health of the Indian public sector manufacturing enterprises in pre-liberalisation period:

(1) The enterprises faced the problem of under trading owing to the excess working capital.

(2) The negative operating profit / small portion of profit during the pre-liberalisation period was a serious concern.

(3) The enterprises failed to achieve the sales target/adequate sales. This was due to under–utilization of available capacity, which contributed to the deterioration of financial health.

(4) The excess debt was a serious concern as it carries with it interest burden. This also affected financial health.

(5) Some type of managerial incompetence might have accounted for almost all failures.

Table 18.5

'Z' Score of Petroleum Sector (Before Liberalisation)

Year	X_1	X_2	X_3	X_4	X_5	'Z' SCORE
1981-1982	19.41	3.95	20.04	0.30	2.48	3.43
1982-1983	13.99	5.03	22.21	0.24	2.35	3.32
1983-1984	13.49	4.95	20.42	0.19	1.96	2.86
1984-1985	13.92	5.03	16.83	0.20	1.67	2.46
1985-1986	17.95	6.86	16.00	0.18	1.43	2.27
1986-1987	13.22	9.16	16.01	0.29	1.26	2.08
1987-1988	11.64	7.75	12.59	0.28	1.24	1.90
1988-1989	16.85	8.07	11.32	0.21	1.38	2.07
1989-1990	17.02	7.97	10.28	0.14	1.20	1.85
1990-1991	20.08	5.63	8.88	0.11	1.17	1.78

X_1 : Working capital to total assets
X_2 : Net operating profit to net assets
X_3 : Earning before interest and taxes to total assets
X_4 : Market value of equity to book value of debt
X_5 : Sales to total assets
Source: *Computed*

Table 18.6

'Z' Score of Petroleum Sector (After Liberalisation)

Year	X_1	X_2	X_3	X_4	X_5	'Z' SCORE
1991-1992	21.24	4.22	8.04	0.11	1.22	1.80
1992-1993	24.87	4.69	7.45	0.10	1.23	1.84
1993-1994	21.94	7.55	8.45	0.08	1.10	1.75
1994-1995	17.42	7.45	9.38	0.11	1.16	1.78
1995-1996	18.92	6.16	10.01	0.15	1.39	2.03
1996-1997	24.83	6.97	11.22	0.15	2.28	3.04
1997-1998	10.74	7.10	10.17	0.13	1.55	2.11
1998-1999	19.75	6.90	15.32	0.15	2.20	3.04
1999-2000	21.54	4.53	15.95	0.13	2.25	3.10
2000-2001	21.05	5.10	16.20	0.13	2.27	3.13

X_1 : Working capital to total assets
X_2 : Net operating profit to net assets
X_3 : Earning before interest and taxes to total assets
X_4 : Market value of equity to book value of debt
X_5 : Sales to total assets
Source: Computed

Conclusion

Financial health plays a significant role in the successful functioning of a firm. Poor financial health threatens the very survival and leads to business failure. The analysis of operational efficiency using Altman's 'Z' score reveals that the financial health of selected public sector manufacturing enterprises was never in the healthy zone in pre-liberalisation period. This may be due to excessive use of working capital over the years, failure to earn adequate surplus to meet non-operating activities, or increase in EBIT, which did not match, with an increase of total assets and increased Debt-Equity mix. However, in post-liberalisation period financial health of all the selected public sector manufacturing enterprises has improved and they are lying on the healthy zone. Further, none of the selected public sector manufacturing enterprises has ever touched the 'too healthy zone' as per 'Z' score in the post-liberalisation period.

The estimated discriminant function could be of great use for the management in attaining the financial health. This study would also be useful to all companies, policy makers and researchers for appraising financial health of corporate sector.

REFERENCES

1. Edwin I. Altman (1968), 'Financial Ratios, Discriminant Analysis and Prediction of Corporate Bankruptcy', *Journal of Finance*, Vol.9, pp.589-609.
2. Bevar, W.H. (1966), 'Financial Ratios as Prediction of Failure', *Journal of Accounting Research*, pp. 71-111.
3. Argenti John (1976), *Corporate Collapse: The Causes and Symptoms*, McGraw-Hill, New York, p.91.
4. Gupta, L.C. (1979), *Financial Ratios as Forwarding Indicators of Sickness, ICICI,* Bombay, pp.65 – 69.
5. Ohlson, J. (1980), 'Financial Ratios and the Prediction of Bankruptcy', *Journal of Accounting Research*, pp.109 – 131.
6. Etebari, A. (1987), 'Financial Ratio Criteria: a Hypothesis and Empirical Test', *Working Paper*, University of New Hampshire, pp.27 – 32.
7. Makridakis, S. (1991), 'What Can be Learnt from Corporate Failure', *Long Range Planning*, Vol. 24(4), pp.115 – 126.

8. Sastry, K.S. (1994), 'Uses of 'Z' Score in Selective Privatization in Mauritius – A Note', *Indian Journal of Finance and Research*, New Delhi, pp.85 – 88.
9. Richard D Gritta (1998), 'Assessing the Financial Strength of Firms Listed on the Warsaw Stock Exchange: A Preliminary Approach Using an MDA Model', *Journal of Foreign Exchange and International Finance,* Vol, XII, No.3, pp.209 – 216.

19

PERFORMANCE OF INDIAN AUTOMOBILE INDUSTRY— ECONOMIC VALUE ADDED (EVA) APPROACH

Maximizing shareholders value is becoming the new corporate standard in India. The corporate, who gave the lowest preference to the shareholders' inquisitiveness, are now bestowing the utmost inclination to it. Shareholders' wealth is measured in terms of the returns they receive on their investment. The returns can either be in the form of dividends or in the form of capital appreciation or both. Capital appreciation in turn depends on the subsequent changes in the market value of the shares. This market value of shares is influenced by a number of factors, which can be company specific, industry specific and macro-economic in nature[1].

An important goal of financial management is to maximise the wealth of the organisation highest capital employees' wealth and consequently enhance the value of the firm. Shareholder wealth is traditionally reflected by either standard accounting parameters (such as profits, earnings and cash flow from operations) or financial ratios (including earnings per share, return on capital employed, return on net worth, net profit margin, operating profit margin etc). All these indicators failed to measure the true economic worth due to manipulative accounting techniques to state higher or lower earnings, depending on non meaningful decision on how to record revenues or expenses. Further, financial information is used by managers, shareholders and other interested parties to access their firm's current performance, and also by stakeholders to predict its future performance. The question that then arises is, whether these measures of corporate performance are linked to the expectation of the shareholders or not. To help corporate to generate value for shareholders, value-based management system has been developed[2].

Over the past several years, an alternative performance measure called Economic Value Added (EVA) has been gaining acceptance around the globe and has also been acknowledged by institutional firms as a credible performance measure. In order to overcome the limitations of accounting based measures of financial performance, Joel M Stern and G. Bennett Stewart & Co., introduced a modified concept of economic profit in 1990, in the name of Economic Value-Added as a measure of business performance. Stern Stewart has claimed that EVA, as a tool of financial management, was neither 'just a phenomenon' nor was it limited to 'for profit' organizations. Economic Value Added has been put to use for management performance evaluation, and more than just a measure of performance, it is the framework for a complete financial management (for improving scarce capital allocation; and valuation of a target company at the time of acquisition).

EVA - Tool of Financial Performance Measurement

Shareholder value creation is the new buzzword today and Economic Value Added is its most popular measure. In simple terms EVA is nothing but returns generated above cost of capital. It is the Net Operating Profit After Tax (NOPAT) minus an appropriate change for the opportunity cost of all capital invested (WACC) in an organisation. EVA is an estimate of "economic profit" or the amount by which earnings exceed or fall short of the required minimum rate of return that shareholders and lenders could get by investing capital in other securities of analogous risk[3].

EVA as a tool of financial measurement enlightens whether the operating profit is enough to cover the cost of capital. Shareholders must earn sufficient returns for the risk they have taken in investing their funds in company's capital. According to Business Standard - KPMG, if a company's EVA is negative, the firm is destroying shareholders' wealth even though it may be reporting a positive and growing earning per share and return on capital employed[4]. The EVA framework, which is becoming more and more admired tool for measuring the financial performance of corporate, offers a consistent approach to set goals and measure performance, communicate with investors, evaluate strategies, allocate capital valuing acquisitions and determine incentive bonuses. It is one of the several ongoing initiatives for a new corporate.

The evaluation and growth of the concept EVA, which may be realistically young age in the west, has been going through its childhood in country like India. It may be quite and emerging concept in the mind of the Indian corporate policy makers and managers. Hence, this paper examines in detail the EVA of selected automobile industry. It consists of sub-parts like EVA - based ranking of selected companies, industry - wise and sector - wise trends in EVA - based ranking, results and discussion on statistically established trends.

Economic Value Added (EVA)

EVA introduced by Stern Stewart & company is an incarnation of Residual Income Concept. The EVA model is based on the hypothesis that a rational investor takes into account just two things; the cash to be generated over the life of a business; and the risk of the cash receipts. Stewart defined 'EVA as an estimate of true economic profit, the amount by which earnings exceed or fall short of required minimum rate of return investors could get by investing in other securities of comparable risk'. It is the net operating profit minus the appropriate charge for the opportunity cost of capital invested in an enterprise (both debt and equity).

Expressed as a formula, EVA for a given period can be written as:

EVA = NOPAT - COST OF CAPITAL EMPLOYED
= NOPAT – (WACC x CE)

Where

NOPAT - Net Operating Profit After Taxes but before financing costs

WACC - Weighted Average Cost of Capital; and

CE - Capital Employed

(or)

equivalently, if rate of return is defined as NOPAT / CAPITAL EMPLOYED, this turns into a perhaps more revealing formula:

EVA = (RATE OF RETURN – COST OF CAPITAL) X CAPITAL EMPLOYED

Where

RATE OF RETURN	-	NOPAT / CAPITAL EMPLOYED
CAPITAL EMPLOYED	-	Total of balance sheet minus non-interest bearing debt in the beginning of the year.
COST OF CAPITAL	-	[Cost of equity X proportion of equity from capital] + [cost of debt X proportion of debt from capital X (1-tax rate)]

Cost of capital or Weighted Average Cost of Capital (WACC) is the average cost of both equity capital and interest bearing debt.

Cost of debt (K_d)

Cost of debt refers to the average rate of interest the company pays for its debt obligations. Cost of debt (K_d) has been computed as:

K_d = **Total interest expenses X (1-Effective tax rate) / Beginning total borrowings**

While calculating beginning borrowing all short-term as well as long-term borrowings has to be included as all debts are interest bearing. Therefore, interest paid in the financial year has been considered as total interest expenses.

Cost of equity (K_e)

To scribble down cost of equity (K_e), Capital Assets Pricing Model (CAPM) has been used. This model holds that firms' equity cost is the composition of risk free rate of return for a stock plus premium representing the volatility of share prices. According to this model, K_e is the shareholders' expected rate of return and this expected rate of return (R_j) is as follows:

$$R_j = R_f + \beta \times (R_m - R_f)$$

Where, Rf = Risk free rate of return,

R_m = Market rate of return, and

β = Sensitivity of the share price in relation to the market index

The interest rate of Government securities has been considered as a proxy for risk free rate of return. The market rate of return has been calculated by using Index Numbers of Security Prices (Bombay Stock Exchange) from year to year (on monthly average basis) base. The yearly return of the index numbers has been computed by using the following formula:

Rm = [(Index number for current year – Index number for previous year / Index number of previous year)] x 100

Beta (β) is the risk-free co-efficient which measures the volatility of a given script of a company with respect to volatility of market. It is calculated by comparing return on a share to return in the stock market. Mathematically, beta is the statistical measure of volatility. It is calculated as covariance of daily return on the stock market indices and the return on daily share prices of a particular company, divided by variance of return on daily stock market indices. The Beta co-efficient has been calculated as follows:

$$\beta_j = COV_{im} / \sigma^2 m$$

where, β_j = is the Beta of the security in the question

COV_{im} = Stands for co-variance between the return of security and return of market, and

$\sigma^2 m$ = Stands for the variance of market return

Inferences on EVA – Re-visiting the Existing Researches

Stern (1990)[5] observed that EVA as a performance measure captures the true economic profit of an organisation. EVA-based financial management and incentive compensation scheme gives manager better quality information and superior motivation to make decisions that will create the maximum share holders wealth in an organisation. **Stewart (1994)**[6] has expanded that adoption of EVA system by more and more companies throughout the world clearly depicts that it provides an integrated decision making framework, can reforms energies and redirect resources to create sustainable value for companies, customers, employees, shareholders and for management. **Grant (1996)**[7] found that EVA concept may have everlastingly changed the way real profitability is measured. EVA is a financial tool that focuses on the difference between company's after tax operating profit and its total cost of capital. **Luber (1996)**[8] confirmed that a positive EVA over a period of time will also have an increasing MVA while negative EVA will bring down MVA as the market looses confidence in the competence of a company to ensure a handsome return on the invested capital.

Banerjee (1997)[9] has conducted an empirical research to find the superiority of EVA over other traditional financial performance measures. ROI and EVA has been calculated for sample companies and a comparison of both showing the superiority of EVA over ROI. **Ethiraj (1998)**[10] derived those stock prices move up as a company adopts EVA as an internal performance criterion. **Anand, et al. (1999)**[11] revealed that EVA and MVA are better measures of business performance that NOPAT and EPS in terms of shareholders' value creation and competitive advantage of a firm. **Bao and Bao (1999)**[12] revealed that the EVA is positively and significantly correlated with the firm value. **Harihar (1999)**[13] highlighted some myths regarding EVA. According to him, EVA calculations are not simple and need a lot of adjustments in the financial books. Further, EVA figures can be manipulated to suit the needs of management. **Thenmozhi (1999)**[14] compared EVA with some other traditional measure of corporate performance viz. ROI, EPS, RONW, ROE, ROCE etc... she has referred to some of the short comings of the concept of EVA but maintain that EVA is a better measure of corporate performance. **Riceman, et al. (2002)**[15] argued that the EVA is a performance measure that is being used by an increasing number of companies, but academic research on EVA is limited.

Bardia, S.C. (2002)[16] revealed that in a dynamic environment a common investor finds it increasingly difficult to monitor his investments. EVA guides the investors in evaluating the performance of the company and monitoring their investments. **Stern, Joel (2003)**[17] presented the results of Stern Stewart's research on Indian companies, which shows considerable need to improve the wealth creation performance and allocation of capital in the Indian economy. He explained how the effective implementation of the EVA framework could be a solution to address this problem. EVA, as an emerging concept of financial management appears that the concept is fairly clear in the minds of almost all these researchers whose studies have been reviewed above. In a fast changing business envircnment, the investor friendly financial performance measures may, perhaps, compose this corridor full of spanking new air.

Research Design

Keeping in view the scope of the study, it is decided to include all the companies under Automobile Industry working before or from the year 1991-92 to 2003-04. But, owing to several constraints such as non-availability of financial statements or non-working of a company in a particular year etc., it is compelled to restrict the number of sample companies to 18. Therefore, this study is ex post facto based on survey method making a survey of eighteen companies in Indian Automobile Industry. There are 26 companies operating in the Indian Automobile Industry. The companies under Automobile Industry are classified into three sectors namely; Commercial Vehicles, Passenger Cars and Multiutility Vehicles and Two and Three wheelers.

For the purpose of the study all the three sectors have been selected. The selected sectors include 26 companies. Out of 26 companies, 5 are under commercial vehicles, 8 under passenger cars and multiutility vehicles and 13 under two and three wheelers sector. Out of 26 companies of the selected sectors, 13 years data is available for 18 companies only. Therefore, all the 18 companies are included in the sample. It accounts for 69.23 per cent of the total companies available in the Indian Automobile Industry. The selected 18 companies include 5 under commercial vehicles, 4 under passenger cars and multiutility vehicles and 9 under two and three wheeler sectors. It is inferred that sample company represents 98.74 percentage of market share in Commercial Vehicles, 89.76

percentage of market share in Passenger Cars and Multiutility Vehicles and 99.81 percentage of market share in Two and Three Wheelers. Thus, the findings based on the occurrence of such representative sample may be presumed to be true representative of Automobile Industry in the country.

Period of study

The period 1991-92 to 2003-04 is selected for this study of Indian Automobile Industry. This 13 years period is chosen in order to have a fairly long, cyclically well balanced period, for which reasonably homogeneous, reliable and up to date financial data would be available. Further, the span chosen for the study is the period of the beginning of liberalization measures introduced by the Government of India. Hence, the period 1991-92 to 2003-04 is an era of growth of corporate performance in the manufacturing sector, particularly Automobile Industry and has got genuine economic significance of its own.

Source of Data

The study is mainly based on secondary data. The major source of data analysed and interpreted in this study related to all those companies selected is collected from "PROWESS" database, which is the most reliable on the empowered corporate database of Centre for Monitoring Indian Economy (CMIE). Besides Prowess database, relevant secondary data have also been collected from BSE Stock Exchange Official Directory, CIME Publications, Annual Survey of Industry, Business newspapers, Reports on Currency and Finance, Libraries of various Research Institutions, through Internet etc. The study required variety of data; therefore, websites like http://indiainfoline.com, www.indiastat.com and www.google.com have been comprehensively searched.

EVA of selected companies

EVA - based performance framework not only provides a far more accurate report card on corporate financial performance than conventional measures, but also has considerable implications for companies on how to make strategic decisions and manage the healthier financial performance in their pursuit of shareholder value. EVA created by the selected Automobile industry during the study period is depicted in Table 19.0. The table shows that out of eighteen industry, sixteen industry has generated positive EVA during the study period except in the year 1992-93, 1994-95, 1996-97, 1998-99,

Table 19.0
EVA of Sample Companies

(Rs. in crores)

Sl. No	Companies	91-92	92-93	93-94	94-95	95-96	96-97	97-98	98-99	99-00	00-01	01-02	02-03	03-04
1	Ashok Leyland Ltd	193.33 (5)	-200.47 (17)	178.07 (5)	121.34 (5)	226.19 (4)	244.25 (3)	249.12 (6)	134.05 (2)	250.08 (8)	283.39 (4)	222.16 (6)	129.23 (4)	234.91 (4)
2	Tata Motors Ltd	272.29 (1)	-343.86 (18)	467.12 (1)	477.77 (1)	777.68 (1)	433.04 (1)	961.36 (1)	-900.70 (18)	1888.03 (1)	199.99 (6)	25.98 (10)	-1937.03 (17)	360.56 (3)
3	Bajaj Tempo Ltd	30.84 (9)	-14.37 (9)	20.79 (11)	13.21 (11)	28.86 (11)	-4.88 (15)	11.12 (13)	-53.81 (12)	-14.84 (17)	-4.04 (16)	1.59 (16)	30.78 (6)	24.88 (11)
4	Eicher Motors Ltd	5.63 (15)	-1.62 (5)	4.06 (15)	15.63 (10)	18.21 (12)	14.28 (10)	8.58 (16)	3.33 (5)	22.81 (13)	23.00 (9)	22.82 (13)	5.21 (8)	38.26 (8)
5	Swaraj Mazda Ltd	-2.47 (18)	-0.25 (3)	-0.08 (17)	4.52 (14)	11.60 (15)	10.71 (11)	10.46 (14)	4.54 (4)	7.08 (16)	8.85 (11)	12.48 (14)	7.43 (7)	18.62 (12)
6	Hindustan Motors Ltd	98.51 (7)	-82.42 (14)	120.30 (7)	78.29 (7)	116.58 (7)	47.50 (7)	134.10 (7)	-66.55 (13)	138.27 (9)	6.58 (14)	68.64 (8)	-167.24 (14)	-44.35 (17)
7	Mahindra and Mahindra Ltd	122.47 (6)	-77.17 (13)	195.48 (4)	125.50 (4)	216.76 (5)	113.71 (6)	423.90 (4)	-178.50 (15)	961.95 (4)	307.59 (3)	395.52 (5)	-104.02 (16)	139.67 (5)
8	Maruti Udyog Ltd	266.56 (2)	-158.32 (15)	256.63 (2)	414.49 (2)	584.49 (2)	311.83 (2)	834.13 (2)	-452.34 (17)	1419.86 (3)	-39.45 (17)	621.12 (2)	-2852.98 (18)	30.86 (9)
9	Dalwoo Motors India Ltd	-0.86 (17)	-1.21 (4)	2.45 (16)	-6.80 (17)	62.03 (8)	-48.81 (18)	-87.12 (18)	-161.33 (14)	-15.29 (18)	-91.12 (18)	-185.09 (18)	-101.02 (13)	-58.01 (18)
10	Bajaj Auto Ltd	242.82 (4)	-175.98 (16)	231.55 (3)	278.45 (3)	414.44 (3)	237.60 (4)	535.21 (3)	-425.16 (16)	1452.88 (2)	422.51 (1)	811.70 (1)	2223.75 (1)	87.48 (7)

Table 19.0 (cont ......)
EVA of Sample Companies

(Rs. in crores)

Sl. No	Companies	91-92	92-93	93-94	94-95	95-96	96-97	97-98	98-99	99-00	00-01	01-02	02-03	03-04
11	LML Ltd	256.28 (3)	130.25 (1)	123.90 (6)	110.86 (6)	118.75 (6)	166.24 (5)	255.71 (5)	276.42 (1)	462.71 (5)	401.60 (2)	410.00 (4)	290.32 (2)	362.97 (2)
12	Maharastra Scooters Ltd	36.69 (8)	-29.20 (10)	21.97 (10)	9.65 (12)	15.66 (13)	-2.29 (14)	19.08 (10)	-28.90 (11)	69.39 (10)	7.58 (12)	23.43 (11)	135.48 (3)	25.14 (10)
13	TVS Motors India Ltd	22.44 (11)	0.15 (2)	31.50 (8)	39.35 (8)	43.23 (9)	38.87 (8)	103.30 (8)	3.07 (6)	252.27 (7)	112.90 (7)	129.29 (7)	-304.01 (15)	117.14 (6)
14	Kinetic Motors Company Ltd	9.14 (14)	-7.98 (8)	6.57 (13)	4.14 (15)	7.01 (16)	-0.15 (13)	9.10 (15)	-1.65 (9)	27.00 (12)	19.09 (10)	28.47 (9)	-33.18 (10)	-21.16 (15)
15	Hero Honda Motors Ltd	2.31 (16)	-5.59 (7)	28.46 (9)	22.32 (9)	29.46 (10)	37.81 (9)	85.38 (9)	39.97 (3)	278.14 (6)	254.86 (5)	496.11 (3)	-34.30 (11)	494.32 (1)
16	Kinetic Engineering Ltd	12.78 (13)	-4.96 (6)	9.09 (12)	6.83 (13)	12.15 (14)	5.98 (12)	15.03 (11)	-1.09 (8)	36.60 (11)	23.11 (8)	22.93 (12)	-38.55 (12)	-40.10 16)
17	Majestic Auto Ltd	28.41 (10)	-49.00 (12)	5.45 (14)	-5.97 (16)	-4.18 (17)	-15.16 (17)	-1.07 (17)	-1.97 (10)	14.78 (14)	6.99 (13)	-5.47 (17)	-27.78 (9)	6.31 (13)
18	Scooters India Ltd	15.46 (12)	-37.27 (11)	-0.38 (18)	-7.88 (18)	-7.27 (18)	-14.68 (16)	12.05 (12)	1.05 (7)	10.24 (15)	3.72 (15)	3.55 (15)	94.98 (5)	-1.90 (14)

Figures in parenthesis denote EVA based ranking of selected companies.

Source: Computed

2002-03 and 2003-04 and two companies have destroyed their shareholder wealth during the same period. In the year 1992-93 the number of companies generating negative EVA went up to sixteen, eleven in the year 1998-99 and ten in the year 2002-03. It would be worthwhile to mention here that during this period the economy of the nation faced showery time. Political instability at Union Government level and Kargil War may be the qualified grounds to such downhill state of affairs in the economy. In the year 2001-02 in which Indian economy revealed the optimistic wind, witnessed that sixteen companies are created wealth for the shareholders and only two have destroyed the same. However the number of companies generates negative EVA increased to ten in the year 2002-03. It may be extrapolated that the year 2003-04 may be able to see the economy in a slightly good health yet again.

It may be observed from Table 19.0 that LML Ltd was the only company out of eighteen companies who have been constantly generating the positive EVA all the way throughout the period of study. On the other hand, Daewoo Motors India Ltd was the only company who has been annihilating the wealth of shareholders right through the period under reference except in the year 1993-94 and 1995-96. Ashok Leyland Ltd, Eicher Motors Ltd, TVS Motors India Ltd, Bajaj Auto Ltd and Hero Honda Motors Ltd created positive EVA during the major part of thirteen years period. Rest of the companies displayed high instability on this front. On the whole Table 19.0 concludes that about one-third (6 out 18), of the sample companies have been able to govern affirmative EVA during period under study whereas remaining companies make feasible to append a very little to the value of shareholders.

EVA based Ranking of Selected Companies

Table 19.0 also presents EVA based ranking of sample companies. It is evident from the table that companies like LML Ltd, Bajaj Auto Ltd, Maruti Udyog Ltd and Tata Motors Ltd are toping in the list during this study period. On the other hand, companies like Swaraj Mazda Ltd, Daewoo Motors India Ltd, Kinetic Engineering Ltd, Majestic Auto Ltd and Scooter India Ltd has been loosing the grounds. Rest of the companies has indexed unsteady position during the period of study period.

EVA based frequencies distribution of sample companies are shown in Table 19.1. It is clear from the table that 16 companies in 1992-93, 11 in 1998-99 and 10 in 2002-03 are reporting negative EVA and the remaining companies generating positive EVA during the study period. It is also observed that 331/3 per cent of the

Table 19.1

EVA - Based Frequencies Distribution of Sample Companies

EVA	91-92	92-93	93-94	94-95	95-96	96-97	97-98	98-99	99-00	00-01	01-02	02-03	03-04
Negative	2	16	2	3	2	6	2	11	2	3	2	10	5
Up to Rs.10 crores	3	1	5	4	1	1	2	4	1	5	2	2	1
Rs.10-25 crores	3		2	3	4	2	5		3	3	4		2
Rs.25-50 crores	3		2	1	3	3		1	2		2	1	3
Rs.50-100 crores	1			1	1		1		1		1	1	1
Rs.100-500 crores	6	1	7	6	5	6	5	2	5	7	5	3	6
Above Rs. 500 crores					2		3		4		2	1	
Total	18	18	18	18	18	18	18	18	18	18	18	18	18

Source: Computed

company have added to the economic value between Rs.100 crores to Rs.500 crores during the study period and only two companies in 1995-96, 3 in 1997-98, 4 in 1999-00, 2 in 2001-02 and 1 in 2002-03 reported an EVA of over Rs.500 crores.

Sector-wise Trends in EVA

Table 19.2 and Figure 1 presents sector-wise EVA of sample companies. It is evident from Table 19.2 that the mean EVA generated for the automobile industry was Rs.79.53 crores during the study period. The mean EVA generated was the highest in two and three wheelers sector followed by commercial vehicles and passenger cars and multiutility vehicles sector. Two and Three wheeler sector and commercial vehicles sector should perform well in this regard because their average was more than the industry average. It is also evident from the table that all the selected sectors and the whole industry witnessed very high fluctuation in their EVA during the study period. Table 19.2 further reported that the commercial vehicles, passenger cars and multiutility vehicles sectors and whole industry registered negative compound annual growth rate of EVA during the study period.

The economic value added of selected industry under commercial vehicles sector during the study period is also presented in Table 19.2. The mean EVA was the highest in Tata Motors Ltd, followed by Ashok Leyland Ltd, Eicher Motors Ltd, Swaraj Mazda Ltd and Bajaj Tempo Ltd. All the industry under the sector had registered very high fluctuation in their EVA during the study period. It is also evident from the table that two companies namely Tata Motors Ltd and Bajaj Tempo Ltd registered negative compound annual growth rate of EVA during the study period.

Table 19.2 depicts the EVA generated by the selected companies under passenger cars and multiutility vehicles sector during the study period. Table 19.2 portrays that Daewoo Motors India Ltd showed negative EVA throughout the study period except in the year 1993-94 and 1995-96. The mean EVA generated was the highest in Mahindra and Mahindra Ltd followed by Maruti Udyog Ltd and Hindustan Motors Ltd. All the companies registered a very high fluctuation in their EVA during the study period. Only Mahindra and Mahindra Ltd witnessed positive compound annual growth rate of EVA and the rest of the company showed negative compound annual growth rate of EVA.

The EVA generated by the companies under two and three wheeler sectors during the study period is presented in Table 19.2. It is evident from the Table 19.2 that Majestic Auto Ltd generated negative EVA in majority of the years, followed by Scooters India Ltd. The rest of the companies had registered a mixed trend of EVA during the study period. Among the selected companies, Bajaj Auto Ltd, LML Ltd, Hero Honda Motors Ltd and TVS Motors India Ltd had shown improved performance with record to EVA generation during the study period. All the selected companies under this sector had registered very high fluctuation in their EVA during the study period. Kinetic Motors Company Ltd, Kinetic Engineering Ltd and

Table 19.2

EVA Sector – wise Trends (1991-92 - 2003-04)

Sl. No.	Industry	Mean (Rs.Crores)	CV	CAGR
1.	Ashok Leyland Ltd	174.28	0.71	15.70
2.	Tata Motors Ltd	206.33	4.45	-9.22
3.	Bajaj Tempo Ltd	5.39	4.50	-4.89
4.	Eicher Motors Ltd	13.86	0.80	14.70
5.	Swaraj Mazda Ltd	7.19	0.82	20.80
	Commercial Vehicles Sectors	**81.41**	**2.42**	**-3.16**
6.	Hindustan Motors Ltd	34.48	2.82	-22.40
7.	Mahindra & Mahindra Ltd	131.30	3.41	2.50
8.	Maruti Udyog Ltd	95.14	10.55	-17.30
9.	Daewoo Motors India Ltd	-53.24	-1.32	-8.77
	Passenger Cars and Multiutility Vehicles Sectors	**51.92**	**7.42**	**-9.01**
10.	Bajaj Auto Ltd	487.47	1.42	19.60
11.	LML Ltd	258.92	0.48	9.88
12.	Maharastra Scooters Ltd	23.36	1.81	13.60
13.	TVS Motors Company Ltd	45.35	2.77	16.00
14.	Kinetic Motors Co. Ltd	3.57	4.87	-0.73
15.	Hero Honda Motors Ltd	133.02	1.40	30.50
16.	Kinetic Engineering Ltd	4.60	4.84	-4.13
17.	Majestic Auto Ltd	-3.74	-5.15	-2.53
18.	Scooters India Ltd	5.51	5.46	11.00
	Two and Three Wheelers Sectors	**105.27**	**0.92**	**20.80**
	Whole Automobile Industry	**79.53**	**2.45**	**-1.24**

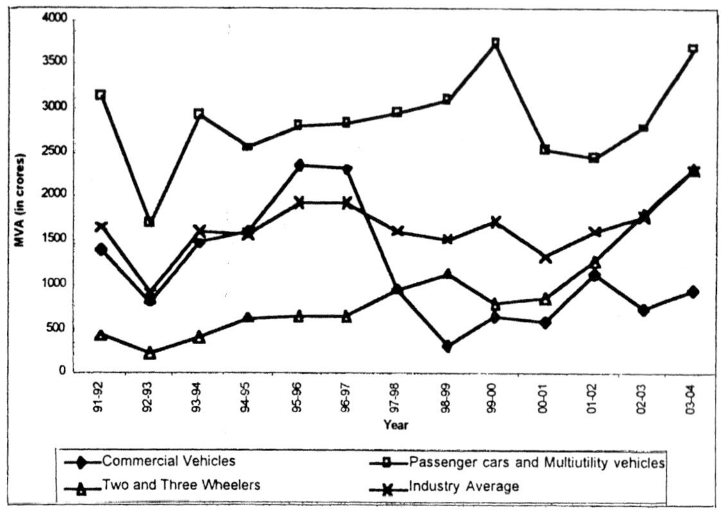

Figure 1. Sector-Wise trend in EVA

Majestic Auto Ltd had registered negative compound annual growth rate of EVA and the rest of the companies showed positive compound annual growth rate of EVA during the study period.

The sector wise paired test provided the value of t test in Table 19.3. The table exhibits that there has been significant deviation (at 5% level) in the EVA of respective years except for the year 1994-95 and 2001-02 to 2003-04.

Comparison of EVA and Conventional Method of Financial performance

Analysing the corporate performance of Indian Automobile Industry based on Return on Capital Employed (ROCE)- the conventional benchmarks and on the new "trendier" one i.e., EVA, the results can be well exhibited in Table 19.4. From the table, it can be inferred that Indian Automobile Industry depicts a rosy picture in terms of return on capital employed. The mean value of return on capital employed of Automobile Industry during the study period 18.40 per cent i.e. for every Rs.100 investment, the return is Rs. 18.40 whereas EVA as a percentage of capital employed is only 14.07 i.e. for every Rs. 100 investment, the company has added value of Rs. 14.07. The same picture is reflected as in the case of commercial vehicles sector and passenger cars and multiutility vehicles sector during the study period. But in case of two and three wheeler sectors, EVA as a percentage of capital employed showed better

Table 19.3

Paired Test of Sector-wise EVA of Sample Companies

Paired Sample Test	Paired Differences							Sig
	Mean	Std Deviation	Std Error Mean	95% Confidence Level Lower	Upper	t	df	(2 -tailed)
EVA 91-92 – EVA 92-93	148.49	187.69	44.24	55.10	241.78	3.36	17	.004
EVA 92-93 – EVA 93-94	-153.46	222.50	52.44	-264.10	-42.81	-2.93	17	.009
EVA 93-94 – EVA 94-95	-6.33	47.30	11.15	-23.45	23.59	.016	17	.995
EVA 94-95 – EVA 95-96	-53.89	80.84	19.05	-94.09	-13.68	-2.83	17	.012
EVA 95-96 – EVA 96-97	60.88	105.66	24.90	8.34	113.42	2.45	17	.026
EVA 96-97 – EVA 97-98	-111.31	178.05	41.97	-199.85	-22.77	-2.65	17	.017
EVA 97-98 – EVA 98-99	299.39	535.38	126.19	33.15	565.63	2.37	17	.030
EVA 98-99 – EVA 99-00	-503.97	832.52	196.23	-917.85	-89.97	-2.57	17	.020
EVA 99-00 – EVA 00-01	295.27	539.71	127.21	26.88	563.66	2.32	17	.033
EVA 00-01 – EVA 01-02	-64.34	192.02	45.26	-159.83	31.15	-1.42	17	.173
EVA 01-02 – EVA 02-03	373.56	1030.43	242.88	-138.86	885.99	1.54	17	.142
EVA 02-03 – EVA 03-04	-299.70	1041.73	245.54	-817.74	218.34	-1.22	17	.239
EVA 91-92 – EVA 03-04	-9.05	149.57	35.25	-83.43	65.33	-0.26	17	.800

Sources: Computed

Table 19.4
Comparison of EVA Vs Conventional Method of Financial Performance

(in percentage)

Year	Commercial Vehicles		Passengers Cars and Multiutility Vehicles		Two and Three Wheelers		Industry Average	
	ROCE	EVA/CE	ROCE	EVA/CE	ROCE	EVA/CE	ROCE	EVA/CE
1991-92	16.09	13.12	8.13	20.18	17.94	36.67	14.05	23.32
1992-93	7.78	-4.10	6.82	-11.82	16.82	8.67	10.47	-2.42
1993-94	17.63	13.40	15.33	19.07	27.88	33.78	20.28	22.08
1994-95	23.47	16.98	21.96	15.96	28.36	26.62	24.60	19.85
1995-96	27.15	21.55	33.75	20.40	26.90	25.89	29.27	22.61
1996-97	20.18	10.49	26.30	7.72	28.74	16.72	25.28	11.64
1997-98	13.43	13.64	16.61	17.21	21.77	28.18	17.27	19.68
1998-99	8.72	1.56	9.48	-8.52	22.94	7.98	13.71	0.34
1999-00	11.23	10.86	5.53	22.56	27.29	42.45	14.68	25.29
2000-01	12.90	10.48	-0.67	2.31	16.55	24.98	9.59	12.59
2001-02	17.63	10.98	3.72	9.98	19.09	30.18	13.48	17.05
2002-03	33.07	19.65	8.72	-38.25	19.57	15.73	20.45	-0.96
2003-04	41.31	16.26	23.33	1.60	13.47	17.69	26.04	11.85
Mean	**19.32**	**11.91**	**13.81**	**6.03**	**22.10**	**24.22**	**18.40**	**14.07**
CV	**0.51**	**0.58**	**0.73**	**2.88**	**0.24**	**0.43**	**0.35**	**0.69**
CAGR	**4.65**	**5.09**	**-6.60**	**- 14.00**	**-2.36**	**-0.96**	**0.33**	**-5.37**

Source: Computed

performance than the return on capital employed. Thus, the comparison shows that divergence exists between the performance results given by traditional measure and EVA. The traditional measures do not reflect the real value addition to shareholders' wealth and thus EVA has to be measured to have an idea about the shareholders value addition.

Conclusion

The company has been successfully able to create value for its shareholders. On comparing industry-wise composite frequencies for EVA for all years, it was found that there has been a significant increasing trend in EVA of the Automobile Industry firms which means that companies have a positive trend to improve their firm values. The recognition of EVA concept in India shows to some extent, diverse trends. A majority of the companies are still not prepared to employ the EVA technique to evaluate their financial performance because of certain inherent difficulties associated with the computation. In view of the above facts, the competent authorities in India should issue necessary guidelines for the computation of EVA and its practices in financial reporting, to the appropriate bodies in India, so that it becomes obligatory for all companies to disclose their EVA in their financial statement and to meet the expectations of shareholders in the country.

References

1. Mangala, Deepa and Joura Simpy, "Linkage between Economic Value Added and Market Value: An Analysis in Indian context", *Indian Management Studies Journal*, June 2002, pp.55-56.
2. Mc Taggart, James et al., "The Value imperative", published by Free Press, New York, 1994, pp. 4-6.
3. Jani Shweta, "Godrej Retools for Value" *Business Standard*, Jan 21, 2003, p. 6.
4. Purikh, Parag, "The Universe of Wealth Creation", PPFAS-Financial Advisory Services Ltd-Online, June 2000, p.2.
5. Stern, Joel (1990), "One way to build value in your firm, Executive compensation", *Financial Executive*, pp. 51-54.
6. Stewart, G. Bennet, (1994), "EVATM Fact and Fantasy", *Journal of Applied Corporate Finance*, pp. 71-84.
7. Grant, J. (1996). "Foundation of EVA for investment Managers: Just in time, EVA", *Journal of Financial Management*, Vol.23, No.1, p.41(8).

8. Luber, R. B. (1996), "Who are the Real Wealth Creators". *Fortune*, pp.2-3.
9. Banerjee, Ashok (1997), "Economic Value Added (EVA): A Better Performance Measure", *The Management Accountant*, pp.86-88.
10. Ethiraj, Govindaraj (1998), 'The EVA Feather in the Market Cap', *The Economic Times*, p. 1.
11. Anand, Manoj, Garg, Ajay, and Arora, Asha (1999), "Economic value added : Business Performance Measure of Shareholder value', *The Management Accountant*, pp.351-56.
12. Bao, B.H. and Bao, D.H., 'The Association between Firm Value and Economic Value Added', *Indian Accounting Review*, Vol.3, No.2, pp.161-64.
13. Harihar,T.S.(1999), 'EVA Prorating Myths', *Chartered Finance Analyst*, pp.8-9.
14. Thenmozhie, M. (1999), 'Economic Value Added as a Measure of Corporate Performance', *The Indian Journal of Commerce*, Vol.52, No.4, pp. 72-85.
15. Riceman, S.S. and Cahan, S.F. (2002), "Do Managers Perform Better under EVA Bonus Schemes", Social Science Research Network Electronic Paper Collection, at http://oaoers.ssrb.cin.
16. Bardia, S.C.,(2002) "Economic Value Added: Overall Consideration", *Economic Challenger*, pp. 1-7.
17. Stern, Joel, (2003) " Workshop on Value – based Management," Organised by the ASCI, Hyderabad, pp. 21-22.

20

EVA AND MVA OF INDIAN AUTOMOBILE INDUSTRY—AN EMPIRICAL STUDY OF RELATIONSHIP

Corporate organizations that are increasingly moving into globalization and towards a perfect market place describe the internationally viable working environment at the very outset. At present, the industry is faced with stiff competition, consolidation, rapid technological advancement and obsolescence, high R&D costs and talent retention. Some strategy – focused organizations are looking at growth beyond competition, defining for their expansion path that would sustain their leadership in a world shaped by continuously evolving market forces. They thus have to think over the operational excellence through product innovation to evolve future projections for long-standing growth framework. Economic Value Added (EVA) appears to provide the modus operandi for this self- propelling growth model. EVA holds a company accountable for the cost of capital it used to expand and operate its business and attempts to show whether a company is creating a real value for its shareholders. Maximising EVA consistently would lead to maximisation of market capitalization.

Market Value Added (MVA) is a measure of shareholder's wealth. If the corporate objective is to enhance shareholder's wealth, it can be achieved by improving MVA. MVA is the difference between the market value of invested capital and book value of invested capital. MVA is the absolute rupee spread between a company's market value and its capital. It represents the stock markets assessment as of a particular time of the net present value of all the company's past and projected capital projects. Therefore, maximizing MVA should be the primary objective for any company that is concerned about its shareholders welfare. A company's EVA is the fuel that fires up its MVA. Thus, EVA is the internal measure of corporate performance and MVA is the external measure of corporate performance.

The evidence of the majority of the empirical studies regarding EVA suggests that there is a positive relationship between EVA and shareholder value creation, measured by Market Value Added (MVA). However, when the explaining power of EVA versus traditional performance measures regarding equity market value or returns is considered, the results are mixed. Thus, an attempt has been made in this paper to find the relevance of Stern and Stewart's claim and the hypothesis that MVA of the firm is largely positive associated with or driven by its EVA generating capacity in Indian context.

Section I discusses the methodology on which the empirical analysis is based. Section II gives analysis of EVA and MVA trends for the full sample companies. Section III comprises of empirical relationship between EVA, MVA and other financial variables. Section IV summarises the main findings and policy perspective in the context of the Indian Automobile industry.

SECTION I

Methodology

Market Value Added (MVA)

While EVA measures shareholder value addition of firm in terms of its real economic performance, MVA measures market's assessment of firm's value. MVA thus measures value by the management over and above the capital invested in the company by investors.

Market Value Added (MVA) = Market Value of Company - Capital Employed

For a public limited company, its market value is calculated as market value of its equity (number of shares outstanding times their share price) plus book value of debt (since market value of debt is generally not available). Capital employed is effectively the book value of investments in the business made-up of debt and equity. Effectively, the formula becomes

Market Value Added (MVA) = Market Value of Equity - Book Value of Equity

These items have been obtained from balance sheet statement of companies. Data for the market price existing on the close of financial year has been collected from the Economic Times, CMIE Prowess and Capitaline databases.

Economic Value Added (EVA)

EVA introduced by Stern Stewart & company is an incarnation of Residual Income Concept. Stewart defined 'EVA as an estimate of true economic profit, the amount by which earnings exceed or fall short of required minimum rate of return investors could get by investing in other securities of comparable risk'. It is the net operating profit minus the appropriate charge for the opportunity cost of capital invested in an enterprise (both debt and equity).

Expressed as a formula, EVA for a given period can be written as:

EVA = NOPAT - COST OF CAPITAL EMPLOYED
= NOPAT – (WACC x CE)

Where

NOPAT - Net Operating Profit After Taxes but before financing costs

WACC - Weighted Average Cost of Capital; and

CE - Capital Employed

(or)

equivalently, if rate of return is defined as NOPAT / CAPITAL , this turns into a perhaps more revealing formula:

EVA = (RATE OF RETURN – COST OF CAPITAL) X CAPITAL

Where

Rate of return	-	NOPAT / CAPITAL
Capital Employed	-	Total of balance sheet minus non-interest bearing debt in the beginning of the year.
Cost of Capital	-	[Cost of equity *X* proportion of equity from capital] + [(cost of debt *X* proportion of debt from capital) *X* (1-tax rate)]

Cost of capital or weighted average cost of capital is the average cost of both equity capital and interest bearing debt.

Cost of debt (K_d)

Cost of debt refers to the average rate of interest the company pays for its debt obligations. Cost of debt (K_d) has been computed as:

K_d = Total interest expenses X (1-Effective tax rate) / Beginning total borrowings

While calculating beginning borrowing, all short-term as well as long-term borrowings has to be included as all debts are interests bearing. Therefore, interest paid in the financial year has been considered as total interest expenses.

Cost of equity (K_e)

To find out cost of equity (K_e), Capital Assets Pricing Model (CAPM) has been used. This model holds that firms' equity cost is the composition of risk free rate of return for a stock plus premium representing the volatility of share prices. According to this model, K_e is the shareholders' expected rate of return and this expected rate of return (R_j) is as follows:

$$R_j = R_f + \beta \text{ X } (R_m - R_f)$$

Where, R_f = Risk free rate of return,

R_m = Market rate of return, and

β = Sensitivity of the share price in relation to the market index

The interest rate of Government securities has been considered as a proxy for risk free rate of return. The market rate of return has been calculated by using Index Numbers of Security Prices (Bombay Stock Exchange) from year to year basis. The yearly return of the index numbers has been computed by using the following formula:

R_m = [(Index number for current year – Index number for previous Year) / (Index number of previous year)] x 100

Beta (β) is the risk-free co-efficient which measures the volatility of a given script of a company with respect to volatility of market. It is calculated by comparing return on a share to return in the stock market. Mathematically, beta is the statistical measure of volatility. It is calculated as covariance of daily return on the stock market indices and the return on daily share prices of a particular company, divided by variance of return on daily stock market indices. The Beta co-efficient has been calculated as follows:

$$\beta_j = COV_{im} / \sigma_m^2$$

where, β_j - is the Beta of the security in the question

COV_{im} - stands for co-variance between the return of security and return of market, and

σ_m^2 - stands for the variance of market return

Keeping in view the scope of the study, it is decided to include all the companies under automobile industry working before or from the year 1991-92 to 2003-04. There are 26 companies operating in the Indian automobile industry. But, owing to several constraints such as non-availability of financial statements or non-working of a company in a particular year etc., it is compelled to restrict the number of sample companies to 18. The companies under automobile industry are classified into three sectors namely; Commercial vehicles, Passenger cars and multiutility vehicles and Two and three wheelers. For the purpose of the study all the three sectors have been selected. It accounts for 69.23 per cent of the total companies available in the Indian automobile industry. The selected 18 companies include 5 under commercial vehicles, 4 under passenger cars and multiutility vehicles and 9 under two and three wheeler sectors. It is inferred that sample company represents 98.74 percentage of market share in commercial vehicles, 89.76 percentage of market share in passenger cars and multiutility vehicles and 99.81 percentage of market share in two and three wheelers. Thus, the findings based on the occurrence of such representative sample may be presumed to be true representative of automobile industry in the country.

The period 1991-92 to 2003-04 is selected for this study. The span chosen for the study is the period of the beginning of liberalization measures introduced by the Government of India. Hence, the period 1991-92 to 2003-04 is an era of growth of corporate performance in the manufacturing sector, particularly automobile industry and has got genuine economic significance of its own. The study is mainly based on secondary data. The major source of data analysed and interpreted in this study related to all those companies selected is collected from "PROWESS" database, which is the most reliable on the empowered corporate database of Centre for Monitoring Indian Economy (CMIE). Besides prowess database, relevant secondary data have also been collected from BSE Stock Exchange Official Directory, CIME Publications, Annual Survey of Industry, Business newspapers, Reports on Currency and Finance, Libraries of various Research Institutions, through Internet etc.

SECTION II

Analysis of EVA and MVA trends

EVA Trends

EVA - based performance framework not only provides a far more accurate report card on corporate financial performance than conventional measures, but also has considerable implications for companies on how to make strategic decisions and manage the healthier financial performance in their pursuit of shareholder value. EVA created by the selected Automobile industry during the study period. i.e. 1991-92 to 2003-04 is depicted in Table 20.0. The table shows that out of eighteen industry, sixteen industry has generated positive EVA during the study period except in the year 1992-93, 1994-95, 1996-97, 1998-99, 2002-03 and 2003-04 and two companies have destroyed their shareholders' wealth during the same period. In the year 1992-93 the number of companies generating negative EVA went up to sixteen, eleven in the year 1998-99 and ten in the year 2002-03. It would be worthwhile to mention here that during this period the economy of the nation faced showery time. Political instability at Union Government level and Kargil War may be the qualified grounds to such downhill state of affairs in the economy. In the year 2001-02 in which Indian economy revealed the optimistic wind, witnessed that sixteen companies are created wealth for the shareholders and only two have destroyed the same. However the number of companies generating negative EVA increased to ten in the year 2002-03. It may be extrapolated that the year 2003-04 may be able to see the economy in a slightly good health yet again.

It may be observed from Table 20.0 that LML Ltd was the only company out of eighteen companies who has been constantly generating the positive EVA all the way throughout the period of study. On the other hand, Daewoo Motors India Ltd was the only company who has been annihilating the wealth of shareholders right through the period under reference except in the year 1993-94 and 1995-96. Ashok Leyland Ltd, Eicher Motors Ltd, TVS Motors India Ltd, Bajaj Auto Ltd and Hero Honda Motors Ltd created positive EVA during the major part of thirteen years period. Rest of the companies displayed high instability on this front. On the whole the Table 20.0 concludes that about one-third (6 out 18), of the sample companies have been able to govern affirmative EVA during period under study whereas remaining companies make feasible to append a very little to the value of shareholders.

Table 20.0 also presents EVA - based ranking of sample companies. It is evident from the table that companies like LML Ltd, Bajaj Auto Ltd, Maruti Udyog Ltd and Tata Motors Ltd are toping in the list during this study period. On the other pass, companies like Swaraj Mazda Ltd, Daewoo Motors India Ltd, Kinetic Engineering Ltd, Majestic Auto Ltd and Scooter India Ltd has been loosing the grounds. Rest of the companies has indexed unsteady position during the period of study period.

Table 20.0
EVA of sample companies

(Rs. in crores)

Sl. No	Companies	91-92	92-93	93-94	94-95	95-96	96-97	97-98	98-99	99-00	00-01	01-02	02-03	03-04
1	Ashok Leyland Ltd	193.33 (5)	-200.47 (17)	178.07 (5)	121.34 (5)	226.19 (4)	244.25 (3)	249.12 (6)	134.05 (2)	250.08 (8)	283.39 (4)	222.16 (6)	129.23 (4)	234.91 (4)
2	Tata Motors Ltd	272.29 (1)	-343.86 (18)	467.12 (1)	477.77 (1)	777.68 (1)	433.04 (1)	961.36 (1)	-900.70 (18)	1888.03 (1)	199.99 (6)	25.98 (10)	-1937.03 (17)	360.56 (3)
3	Bajaj Tempo Ltd	30.84 (9)	-14.37 (9)	20.79 (11)	13.21 (11)	28.86 (11)	-4.88 (15)	11.12 (13)	-53.81 (12)	-14.84 (17)	-4.04 (16)	1.59 (16)	30.78 (6)	24.88 (11)
4	Eicher Motors Ltd	5.63 (15)	-1.62 (5)	4.06 (15)	15.63 (10)	18.21 (12)	14.28 (10)	8.58 (16)	3.33 (5)	22.81 (13)	23.00 (9)	22.82 (13)	5.21 (8)	38.26 (8)
5	Swaraj Mazda Ltd	-2.47 (18)	-0.25 (3)	-0.08 (17)	4.52 (14)	11.60 (15)	10.71 (11)	10.46 (14)	4.54 (4)	7.08 (16)	8.85 (11)	12.48 (14)	7.43 (7)	18.62 (12)
6	Hindustan Motors Ltd	98.51 (7)	-82.42 (14)	120.30 (7)	78.29 (7)	116.58 (7)	47.50 (7)	134.10 (7)	-66.55 (13)	138.27 (9)	6.58 (14)	68.64 (8)	-167.24 (14)	-44.35 (17)
7	Mahindra and Mahindra Ltd	122.47 (6)	-77.17 (13)	195.48 (4)	125.50 (4)	216.76 (5)	113.71 (6)	423.90 (4)	-178.50 (15)	961.95 (4)	307.59 (3)	395.52 (5)	-104.02 (16)	139.67 (5)
8	Maruti Udyog Ltd	266.56 (2)	-158.32 (15)	256.63 (2)	414.49 (2)	584.49 (2)	311.83 (2)	834.13 (2)	-452.34 (17)	1419.86 (3)	-39.45 (17)	621.12 (2)	-2852.98 (18)	30.86 (9)
9	Daewoo Motors India Ltd	-0.86 (17)	-1.21 (4)	2.45 (16)	-6.80 (17)	62.03 (8)	-48.81 (18)	-87.12 (18)	-161.33 (14)	-15.29 (18)	-91.12 (18)	-185.09 (18)	-101.02 (13)	-58.01 (18)

Figures in parenthesis denote EVA based ranking of selected companies.

Source: Computed

Table 20.0 (cont ......)
EVA of sample companies

(Rs. in crores)

Sl. No	Companies	91-92	92-93	93-94	94-95	95-96	96-97	97-98	98-99	99-00	00-01	01-02	02-03	03-04
10	Bajaj Auto Ltd	242.82 (4)	-175.98 (16)	231.55 (3)	278.45 (3)	414.44 (3)	237.60 (4)	535.21 (3)	-425.16 (16)	1452.88 (2)	422.51 (1)	811.70 (1)	2223.75 (1)	87.48 (7)
11	LML Ltd	256.28 (3)	130.25 (1)	123.90 (6)	110.86 (6)	118.75 (6)	166.24 (5)	255.71 (5)	276.42 (1)	462.71 (5)	401.60 (2)	410.00 (4)	290.32 (2)	362.97 (2)
12	Maharastra Scooters Ltd	36.69 (8)	-29.20 (10)	21.97 (10)	9.65 (12)	15.66 (13)	-2.29 (14)	19.08 (10)	-28.90 (11)	69.39 (10)	7.58 (12)	23.43 (11)	135.48 (3)	25.14 (10)
13	TVS Motors India Ltd	22.44 (11)	0.15 (2)	31.50 (8)	39.35 (8)	43.23 (9)	38.87 (8)	103.30 (8)	3.07 (6)	252.27 (7)	112.90 (7)	129.29 (7)	-304.01 (15)	117.14 (6)
14	Kinetic Motors Company Ltd	9.14 (14)	-7.98 (8)	6.57 (13)	4.14 (15)	7.01 (16)	-0.15 (13)	9.10 (15)	-1.65 (9)	27.00 (12)	19.09 (10)	28.47 (9)	-33.18 (10)	-21.16 (15)
15	Hero Honda Motors Ltd	2.31 (16)	-5.59 (7)	28.46 (9)	22.32 (9)	29.46 (10)	37.81 (9)	85.38 (9)	39.97 (3)	278.14 (6)	254.86 (5)	496.11 (3)	-34.30 (11)	494.32 (1)
16	Kinetic Engineering Ltd	12.78 (13)	-4.96 (6)	9.09 (12)	6.83 (13)	12.15 (14)	5.98 (12)	15.03 (11)	-1.09 (8)	36.60 (11)	23.11 (8)	22.93 (12)	-38.55 (12)	-40.10 (16)
17	Majestic Auto Ltd	28.41 (10)	-49.00 (12)	5.45 (14)	-5.97 (16)	-4.18 (17)	-15.16 (17)	-1.07 (17)	-1.97 (10)	14.78 (14)	6.99 (13)	-5.47 (17)	-27.78 (9)	6.31 (13)
18	Scooters India Ltd	15.46 (12)	-37.27 (11)	-0.38 (18)	-7.88 (18)	-7.27 (18)	-14.68 (16)	12.05 (12)	1.05 (7)	10.24 (15)	3.72 (15)	3.55 (15)	94.98 (5)	-1.90 (14)

Figures in parenthesis denote EVA based ranking of selected companies.

Source: Computed

Table 20.1 presents sector - wise EVA of sample companies. It is evident from Table 20.1 that the mean EVA generated for the automobile industry was Rs.79.53 crores during the study period. The mean EVA generated was the highest in two and three wheelers sector followed by commercial vehicles and passenger cars and multiutility vehicles sector. Two and three wheelers sector and commercial vehicles sector should perform well in this regard because their average was more than the industry average. It is also evident from the table that all the selected sectors and whole industry witnessed very high fluctuation in their EVA during the study period. Table 20.1 further reported that the commercial vehicles, passenger cars and multiutility vehicle sectors and whole industry registered negative compound annual growth rate of EVA during the study period.

The economic value added of selected industry under commercial vehicles sector during the study period is also presented in Table 20.1. The mean EVA was the highest in Tata Motors Ltd, followed by Ashok Leyland Ltd, Eicher Motors Ltd, Swaraj Mazda Ltd and Bajaj Tempo Ltd. All the industry under the sector had registered very high fluctuation in their EVA during the study period. It is also evident from the table that two companies namely Tata Motors Ltd and Bajaj Tempo Ltd registered negative compound annual growth rate of EVA during the study period.

Table 20.1 depicts the EVA generated by the selected companies under passenger cars and multiutility vehicles sector during the study period. Table 20.1 portrays that Daewoo Motors India Ltd showed negative EVA throughout the study period except in the year 1993-94 and 1995-96. The mean EVA generated was the highest in Mahindra and Mahindra Ltd followed by Maruti Udyog Ltd and Hindustan Motors Ltd. All the companies registered very high fluctuation in their EVA during the study period. Only Mahindra and Mahindra Ltd witnessed positive compound annual growth rate of the EVA and rest of the company showed negative compound annual growth rate of EVA.

The EVA generated by the companies under two and three wheeler sectors during the study period is presented in Table 20.1. It is evident from the Table 20.1 that Majestic Auto Ltd generated negative EVA in majority of the years, followed by Scooters India Ltd. The rest of the companies had registered a mixed trend of EVA during the study period. Among the selected companies, Bajaj Auto

Ltd, LML Ltd, Hero Honda Motors Ltd and TVS Motors India Ltd had shown improved performance with record to EVA generation during the study period. All the selected companies under this sector had registered very high fluctuation in their EVA during the study period. Kinetic Motors Company Ltd, Kinetic Engineering Ltd and Majestic Auto Ltd had registered negative compound annual growth rate of EVA and the rest of the companies showed positive compound annual growth rate of EVA during the study period.

Table 20.1

EVA Sector – wise Trends (1991-92 - 2003-04)

Sl. No	Industry	Mean (Rs.in crores)	CV	CAGR
1.	Ashok Leyland Ltd	174.28	0.71	15.70
2.	Tata Motors Ltd	206.33	4.45	-9.22
3.	Bajaj Tempo Ltd	5.39	4.50	-4.89
4.	Eicher Motors Ltd	13.86	0.80	14.70
5.	Swaraj Mazda Ltd	7.19	0.82	20.80
	Commercial Vehicles Sectors	**81.41**	**2.42**	**-3.16**
6.	Hindustan Motors Ltd	34.48	2.82	-22.40
7.	Mahindra & Mahindra Ltd	131.30	3.41	2.50
8.	Maruti Udyog Ltd	95.14	10.55	-17.30
9.	Daewoo Motors India Ltd	-53.24	-1.32	-8.77
	Passenger Cars and Multiutility Vehicles Sectors	**51.92**	**7.42**	**-9.01**
10.	Bajaj Auto Ltd	487.47	1.42	19.60
11.	LML Ltd	258.92	0.48	9.88
12.	Maharastra Scooters Ltd	23.36	1.81	13.60
13.	TVS Motors Company Ltd	45.35	2.77	16.00
14.	Kinetic Motors Co. Ltd	3.57	4.87	-0.73
15.	Hero Honda Motors Ltd	133.02	1.40	30.50
16.	Kinetic Engineering Ltd	4.60	4.84	-4.13
17.	Majestic Auto Ltd	-3.74	-5.15	-2.53
18.	Scooters India Ltd	5.51	5.46	11.00
	Two and Three Wheelers Sectors	**105.27**	**0.92**	**20.80**
	Whole Automobile Industry	**79.53**	**2.45**	**-1.24**

MVA Trends

Table 20.2 presents MVA calculation of selected companies of Indian Automobile industry. On the base of the table, it may be observed that out of 18 companies 15 companies have registered positive MVA throughout the study period. It indicates that the market value of these companies is dominating over the book value. On the other hand Hindustan Motors Ltd (1997-98, 1999-00, 2000-01 and 2001-02), Daewoo Motors Ltd (1997-98 and 1999-2004) and Scooters India Ltd (except 1998-99, 1999-00, 2001-02 and 2003-04) have registered negative MVA during the study period. It shows that the book value of these companies is dominated over the market value.

Table 20.2 also provides MVA based ranking. Glancing all the way through the table, it is noticed that companies like Maruti Udyog Ltd, Bajaj Auto Ltd, Tata Motors Ltd, Ashok Leyland Ltd, Mahindra and Mahindra Ltd and TVS Motors India Ltd are topping the list and on the other side companies like Scooters India Ltd, Daewoo Motors India Ltd, Hindustan Motors Ltd, Majestic Auto Ltd and Kinetic Engineering Ltd are struggling in terms of MVA over the period.

Table 20.3 portrays whole automobile industry and sector wise information pertaining to MVA. It is evident from Table 20.3 that among the three sectors, passenger cars and multiutility vehicles sector have been generating highest market value added throughout the study period. This was due to the better market value added of Maruti Udyog Ltd and Mahindra and Mahindra Ltd. It was followed by commercial vehicles sector and two and three wheelers. Table 20.3 also shows that all the selected sectors of automobile industry have been generating positive aggregate MVA throughout the period. The growth of MVA is more confident in case of passenger cars and multiutility vehicles whereas less consistent in case of commercial vehicles and two and three wheelers sector. Table also brings out that only the commercial vehicles sector had registered negative compound annual growth rate of MVA during the study period.

The market value added of selected companies under commercial vehicles sector during the study period is also presented in Table 20.3. Table 20.3 reveals that the mean MVA of Tata Motors Ltd were the highest followed by Ashok Leyland Ltd, Bajaj Tempo Ltd, Eicher Motors Ltd and Swaraj Mazda Ltd. Table 20.3 brings out that all the selected companies under the commercial vehicles sector had registered very high fluctuations in their MVA except Bajaj Tempo Ltd which registered moderate fluctuations during the study period. Further, Table 20.3 provided that the two companies namely

Table 20.2

MVA of sample companies

(Rs. in crores)

Sl. No	Companies	91-92	92-93	93-94	94-95	95-96	96-97	97-98	98-99	99-00	00-01	01-02	02-03	03-04
1	Ashok Leyland Ltd	424.31 (4)	464.71 (4)	917.28 (4)	1190.49 (4)	1233.30 (5)	611.30 (6)	328.25 (7)	1027.56 (5)	511.40 (6)	676.71 (5)	1047.77 (5)	213.17 (4)	2468.99 (5)
2	Tata Motors Ltd	6283.94 (2)	3503.05 (2)	6069.37 (2)	6444.12 (2)	10112.67 (1)	10700.65 (1)	4334.61 (3)	295.41 (7)	2345.58 (4)	2054.88 (4)	4359.15 (4)	727.81 (4)	1206.66 (7)
3	Bajaj Tempo Ltd	305.25 (7)	159.37 (7)	350.98 (6)	344.69 (6)	356.93 (6)	282.64 (7)	184.20 (9)	228.25 (8)	340.08 (8)	219.67 (8)	122.03 (9)	371.03 (9)	340.97 (9)
4	Eicher Motors Ltd	39.60 (16)	16.40 (16)	67.50 (13)	55.50 (14)	57.96 (14)	12.44 (17)	29.20 (14)	55.56 (11)	39.90 (11)	31.74 (11)	128.56 (8)	317.52 (11)	293.49 (10)
5	Swaraj Mazda Ltd	41.27 (15)	17.06 (15)	35.15 (17)	28.90 (17)	30.18 (17)	25.53 (15)	29.55 (13)	42.64 (13)	27.89 (13)	21.88 (13)	62.12 (12)	172.52 (11)	293.49 (10)
6	Hindustan Motors Ltd	110.63 (10)	47.31 (11)	181.07 (10)	142.11 (11)	150.23 (11)	43.35 (14)	-8.39 (16)	9.49 (18)	-28.47 (17)	-84.34 (17)	-23.38 (17)	664.39 (8)	101.49 (13)
7	Mahindra and Mahindra Ltd	384.56 (5)	367.86 (5)	880.37 (5)	841.78 (5)	1575.30 (4)	1685.95 (4)	928.68 (5)	1785.92 (4)	926.04 (5)	417.72 (5)	462.88 (7)	1465.79 (6)	2643.29 (4)
8	Maruti Udyog Ltd	12099.24 (1)	6377.44 (1)	10654.64 (1)	9175.90 (1)	9478.58 (2)	9461.12 (2)	10979.28 (1)	10544.05 (1)	14144.72 (1)	10156.94 (1)	9771.41 (1)	9361.00 (1)	12219.21 (1)
9	Daewoo Motors India Ltd	24.92 (17)	12.48 (17)	60.57 (16)	94.04 (13)	100.11 (12)	188.56 (10)	-21.98 (18)	140.00 (10)	-56.74 (18)	-301.09 (18)	-348.11 (18)	-249.46 (18)	-120.64 (18)

Figures in parenthesis denotes MVA based ranking of selected companies.

Source: Computed

Table 20.2 (Cont ....)
MVA of sample companies

(Rs. in crores)

Sl. No	Companies	91-92	92-93	93-94	94-95	95-96	96-97	97-98	98-99	99-00	00-01	01-02	02-03	03-04
10	Bajaj Auto Ltd	2951.28 (3)	1586.69 (3)	2593.31 (3)	4731.38 (3)	4887.86 (3)	4552.39 (3)	6777.89 (2)	5365.98 (2)	3180.98 (3)	3180.98 (3)	4697.99 (3)	7714.77 (2)	9212.27 (3)
11	LML Ltd	105.47 (11)	78.10 (10)	234.04 (8)	167.32 (9)	187.27 (9)	274.17 (8)	343.08 (6)	190.83 (9)	84.12 (9)	40.16 (9)	114.74 (10)	150.58 (12)	124.08 (12)
12	Maharastra Scooters Ltd	71.83 (14)	35.56 (13)	62.67 (15)	53.29 (16)	55.22 (16)	46.47 (13)	64.08 (10)	54.10 (12)	27.96 (12)	17.10 (14)	70.24 (11)	120.15 (13)	156.58 (11)
13	TVS Motors India Ltd	349.27 (6)	175.10 (6)	305.15 (7)	260.11 (7)	269.35 (7)	268.88 (9)	315.08 (8)	301.92 (6)	411.64 (7)	331.72 (7)	1021.94 (6)	1778.70 (5)	1800.73 (6)
14	Kinetic Motors Company Ltd	130.04 (9)	93.36 (9)	171.23 (11)	145.69 (10)	150.93 (10)	146.01 (11)	64.07 (11)	41.25 (14)	51.53 (10)	36.80 (10)	43.85 (13)	33.80 (14)	38.19 (15)
15	Hero Honda Motors Ltd	264.47 (8)	133.27 (8)	231.39 (9)	246.58 (8)	255.52 (8)	655.81 (5)	1117.02 (4)	4352.66 (3)	3533.09 (2)	4312.72 (2)	5531.69 (2)	6633.43 (3)	9662.88 (2)
16	Kinetic Engineering Ltd	88.51 (12)	45.78 (12)	94.75 (12)	94.72 (12)	98.17 (13)	57.37 (12)	34.87 (12)	32.47 (15)	25.33 (14)	24.42 (12)	29.30 (14)	31.11 (15)	24.24 (16)
17	Majestic Auto Ltd	74.99 (13)	34.84 (14)	64.86 (14)	54.48 (15)	56.61 (15)	21.68 (16)	17.16 (15)	14.86 (17)	6.42 (15)	8.78 (15)	17.20 (15)	24.62 (16)	39.32 (14)
18	Scooters India Ltd	-36.17 (18)	-26.60 (18)	-18.84 (18)	-21.53 (18)	-21.00 (18)	-17.27 (18)	-11.28 (17)	14.97 (16)	3.38 (16)	-7.64 (16)	3.20 (16)	-0.30 (17)	12.68 (17)

Figures in parenthesis denotes MVA based ranking of selected companies.

Source: Computed

Table 20.3

MVA Sector – wise Trends (1991-92 to 2003-04)

Sl. No	Industry	Mean (Rs.in Crores)	CV	CAGR
1.	Ashok Leyland Ltd	1003.02	0.65	8.64
2.	Tata Motors Ltd	4495.22	0.74	-16.70
3.	Bajaj Tempo Ltd	277.39	0.31	-0.54
4.	Eicher Motors Ltd	99.63	1.31	17.00
5.	Swaraj Mazda Ltd	63.71	1.25	13.80
	Commercial Vehicles Sectors	**1187.83**	**0.53**	**-6.34**
6.	Hindustan Motors Ltd	100.43	1.87	-19.00
7.	Mahindra & Mahindra Ltd	1105.09	0.62	7.03
8.	Maruti Udyog Ltd	10340.26	0.18	1.58
9.	Daewoo Motors India Ltd	-36.72	-4.67	-39.30
	Passenger Cars and Multiutility Vehicles Sectors	**2877.27**	**0.18**	**1.85**
10.	Bajaj Auto Ltd	4726.06	0.46	8.36
11.	LML Ltd	161.07	0.53	-2.70
12.	Maharastra Scooters Ltd	64.25	0.58	3.59
13.	TVS Motors Company Ltd	583.81	0.98	15.30
14.	Kinetic Motors Co. Ltd	88.21	0.60	-14.00
15.	Hero Honda Motors Ltd	2840.81	1.09	38.20
16.	Kinetic Engineering Ltd	52.39	0.58	-11.90
17.	Majestic Auto Ltd	33.52	0.68	-11.60
18.	Scooters India Ltd	-9.72	-1.61	13.80
	Two and Three Wheelers Sectors	**948.68**	**0.62**	**14.60**
	Whole Automobile Industry	**1671.26**	**0.20**	**2.41**

Tata Motors Ltd and Bajaj Tempo Ltd had registered negative compound annual growth rate of MVA and rest of the companies had positive compound annual growth rate of MVA during the study period.

Table 20.3 presents MVA of selected companies under passenger's cars and multiutility vehicles sector. The table shows that the companies like Maruti Udyog Ltd and Mahindra and Mahindra Ltd are top in the list and it was followed by Hindustan Motors Ltd and Daewoo Motors Ltd. All the selected companies except Maruti Udyog Ltd had registered very high fluctuation in their MVA during the study period. Table 20.3 also brings out values relating to compound annual growth rate of MVA of selected companies. It is evident from the table that Hindustan Motors Ltd and Daewoo Motors India Ltd had registered negative growth rate and rest of the companies had registered positive growth rate of MVA during the study period.

Table 20.3 brings out the values relating to MVA of selected companies under two and three wheelers. Table 20.3 showed that Bajaj Auto Ltd, Hero Honda Motors Ltd, TVS Motors India Ltd and LML Ltd comparatively top in the list. On the other hand, Scooters India Ltd and Majestic Auto Ltd are struggling on their front with regard to MVA during the study period. It is also noticed that all the selected companies have registered very high fluctuations in their MVA during the study period. The analysis of compound annual growth rate of MVA showed mixed trend among the selected companies under the sector during the study period.

SECTION III

Empirical Relationship

MVA-EVA - Regression Analysis

In this section an attempt to find the relevance of Stern and Stewart's claim that MVA of the firm is largely positive association with or driven by its EVA generating capacity. The result of correlation co-efficient, linear regression, Durbin - Watson model, F - statistics and t - statistics have been determined between dependent variable (MVA) and independent variable(EVA). The values hence obtained have their particular statistical sense. The regression co-efficient for EVA so worked out portrays the temperament of association between the dependent and particular independent variable. The t - statistics and F - statistics so calculated determine the level of significant or insignificant association between the variables. Durbin - Watson model allows the researcher to establish the auto-correlation, if any between dependent and independent variable (the desirable value is two and any value more than two signifies negative auto-correlation and vice versa); values of adjusted R^2 indicate the extent of variation in the dependent variable which may be explicated by independent variable (s) and the standard error speaks about the limits within which the estimated value as the dependent variable is expected to lie.

Table 20.4 offers the explanation about the regression analysis between MVA and EVA during the study period for the whole Automobile industry and its three sectors. Table 20.2 provides the values of R, R-square and adjusted R-square for the whole industry

0.165, 0.03 and – 0.06 respectively. It sounds that there exists poor relationship between MVA and EVA in Automobile industry, as the value of adjusted R-square in negative. Interestingly, the t and F statistics give the identical results but both of them lead to insignificant association between the variables under reference. It is evident from the table that the overall result in passenger cars and multiutility vehicles does not differ from whole industry and statistical association between MVA and EVA is again insignificant. Table 20.4 suggests that EVA is serially correlated in commercial vehicles and two and three wheelers sector and adjusted R-square value is also positive. The t and F statistics are resulting identical values and secure that in commercial vehicles and two and three wheelers sector relationship between MVA and EVA is fairly significant. However, the MVA-EVA analysis supports the hypothesis of Stern and Stewart's that MVA of firm is largely positive associated with EVA in all the selected sectors of Indian Automobile industry.

Table 20.4
MVA - EVA: Linear Regression Analysis
Dependent variable - Market Value Added (MVA)
Independent variable - Economic Value Added (EVA)

Independent Variable	Co-efficient	t	Multiple R	R Square	Adjusted R Square	Std. Error of the Estimate	Durbin-Watson	F Value
Commercial Vehicles : EVA	1.041	1.138	0.325	0.11	0.03'	623.52	0.83	1.30
Passenger Cars and Multiutility Vehicles: EVA	0.321	0.796	0.233	0.06	-0.03	537.98	1.78	0.63
Two and Three wheelers: EVA	2.602	1.562	0.426	0.18	0.11	558.29	0.86	2.44
Whole Industry: EVA	**0.280**	**0.556**	**0.165**	**0.03**	**-0.06**	**339.76**	**1.23**	**0.31**

Source: Computed

Determinants of Market Value Added

The purpose of this analysis whether a particular independent variable or a set of variables emerges as the most explanatory variable of the MVA during the study period. In order to meet this objective, multiple regression analysis has been considered on sector-wise and whole industry during the study period. The results of multiple regression analysis are presented in this section.

Whole industry

Table 20.5 brings out the determinants of market value added for whole Automobile industry during the study period. It is observed from the Table 20.6 that all the selected independent variables exists significant influence on MVA of Automobile industry during the study period. Co-efficient of determination, R^2 in the case is 0.90 implying that changes in MVA are predicated by these independent variables to the extent of 90 per cent. It is also evident from the table that ROCE is found in strong association with MVA followed by NOPAT, EPS and EVA. However, RONW is negatively related with

Table 20.5
Determinants of MVA - Multiple Regression Analysis
(Whole Industry)
Dependent variable: Market Value Added (MVA)

Independent Variables	Co-efficients	t value	Significant / Not significant
Constant	730.11	5.058	
EVA	0.41	1.923	Significant **
EPS	1.28	2.362	Significant **
ROCE	63.02	3.331	Significant *
NOPAT	2.15	2.297	Significant **
RONW	-33.78	2.39	Significant *
R^2 = 0.90			
Adj R^2 = 0.84			
F = 23.12			
DW = 1.53			

EVA - Economic Value Added; ROCE - Return on Capital Employed; EPS - Earnings Per Share; NOPAT - Net Operating Profit After Tax;

RONW- Return On Net Worth.

* - Significant at 0.05 level; * * - Significant at 0.10 level

Source: Computed

MVA during the study period. The value of Adjusted R^2 and F value shows the good fitness of the model. From these regression results it can be concluded that all the selected independent variables have well explained the MVA of Automobile industry during the study period.

Commercial vehicles

Table 20.6 portrays the results of multiple regression analysis for commercial vehicles sector. It is revealed from the Table 20.6 that all the selected independent variables that are found statistically significant with MVA of commercial vehicles sector during the study period. Co-efficient of determination, R^2 in this case is 0.75 implying that change in MVA is predicted by these independent variables to the extent of 75 per cent only. It is also found that EPS is strongly associated with MVA followed by ROCE, RONW, NOPAT and EVA during the study period. The value of F statistic and adjusted R^2 showed the good fitness of the model.

Table 20.6

Determinants of MVA - Multiple Regression Analysis (Commercial Vehicles) Dependent variable: Market Value Added (MVA)

Independent Variables	Co-efficients	t value	Significant / Not significant
Constant	770.31	1.954	
EVA	0.33	2.364	Significant *
EPS	109.77	1.952	Significant **
ROCE	78.99	1.914	Significant **
NOPAT	1.71	2.551	Significant *
RONW	38.51	1.949	Significant **
R^2 = 0.75			
Adj R^2 = 0.56			
F = 17.97			
DW = 1.63			

EVA - Economic Value Added; ROCE - Return On Capital Employed ; EPS - Earnings Per Share; NOPAT - Net Operating Profit After Tax ; RONW- Return On Net Worth.

* - Significant at 0.05 level;

* * - Significant at 0.10 level

Source: Computed

Passenger Cars and Multiutility Vehicles

Table 20.7 gives an account of multiple regression analysis between MVA and other financial variables in respect of passenger cars and multiutility vehicles sector. The result provided by this table witnessed that the variables noticed significantly associated with MVA are EVA, EPS, ROCE and NOPAT. The co-efficient of determination, R^2 in this case is 0.83 implying that changes in MVA is predicted by these independent variables to the extent of 83 per cent. Once again the ROCE has emerged as the most important variable in determining MVA of passenger cars and multiutility vehicles sector followed by NOPAT, EVA and EPS. The value of R^2 and F shows the good fitness of the model.

Table 20.7

Determinants of MVA- Multiple Regression Analysis (Passenger Cars and Multiutility Vehicles)

Dependent variable: Market Value Added (MVA)

Independent Variables	Co-efficients	t value	Significant / Not significant
Constant	2181.88	7.725	
EVA	0.35	2.058	Significant **
EPS	0.34	3.099	Significant *
ROCE	24.15	2.834	Significant *
NOPAT	5.42	3.422	Significant *
RONW	-44.20	1.774	Not significant
R^2 = 0.83			
Adj R^2 = 0.68			
F = 30.37			
DW = 1.94			

EVA - Economic Value Added; ROCE - Return on Capital Employed ; EPS - Earnings Per Share; NOPAT - Net Operating Profit After Tax ; RONW- Return On Net Worth.

* - Significant at 0.05 level;

* * - Significant at 0.10 level

Source: Computed

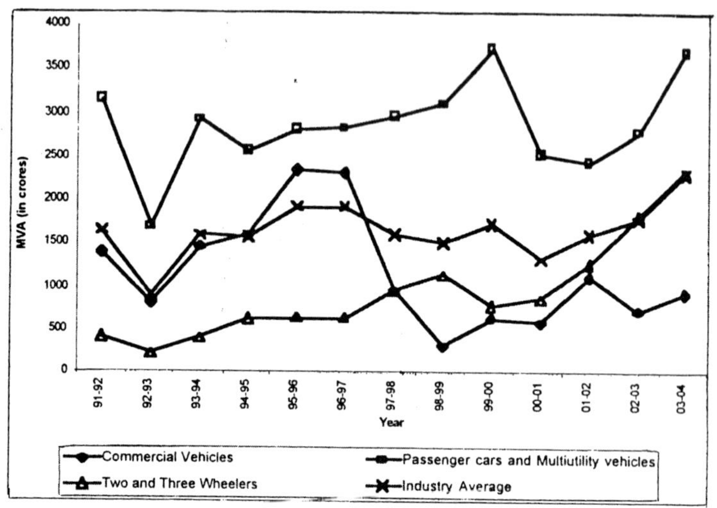

Figure 1. Sector-Wise trend in MVA

Table 20.8

Determinants of MVA- Multiple Regression Analysis

(Two and Three Wheelers)

Dependent variable: Market Value Added (MVA)

Independent Variables	Co-efficients	t value	Significant / Not significant
Constant	-460.41	1.694	
EVA	1.57	2.950	Significant *
EPS	49.36	2.832	Significant *
ROCE	1.04	1.053	Not significant
NOPAT	16.93	10.188	Significant *
RONW	20.99	2.374	Significant **
R^2 = 0.97			
Adj R^2 = 0.95			
F = 49.81			
DW = 1.98			

EVA - Economic Value Added; ROCE - Return on Capital Employed ; EPS - Earnings Per Share; NOPAT - Net Operating Profit After Tax ;
RONW- Return On Net Worth.

* - Significant at 0.05 level;

* * - Significant at 0.10 level

Source: Computed

Two and Three Wheelers

Table 20.8 describes the results of multiple regression for determinants of MVA for two and three wheelers sector during the study period. It is explicit from the table that all the independent variables except ROCE significantly associated with MVA of two and three wheelers sector during the study period. Co-efficient of determination, R^2 in this case is 0.97 implying that changes in MVA is predicted by selected independent variables to the extent of 97 per cent. Among the selected independent variables, EPS is strongly associated with MVA followed by RONW, NOPAT, and EVA. However, the ROCE has not emerged as one of the most important variables explaining MVA in case of two and three wheelers sector. The value of t, F and adjusted R^2 sounds the good fitness of the model.

SECTION IV

Conclusion

EVA analysis has captivated much attention in the western countries both as a management innovation as well as stock market analysis. The recognition of such technique in Indian context shows to some extent diverse trends. Some corporate houses like Infosys, BPL, HLL, NIIT, TCS, Godrej Soaps, etc. have started publishing EVA in their financial statements. Majority of companies are still not prepared to put in the EVA technique for evaluating their financial performances because of certain inherent difficulties associated with the computation. As the corporate most vital objective at this moment is to maximize shareholder value establishing a relationship between financial variables and the corporate objective is imperative. With this objective in mind, the present study intends to examine the relationship between shareholders wealth and financial variables in the case of Indian Automobile industry. The selected financial measures like EVA, EPS , ROCE, NOPAT and RONW have been compared with MVA. The multiple regression analysis has been carried out and the results revealed ROCM as the most significant related variable with MVA followed by EPS and EVA. This study suggests that the relationship between MVA and EVA is positively associated by supporting Stern Steward claim's and statistically significant. When all is said and done, EVA and MVA itself positions in an appearance as the most outstanding factors in the definitive analysis as having a decisive impact on a firm's value.

Table 20.9
List of sample companies included in the present study

Sl. No.	Sectors / Companies	Year of Incor-poration	Ownership	Market share (%)	Total market share (%)
	Commercial Vehicles (5)				
1.	Ashok Leyland Ltd	1956	Hinduja Group	35.62	
2.	Tata Motors Ltd	1956	Tata Group	34.22	
3.	Bajaj Tempo Ltd	1958	Firodia Group	11.50	
4.	Eicher Motors Ltd	1982	Eicher Group	10.65	
5.	Swaraj Mazder Ltd	1983	State and Private Sector	6.75	98.74
	Passenger Cars and Multiutility Vehicles (4)				
6.	Hindustan Motors Ltd	1942	Birla C.K.Group	8.31	
7.	Mahindra and Mahindra Ltd	1945	Mahindra and Mahindra	42.17	
8.	Maruti Udyog Ltd	1981	Private (Foreign)	36.60	
9.	Daewoo Motors India Ltd	1983	Private (Foreign)	2.68	89.76
	Two and Three Wheelers (9)				
10.	Bajaj Auto Ltd	1945	Bajaj Group	18.80	
11.	LML Ltd	1972	LML Group	11.58	
12.	Maharashtra Scooters Ltd	1975	Bajaj Group	7.80	
13.	TVS Motor Company Ltd	1982	T.V.S. Group	12.93	
14.	Kinetic Motor Company Ltd	1984	Firodia Group	11.75	
15.	Hero Honda Motors Ltd	1984	Hero (Munsals) Groups	10.54	
16.	Kinetic Engineering Ltd	1970	Firodia Group	9.72	
17.	Majestic Auto Ltd	1986	Hero Group	9.04	
18.	Scooters India Ltd	1972	Central Govt. Commercial Enterprise	7.65	99.81

21

FINANCIAL STRUCTURE OF CORPORATE ENTERPRISES IN INDIA—AN EMPIRICAL ANALYSIS

Accounting regarding the "Financial structure of a business consists of three elements: assets, liabilities and capital. The financial structure provides an insight into the various types of sources tapped to finance, the total assets employed in a business enterprise. That part of financial structure which represents long-term sources is known as capital structure. Since the balance sheet is a detailed form of the fundamental, or structure equation, it is set for the financial structure of an enterprise. It states the nature and amount of each of the various assets, liabilities and property interest of the owner or owners. Stating the nature of the assets, liabilities and capital is not as difficult as stating their amounts. The financial structure can be made initially from the point of view of the time for which funds are needed. It includes both the sources of finance, i.e., long term and short term. Thus financial structure refers to the makeup of permanent capital of firm.

Over the past, many researchers have tried to establish the factors which influence a firm's financial structure. The association between a firm's financial structure and its size, profitability similar other operating characteristics have gained considerable importance. Some of them have presented affirmative evidences in respect of a particular factor or a group of factors as determinant of corporate financial structure, others have presented dissenting evidences in respect of the same factor or factors to be a clear determinant of financial structure. Scott and Scott et al[1&2] presented empirical evidences claiming that industrial class has got influence on the firm's financial structure. Remmers et al[3] in their study, however, presented dissenting evidence arguing that neither size nor industry class is a clear determinant of the firm's financial structure. Therefore in this part an attempt has been made to study the corporate financial structure relationship with reference to size, profitability, operating leverage, external financing and income gearing. Testing of the hypothesis, formulated for this study thus falls within the scope of the study.

Hypothesis

Hypothesis means the researcher must select from the intricacy of observed events such considerable and pertinent facts that would most effectively elucidate the problem under study. It gives us an idea about indispensable associations, which exist between the different fundamentals within the complexity. Therefore, the hypotheses of the present study are:

(i) Financial leverage is independent of industry class.

(ii) Financial leverage is independent of industry size.

(iii) Financial leverage and profitability are independent of each other.

(iv) Financial leverage and operating leverage have got no association between them.

(v) Financial leverage and external financing are independent of each other.

(vi) Financial leverage has got no association with income gearing.

Research Design

Keeping in view the scope of the study, it is decided to include all the companies under automobile industry working before or from the year 1991-92 to 2003-04. There are 26 companies operating in the Indian automobile industry. But, owing to several constraints such as non-availability of financial statements or non-working of a company in a particular year etc., it is compelled to restrict the number of sample companies to 18. The companies under automobile industry are classified into three sectors namely; Commercial vehicles, Passenger cars and multiutility vehicles and Two and three wheelers. For the purpose of the study all the three sectors have been selected. It accounts for 69.23 per cent of the total companies available in the Indian automobile industry. The selected 18 companies include 5 under commercial vehicles, 4 under passenger cars and multiutility vehicles and 9 under two and three wheeler sectors. It is inferred that sample company represents 98.74 percentage of market share in commercial vehicles, 89.76 percentage of market share in passenger cars and multiutility vehicles and 99.81 percentage of market share in two and three wheelers. Thus, the findings based on the occurrence of such representative sample may be presumed to be true representative of automobile industry in the country.

The period 1991-92 to 2003-04 is selected for this study. The span chosen for the study is the period of the beginning of liberalization measures introduced by the Government of India. Hence, the period 1991-92 to 2003-04 is an era of growth of corporate performance in the manufacturing sector, particularly automobile industry and has got genuine economic significance of its own. The study is mainly based on secondary data. The major source of data analysed and interpreted in this study related to all those companies selected is collected from "PROWESS" database, which is the most reliable on the empowered corporate database of Centre for Monitoring Indian Economy (CMIE). Besides prowess database, relevant secondary data have also been collected from BSE Stock Exchange Official Directory, CIME Publications, Annual Survey of Industry, Business newspapers, Reports on Currency and Finance, Libraries of various Research Institutions, through Internet etc.

ANALYSIS

Financial leverage and Industry class

The first hypothesis relates to the possible association between industry class and financial structure. Firms in the same industry should experience similar amount of business risk because they produce similar products, incur similar set of rules, regulations, guidelines and environment. Since business risk has got relationship with the types of product, and the product with types of industries, there is reason to believe that a firm's financial structure is influenced by its industrial classification. The same logic should also hold good for inter-industry comparison. Since industries deal with different products, operate under different environment, rely on different technology, have different cost structure, their business risks should essentially be different. As such, their financial structures should also be different.

To test whether the financial leverage of selected sectors of Indian automobile industry significantly differs, Analysis of Variance (ANOVA) has been applied and result of which is displayed in Table 21.0 It is evident from Table 21.0 that F ratio (82.62) is much higher than the table value of F (3.40) at 5 per cent level of significance. This indicates that the means of the financial leverages of the selected sectors of Indian automobile industry differ significantly. Thus the null hypothesis that financial leverage is independent of industrial class is rejected leading to the conclusion that financial leverage depends upon industrial class.

Table 21.0

Analysis of Variance (ANOVA) for financial leverages of Indian automobile industry

Sectors			Mean		No. of items
Commercial Vehicles			0.468		13
Passenger Cars and Multiutility Vehicles			0.542		13
Two and Three Wheelers			0.268		13
Mean			0.425		13
Source of variations	**Sum of squares**	**Df**	**Mean square**	**F ratio**	**F Value (at 5%)**
Between the years	0.238	12	0.019	6.27	2.18
Between the sectors	0.522	2	0.261	82.62	3.40
Error	0.076	24	0.003		
Total	0.836	38			

Source : Computed

Financial leverage and Size

Large firms are generally more diversified, enjoy easier access to capital markets, receive higher credit ratings, and pay lower rates of interest on borrowed capital. Moreover as the level of activity increases with size, more debt is expected in the financial structure of large corporations. Hence, size of the firm should be positively related to its financial structure. The same logic should also hold good for inter-industry variations. In order to test the validity of the second null hypothesis that financial leverage and industry size are independent, correlation co-efficient between financial leverage and industry size have been calculated for all the three sectors namely commercial vehicles, passenger cars and multiutility vehicles, two and three wheelers and whole industry during the study period. To test the significance of correlation co-efficient, t values have also been computed.

Table 21.1 exhibits details of empirical results found in respect of the hypothesis concerning financial leverage and industry size. It is apparent from Table 21.1 that not only there exists positive correlations between financial leverages and industry size but also the relations are statistically significant at 5 per cent level in case of all the sectors and whole industry during the study period.

Therefore, the null hypothesis that leverage is independent of industry size is rejected and hence concluded that size has got bearing on financial structure.

Table 21.1

Statement showing correlation coefficients, t-values and levels of significance of financial leverage and different factors

Industry class	Correlation between	r-value	t value	Significant / Not significant
Commercial Vehicles	FL and size	0.475	9.36*	Significant
	FL and profit	-0.641	2.73*	Significant
	FL and ol	-0.440	2.42*	Significant
	FL and ef	0.694	11.28*	Significant
	FL and ig	0.280	1.38	Not significant
Passenger Cars and Multiutility Vehicles	FL and size	0.028	6.51*	Significant
	FL and profit	-0.795	1.11	Not significant
	FL and ol	-0.429	1.87*	Significant
	FL and ef	-0.192	8.71*	Significant
	FL and ig	0.570	2.14	Significant
Two and Three Wheelers	FL and size	0.566	5.96*	Significant
	FL and profit	-0.705	7.65*	Significant
	FL and ol	0.064	0.58	Not significant
	FL and ef	0.933	7.43*	Significant
	FL and ig	0.479	6.17*	Significant
Whole Industry	FL and size	0.540	7.61*	Significant
	FL and profit	-0.733	3.72*	Significant
	FL and ol	-0.402	2.23*	Significant
	FL and ef	0.565	9.58*	Significant
	FL and ig	0.591	2.59*	Significant

FL - Financial Leverage　　profit - profitability

ol - operating leverage　　ef - external financing

ig - income gearing

* - Significant of at 0.05 level

Source: Computed

Financial leverage and Profitability

The third hypothesis is pertaining to the relationship between a firm's profitability and its financial structure. A firm's ability to generate internal surpluses for business expansion depends upon its earning capacity. A more profitable firm may be considered to be in a better position to generate internal funds by way of reserves and surpluses. As reserves and surpluses will grow, the firm's dependence on external financing will decline, and consequently its dependence on dept capital too. This is because, a firm going for external funds will certainly prefer low-cost source and debt will be the first choice. Hence, a negative relationship should exist between a firm's financial leverage and its profitability. This phenomenon should also be true for industry level comparison, for profitability differs from industry to industry. In order to test the validity for the null hypothesis that financial leverage and profitability are independent of each other, correlation co-efficient between financial leverage and profitability have been calculated along with t value for all the three sectors and whole industry and empirical results are presented in Table 21.1.

It is evident from the Table 21.1 that the existence of negative correlation between financial leverage and profitability in commercial vehicles, two and three wheelers and whole industry and also the relation are statistically significant at 5 per cent level. Although empirical evidences indicate the existence of negative correlation between financial leverage and profitability in passenger cars and multiutility vehicles sector the relations could not be found statistically significant. Thus the null hypothesis that financial leverage is independent of profitability is rejected and concluded that there exists negative correlation between them.

Financial leverage and Operating leverage

The fourth hypothesis relates to the suspected influence of operating leverage on financial structure. Ferri and Jones[4] define operating leverage as "the use of fixed costs in the firm's production scheme but is generally associated with the employment of fixed assets". According to them, the use of fixed assets can magnify the variability of the firm's future income and hence, "operating leverage should be negatively related to the firm's financial structure". Determining the validity of this hypothesis in case of Indian automobile industry was thus the purpose of the fourth test. In order to test the validity of the null hypothesis that financial leverage and operating leverage have got no association between them, correlation co-efficient between financial leverages and operating leverages have been calculated along with the value for all the three sectors of automobile industry and whole industry and empirical results are presented in Table 21.1.

In case of Indian automobile industry, however a definite conclusion could not be reached as far as the relationship between operating leverage and financial leverage is concerned. Empirical evidences from Table 21.1 show that there exists negative correlation between operating leverage and financial leverage in case of commercial vehicles, passenger cars and multiutility vehicles and whole industry but also the relationships are statistically significant at 5 per cent level. Interestingly in case of two and three wheelers positive correlation between financial leverage and operating leverage, could not be found statistically significant. Thus, the null hypothesis that operating leverage and financial leverage are independent of each other could not be fully rejected in the sense there exists both negative as well as positive correlation between them in different sectors in the same period.

Financial leverage and External financing

The fifth hypothesis relates to the association between the external financing and financial structure. Generally firms prepare internal to external financing, and they will prefer the safest security first, i.e., they will choose debt before equity financing, in case they seek external financing to finance real investments with a positive net present value. This implies that when external financing will increase, the proportion of debt in the total financing will also increase. Hence there should exist, a positive relationship between external financing and firm's financial leverage. This logic should also be valid for inter- industry comparison.

Empirical evidence from Table 21.1 shows that there exists a strong and statistically significant positive relationship between financial leverage and external financing in case of commercial vehicles, two and three wheelers and whole industry. The Table 21.1 further shows that the existence of negative significant correlation between financial leverage and external financing in case of passenger cars and multiutility vehicles sector. Thus the null hypothesis that financial leverage and external financing are independent of each other could not be fully rejected in the sense there exists both positive as well as negative correlation between them in different industry in the same period.

Financial leverage and Income gearing

The sixth and the last hypothesis relates to the possible association between income gearing and a firm's financial leverage.

Income gearing is considered to be a measure of corporate vulnerability to fluctuations in general economic conditions. Since firms operate under different economic conditions, and economic conditions have bearing on capital as well as debt markets, there should exist relationship between income gearing and a firm's financial leverage.

Empirical evidence from Table 21.1 shows that there exists a statistically significant positive relationship between income gearing and corporate financial structure in case of passenger cars and multiutility vehicles, two and three wheelers and whole industry. In case of commercial vehicles, the relations though positive are found to be statistically insignificant. Thus, while rejecting the null hypothesis that there is no association between income gearing and financial leverage, it may conclude that income gearing and financial leverage are positively correlated.

Conclusion

The analysis of hypotheses reveals that financial leverage is independent of industry class and was rejected leading to the conclusion that financial structure depends upon industry class. Further size and income gearing are positively correlated with financial leverage and got bearing on financial structure. The relationship between financial structure and profitability was found to be negative and profitability could be accepted as a clear determinant of financial structure. The finding also reveals that the relationship between financial structure, operating leverage and external financing exists both positive and negative correlation between them in different industry in the same period, thus, overall results exhibited by the analysis leads to the conclusion that industry class, size and profitability are the most significant factors which influence, to a great extent, the financial structure of Indian Automobile Industry.

Endnote:

In this study at hand, a number of key financial variables have been identified for the purpose of analysis. The computation of these variables has been made for a period of 13 years. An epigrammatic explanation of the selected variable is outlined below.

Financial structure

There exists a great deal of controversy regarding the concept of capital structure, financial structure, capitalization and financial-mix. While some prefer to use these terms as synonymous and hence use them interchangeably, others put a distinction between capital structure and financial structure by including only long-term sources of funds (debt and ownership capital) under the former, and all sources of funds (i.e., both long-term and short-term) under the latter. Thus, in this study the entire liabilities side of the balance sheet has been considered as financial structure for the purpose of the present study.

Financial leverage

Financial leverage, expressed as a ratio between total debt to total assets at book value, i.e., D/TA, has been used as the only measure of capital structure in this study. This is the measure which Remmers et al., have also used in their study. The reason of accepting this ratio (i.e., total debt to total assets at book value) as financial structure or financial leverage lies with the fact of its conceptual simplicity over other measures and its ability to more completely reflect a firm's total reliance on borrowed capital.

Operating leverage

The traditional measure of operating leverage is the ratio of the percentage change in earnings to the percentage change in sales. Because of lack of a unique measure of operating leverage, some even prefer to calculate it, from the balance sheet data, by dividing net fixed assets by total assets at book value and even by dividing the net fixed assets by average total assets at book value. Operating leverage to be called as degree of operating leverage, has been calculated by dividing the percentage change in average earnings before interest and taxes by the percentage change in average sales.

Mathematically, $DOL_t = \dfrac{[(EBIT_t - EBIT_{t-1})/EBIT_{t-1}]}{[(SA_t - SA_{t-1})/SA_{t-1}]}$

Where,

DOL_t = Degree of operating leverage in time 't'

$EBIT_t$ = Earnings Before Interest and Taxes in year 't'

$EBIT_{t-1}$ = Earnings Before Interest and Taxes in the previous year

SA_t = Sales in year 't'

SA_{t-1} = Sales in previous year

Income gearing

The ratio of interest to EBIT has been taken as 'income gearing'. Another measure of income gearing, often used in the literature, is the proportion of interest to cash flows. Singh and Hamid have used both of the measures, what they call the 'flow measures of gearing' in their study.

Payout ratio

The ratio of dividend to profit after tax has been taken as payout ratio.

External financing

Share capital, borrowings, trade dues and other current liabilities and miscellaneous non-current liabilities, constitute to form the external financing.

References

1. Scott, David F. (1972). Evidence on the importance of Financial Structure, Financial Management, Summer, pp.45-50.
2. Scott, David F. and Martin, John D., (1975). Industry influence on Financial structure, Financial Management, Vol.4, Spring, pp. 67-75.
3. Remmers Lee, Stonenill, Arthur Wright Richard and Bekhuisen, Theo (1974). Industry and size as debt ratio determinants in Manufacturing Internationally, Financial Management, pp. 24-32.
4. Ferri, Michael, G., and Jones, Wesley H., (1979). Determination of Financial Structure: A New Methodological Approach, The Journal of Finance, Vol, XXXIV, No.3. June, pp.631-644.
5. Singh, A. and Hamid J., Corporate Financial Structure in Developing countries, IFC Technical paper, No.1, The world Bank, Washington, D.C.

22

LINKAGE BETWEEN MARKET VALUE ADDED (MVA) AND OTHER FINANCIAL VARIABLES : AN ANALYSIS IN INDIAN AUTOMOBILE INDUSTRY

The corporate missions have undergone radical changes during last decade. This is mainly due to the economic reforms implemented in most of the developing countries in the world particularly in India that has invited greater competition and mounting transparencies in the financial working, management, and control of corporation. In such altered circumstances, using conventional accounting measures to elucidate the behaviour of performance is, perhaps, not a suitable built-in approach. But in the shifting economic order, it is now well settled that the aim of every business entity be supposed to maximize the wealth of equity shareholders. Simply with this reason, all economic and non- economic activities of the firm should be aimed at to realize this objective.

The expansion of the capital markets, increased shareholder activism, institutional investors with large equity positions, and more active boards of directors have all contributed to heighten the pressure on companies to consistently maximize shareholder value. In response, and regarding the shortcomings of traditional Profit – related performance measures, consulting companies such as Stern Stewart, The Alcar Group and Strategic planning Associates have developed "New" Value – based Performance measures. Probably, the most popular periodic value – based Performance measure is Stern Stewart's Economic Value Added (EVA).

The evidence of the majority of the empirical studies regarding EVA suggests that there is a Positive relationship between EVA and Shareholder value creation , measured by Market Value Added (MVA). However, when the explaining power of EVA versus traditional performance measures regarding Equity Market Value or Returns is considered, the results are mixed. Hence, an attempt has been made in this article to find out the sector – wise trends as far as the factors affecting MVA are concerned. The purpose of this study was to explore whether any relationship existed between dependent and independent variables and to come across, whether a particular independent variable emerges as the most explanatory variable of MVA during the study period.

Market Value Added

Market Value Added (MVA) is a measure of shareholder's wealth. If the corporate objective is to enhance shareholder's wealth, it can be achieved by improving MVA. MVA is the difference between the market value of invested capital and book value of invested capital. MVA is the absolute rupee spread between a company's market value and its capital. It represents the stock market's assessment as of a particular time of the net present value of all a company's past and projected capital projects. Therefore, maximizing MVA should be the primary objective for any company that is concerned about its shareholder's welfare. Economic Value Added (EVA) is net operating profit after tax minus an appropriate change for the opportunity cost of all capital invested in an organization. A company's EVA is the fuel that fires up its MVA. Thus, EVA is the internal measure of corporate performance and MVA is the external measure of corporate performance.

The present article makes an attempt to find the relevance in Indian context of Stern and Stewart's claim that MVA of the firm is largely positively associated with or driven by its EVA generating capacity. The study also portrays the association between MVA and other selected traditional financial variables like Earnings Per Share (EPS), Return on Capital Employed (ROCE), Net Operating Profit After Tax (NOPAT) and Return on Net Worth (RONW).

Review of Literature

Stern (1990)[1] observed that EVA as a performance measure captures the true economic profit of an organisation. EVA-based financial management and incentive compensation scheme gives managers better–quality information and superior motivation to make decisions that will create the maximum shareholder wealth in an organisation. **Stewart (1994)**[2] has expanded that adoption of the EVA system by more and more companies throughout the world clearly depicts that it provides an integrated decision - making framework, can reform energies and redirect resources to create sustainable value for companies, customers, employees, shareholders and for management. **Grant (1996)**[3] found that EVA concept might have everlastingly changed the way real profitability is measured.

EVA is a financial tool that focuses on the difference between company's after tax operating profit and its total cost of capital. **Luber (1996)**[4] confirmed that a positive EVA over a period of time will also have an increasing MVA while negative EVA will bring down MVA as the market loses confidence in the competence of a company to ensure a handsome return on the invested capital.

Banerjee (1997)[5] has conducted an empirical research to find the superiority of EVA over other traditional financial performance measures. ROI and EVA have been calculated for sample companies and a comparison of both showing the superiority of EVA over ROI. **Ethiraj (1998)**[6] derived those stock prices moves up as a company adopts EVA as an internal performance criterion. **KPMG - BS study (1998)**[7] assessed top 100 companies on EVA, Sales, PAT and MVA criteria. The Survey has used the BS – 1000 list of companies using a composite index comprising sales, profitability and compounded annual growth rate of those companies covering the period 1996-97. Sixty companies have been found able to create positive Shareholder Value whereas 38 companies have been found to destroy it. **Anand, et al (1999)**[8] revealed that EVA and MVA are better measures of business performance that NOPAT and EPS in terms of shareholders' value creation and competitive advantage of a firm. **Bao and Bao (1999)**[9] revealed that the EVA is positively and significantly correlated with the firm value. **Harihar (1999)**[10] highlighted some myths regarding EVA. According to him, EVA calculations are not simple and need a lot of adjustments in the financial books. Further, EVA figures can be manipulated to suit the needs of management. **Thenmozhi (1999)**[11] compared EVA with some other traditional measure of corporate performance viz. ROI, EPS, RONW, ROE, ROCE etc. She has referred to some of the shortcomings of the concept of EVA but maintain that EVA is a better measure of corporate performance. **Banerjee (2000)**[12] attempted to find out whether Market Value of Firm if the function of current operational Value (COV) and Future Growth Value (FGV). Based on the analysis of his data he comes to the conclusion that in many cases there was a considerable divergence between MVA and the sum total of COA and FGV.

Riceman, et al (2002)[13] argued that EVA is a performance measure that is being used by an increasing number of companies, but academic research on EVA is limited. **Mangala and Simpy (2002)**[14] discussed the relationship between EVA and Market Value among various companies in India. The results of the analysis confirm Stern's hypothesis and concluded that the company's current operational value was more significant in contributing to change in market value of share in Indian context. **Bardia (2002)**[15] revealed that in a dynamic environment, a common investor finds it increasingly difficult to monitor his investments. EVA guides investors in evaluating the performance of the company and monitoring their investments. **Stern, Joel (2003)**[16] presented the results of Stern Stewart's research on Indian companies, which shows considerable need to improve the wealth creation performance and allocation of capital in the Indian economy. They explained how the effective implementation of the EVA framework could be a solution to address this problem. **Balachandran and Sriram (2005)**[17] made an attempt to study the value created for the shareholders of the company. They used to determine the relationship between Economic Value Added and dividend paid to the shareholders. The study revealed that the company had utilized the dividend-paying fund ploughing back into the business. The company was very conservative in declaring dividend and always had long-term objective of creating wealth to the shareholders, which has been achieved. **Ali M Ghanbari and Narges Sarlak (2006)**[18] empirically reviewed the trend of EVA of Indian Automobile Companies. The results indicate that there was a significant increasing trend in EVA during the period of study and the firms in the automobile industry are moving towards the improvement of their firm's value.

It appears that the concept of EVA, as an emerging concept of financial management is fairly clear in the minds of almost all these researches whose studies have been reviewed above. In a fast changing business environment, the investor friendly financial performance measures may be the need of hour.

Research Design

Keeping in view the scope of the study, it is decided to include all the companies under automobile industry working before or from the year 1991-92 to 2003-04. There are 26 companies operating in the Indian automobile industry. But, owing to several constraints such as non-availability of financial statements or non-working of a company in a particular year etc., it is compelled to restrict the number of sample companies to 18. The companies under automobile industry are classified into three sectors namely; Commercial vehicles, Passenger cars and multiutility vehicles and Two and three wheelers. For the purpose of the study all the three sectors have been selected. It accounts for 69 per cent of the total companies available in the Indian automobile industry. The selected 18 companies include 5 under commercial vehicles, 4 under passenger cars and multiutility vehicles and 9 under two and three wheeler sectors. It is inferred that sample company represents 99 percentage of market share in commercial vehicles, 90 percentage of market share in passenger cars and multiutility vehicles and 99 percentage of market share in two and three wheelers. Thus, the findings based on the occurrence of such representative sample may be presumed to be true representative of automobile industry in the country.

With a view to present the methodological analysis placed in this study, the selected variables like MVA, EVA, EPS, ROCE, NOPAT and RONW constitute the variable base. Out of these, MVA is considered as dependent variable and other are independents. The rationale of this analysis is to examine that which particular independent variable has been able to explain the dependent variable in superior manner throughout the period. The period 1991-92 to 2003-04 is selected for this study. The span chosen for the study is the period of the beginning of liberalization measures introduced by the Government of India. Hence, the period 1991-92 to 2003-04 is an era of growth of corporate performance in the manufacturing sector, particularly automobile industry and has got genuine economic significance of its own.

The study is based on secondary data. The major source of data analysed and interpreted in this study related to all those companies selected is collected from "PROWESS" database, which is the most reliable on the empowered corporate database of Centre for Monitoring Indian Economy (CMIE). Besides prowess database, relevant secondary data have also been collected from BSE Stock Exchange Official Directory, CMIE Publications, Annual Survey of Industry, business newspapers, Reports on Currency and Finance, Libraries of various Research Institutions, through Internet etc.

Sector wise trends in MVA

Table 22.0 portrays whole automobile industry and sector wise information pertaining to MVA. It is evident from Table 22.0 that among the three sectors, passenger cars and multiutility vehicles sector have been generating highest market value added throughout the study period. This was due to the better market value added of Maruti Udyog Ltd and Mahindra and Mahindra Ltd. It was followed by commercial vehicles sector and two and three wheelers. Table 22.0 also shows that all the selected sectors of automobile industry have been generating positive aggregate MVA throughout the period. The growth of MVA is more in case of passenger cars and multiutility vehicles whereas less consistent in case of commercial vehicles and two and three wheelers sector. Table also brings out that only the commercial vehicles sector had registered negative compound annual growth rate of MVA during the study period.

Table 22.0

MVA Sector - wise Trends (1991-92 to 2003-04)

Sl. No	Industry	Mean (Rs.in crores)	CV	CAGR
1.	Ashok Leyland Ltd	1003.02	0.65	8.64
2.	Tata Motors Ltd	4495.22	0.74	-16.70
3.	Bajaj Tempo Ltd	277.39	0.31	-0.54
4.	Eicher Motors Ltd	99.63	1.31	17.00
5.	Swaraj Mazda Ltd	63.71	1.25	13.80
	Commercial Vehicles Sector	**1187.83**	**0.53**	**-6.34**
6.	Hindustan Motors Ltd	100.43	1.87	-19.00
7.	Mahindra & Mahindra Ltd	1105.09	0.62	7.03
8.	Maruti Udyog Ltd	10340.26	0.18	1.58
9.	Daewoo Motors India Ltd	-36.72	-4.67	-39.30
	Passenger Cars and Multiutility Vehicles Sector	**2877.27**	**0.18**	**1.85**
10.	Bajaj Auto Ltd	4726.06	0.46	8.36
11.	LML Ltd	161.07	0.53	-2.70
12.	Maharastra Scooters Ltd	64.25	0.58	3.59
13.	TVS Motors Company Ltd	583.81	0.98	15.30
14.	Kinetic Motors Co. Ltd	88.21	0.60	-14.00
15.	Hero Honda Motors Ltd	2840.81	1.09	38.20
16.	Kinetic Engineering Ltd	52.39	0.58	-11.90
17.	Majestic Auto Ltd	33.52	0.68	-11.60
18.	Scooters India Ltd	-9.72	-1.61	13.80
	Two and Three Wheelers Sector	**948.68**	**0.62**	**14.60**
	Whole Automobile Industry	**1671.26**	**0.20**	**2.41**

The market value added of selected companies under commercial vehicles sector during the study period is also presented in Table 22.0. Table 22.0 reveals that the mean MVA of Tata Motors Ltd were the highest followed by Ashok Leyland Ltd, Bajaj Tempo Ltd, Eicher Motors Ltd and Swaraj Mazda Ltd. Table 22.0 brings out that all the selected companies under the commercial vehicles sector had registered very high fluctuations in their MVA except Bajaj Tempo Ltd which registered moderate fluctuations during the study period. Further, Table 22.0 provided that the two companies namely Tata Motors Ltd and Bajaj Tempo Ltd had registered negative compound annual growth rate of MVA and rest of the companies had positive compound annual growth rate of MVA during the study period.

Table 22.0 presents MVA of selected companies under passenger's cars and multiutility vehicles sector. The table shows that the companies like Maruti Udyog Ltd and Mahindra and Mahindra Ltd is top in the list and it was followed by Hindustan Motors Ltd and Daewoo Motors Ltd. All the selected companies except Maruti Udyog Ltd had registered very high fluctuation in their MVA during the study period. Table 22.0 also brings out values relating to compound annual growth rate of MVA of selected companies. It is evident from the table that Hindustan Motors Ltd and Daewoo Motors India Ltd had registered negative growth rate and rest of the companies had registered positive growth rate of MVA during the study period.

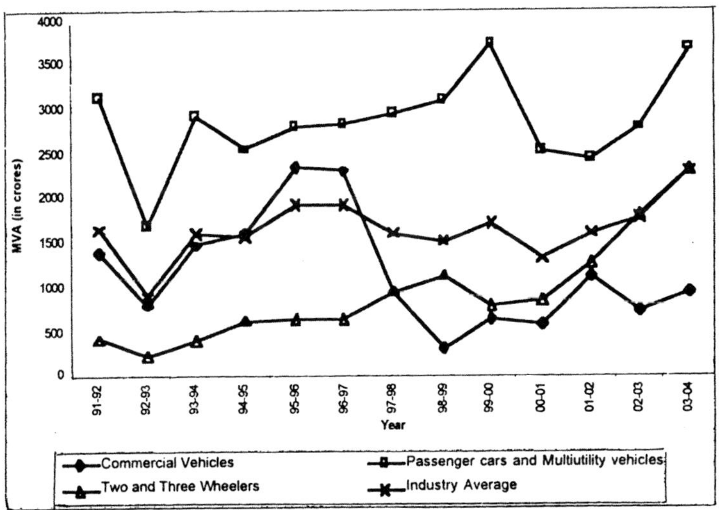

Figure 1. Sector-Wise trend in MVA

Table 22.0 brings out the values relating to MVA of selected companies under two and three wheelers. Table 22.0 showed that Bajaj Auto Ltd, Hero Honda Motors Ltd, TVS Motors India Ltd and LML Ltd comparatively top in the list. On the other hand, Scooters

India Ltd and Majestic Auto Ltd are struggling on their front with regard to MVA during the study period. It is also noticed that all the selected companies have registered very high fluctuations in their MVA during the study period. The analysis of compound annual growth rate of MVA showed mixed trend among the selected companies under the sector during the study period.

MVA vis-à-vis other Financial Variables-Linear Regression

In this section an attempt to find the relevance of Stern and Stewart's claim that MVA of the firm is largely positive association with or driven by its EVA generating capacity and other financial variables like EPS, ROCE, NOPAT and RONW. In this section, result of correlation co-efficient, linear regression, Durbin - Watson model, F - statistics and t - statistics have been determined between dependent variable (MVA) and independent variables. The values hence obtained have their particular statistical sense. The regression co-efficient for independent variables like EVA, EPS, ROCE, NOPAT and RONW so worked out portrays the temperament of association between the dependent and particular independent variable. The t - statistics and F - statistics so calculated determine the level of significant or insignificant association between the variables. Durbin - Watson model allows the researcher to establish the auto-correlation, if any between dependent and independent variable (the desirable value is two and any value more than two signifies negative auto-correlation and vice versa); values of adjusted R^2 indicate the extent of variation in the dependent variable which may be explicated by independent variable (s) and the standard error speaks about the limits within which the estimated value as the dependent variable is expected to lie.

MVA-EVA analysis

Table 22.1 offers the explanation about the regression analysis between MVA and EVA during the study period for the whole automobile industry and its three sectors. Table 22.1 provides the values of R, R-square and adjusted R-square for the whole industry 0.165, 0.03 and – 0.06 respectively. It sounds that there exists poor relationship between MVA and EVA in automobile industry, as the value of adjusted R-square in negative. Interestingly, the t and F statistics give the identical results but both of them lead to insignificant association between the variables under reference. It is evident from the table that the overall result in passenger cars and multiutility vehicles does not differ from whole industry and

Table 22.1
MVA - EVA: Linear Regression Analysis
Dependent variable - Market Value Added (MVA)
Independent variable - Economic Value Added (EVA)

Independent Variable	Co-efficient	t	Multiple R	R Square	Adjusted R Square	Std. Error of the Estimate	Durbin-Watson	F Value
Commercial Vehicles :								
EVA	1.041	1.138	0.325	0.11	0.03	623.52	0.83	1.30
Passenger Cars and Multiutility Vehicles:								
EVA	0.321	0.796	0.233	0.06	-0.03	537.98	1.78	0.63
Two and Three wheelers:								
EVA	2.602	1.562	0.426	0.18	0.11	558.29	0.86	2.44
Whole Industry:								
EVA	0.280	0.556	0.165	0.03	-0.06	339.76	1.23	0.31

Source: Computed

statistical association between MVA and EVA is again insignificant. Table 22.1 suggests that EVA is serially correlated in commercial vehicles and two and three wheelers sector and adjusted R-square value is also positive. The t and F statistics are resulting identical values and secure that in commercial vehicles and two and three wheelers sector relationship between MVA and EVA is fairly significant. However, the MVA-EVA analysis supports the hypothesis of Stern and Stewart's that MVA of firm is largely positive associated with EVA in all the selected sectors of Indian automobile industry.

MVA-EPS analysis

The linear regression analysis between MVA and EPS is presented by Table 22.2 for the study period. It is evident from the Table 22.2 that the correlation co-efficient between MVA and EPS for the whole industry is 0.306 and value of R-square and adjusted R-square is very low and may not be adequate for the fitness of the model. The t and F statistics suggest that the association between MVA and EPS of automobile industry is not significant and EPS does not suitably explain the MVA. It is evident from the table that the correlation co-efficient between MVA and EPS in passenger cars and multiutility vehicles and two and three wheelers 0.223 and 0.246 respectively and value of adjusted R-square is negative. This shows the poor fitness of the model. Both t statistics and F statistics certify that the association between these two variables is insignificant as presented in the table. It is again noticed from the table that the variables are clearly correlated in commercial vehicles sector and adjusted R-square value is also positive. The t and F statistics are resulting identical values and secured that EPS of commercial vehicles sector has been able to describe MVA in best term than the other sectors. The overall results showed that EPS is positively associated with MVA in all the three sectors and the whole industry during the study period.

MVA – ROCE analysis

Table 22.3 offers the explanation about the regression analysis between MVA and ROCE during the study period for the whole automobile industry and its three sectors. Table 22.3 provides the values of R, R – square and adjusted R – square are 0.756, 0.57 and 0.53 respectively. It sounds that the good fitness of the model. Interestingly, t and F statistics give the identical result but both of them lead to significant association between the variable under reference. In two and three wheelers sector the results are just about

Table 22.2

MVA - EPS: Linear Regression Analysis

Dependent variable - Market Value Added (MVA)

Independent variable - Earning Per Share (EPS)

Independent Variable	Co-efficient	t	Multiple R	R-Square	Adjusted R-Square	Std. Error of the Estimate	Durbin-Watson	F Value
Commercial Vehicles:								
EPS	46.84	1.566	0.427	0.18	0.11	596.11	0.84	2.45
Passenger Cars and Multiutility Vehicles:								
EPS	2.67	0.760	0.223	0.05	-0.04	539.28	1.99	0.58
Two and Three Wheelers:								
EPS	30.09	0.840	0.246	0.06	-0.03	598.19	0.34	0.71
Whole Industry:								
EPS	6.53	1.068	0.306	0.09	0.12	327.93	1.37	1.14

Source: Computed

Table 22.3

MVA – ROCE: Linear Regression Analysis

Dependent variable - Market Value Added (MVA)

Independent variable – Return On Capital Employed (ROCE)

Independent Variable	Co-efficient	t	Multiple R	R-Square	Adjusted R -Square	Std. Error of the Estimate	Durbin-Watson	F Value
Commercial Vehicles :								
ROCE	19.587	1.061	0.305	0.09	0.01	627.87	0.78	1.13
Passenger Cars and Multiutility Vehicles:								
ROCE	9.765	0.629	0.186	0.04	-0.05	543.56	1.90	0.40
Two and Three Wheelers:								
ROCE	53.56**	1.804	0.478	0.23	0.16	542.08	0.53	3.26
Whole Industry:								
ROCE	38.99*	3.830	0.756	0.57	0.53	225.51	1.34	14.67

* * - Significant at 0.10 level ; * - Significant at 0.05 level

Source: Computed

similar to whole industry. Table 22.3 suggests that the variables are clearly correlated in two and three wheelers sector and adjusted R – square value is also positive. The t and F statistics are resulting identical values and secure that in two and three wheelers sectors the association between MVA and ROCE is fairly significant. However, in case of passenger cars and multiutility vehicles and commercial vehicles sector the values of R, R-square and adjusted R-square showed that there exists poor relationship between MVA and ROCE in these sectors. Interestingly, t and F statistics give the identical results but both of them lead to insignificant association between the variables under reference. The overall results showed that ROCE is positively associated with MVA in all the three sectors and the whole industry during the study period.

MVA – NOPAT analysis

Linear regression analysis between MVA and NOPAT is presented in Table 22.4. In Table 22.4 the statistical association between MVA and NOPAT of all the three sectors and the whole industry are provided. The table reveals that the value of R, R-square and adjusted R-square are high and it may be adequate for the fitness of the model in case of whole industry, passenger cars and multiutility vehicles sector and two and three wheelers sector. The t and F statistics also suggest that the association between MVA and NOPAT is significant and NOPAT is suitable to explain in the MVA of these sectors and whole industry during the study period. The results regarding the association of MVA and NOPAT in commercial vehicles sector slightly differ. The table reveals that value of adjusted R-square is very low and it may not be adequate for the fitness of the model, the t and F statistics also suggest that the association between the MVA and NOPAT is not significant and NOPAT do not suitably explain the MVA of commercial vehicles sector during the study period. The overall analysis showed that NOPAT is positively associated with MVA in all the three sectors and whole industry.

MVA – RONW analysis

Table 22.5 tenders the elucidation concerning the regression analysis between MVA and RONW during the study period. The Table 22.5 provides the values of R, R-square and adjusted R-square. Table 22.5 suggests that variables are clearly correlated in whole industry, commercial vehicles and two and three wheelers sector and adjusted R-square value is also positive. The t and F statistics are resulting identical values and secured that in these sectors and

Table 22.4

MVA – NOPAT: Linear Regression Analysis

Dependent variable - Market Value Added (MVA)

Independent variable – Net Operating Profit After Tax (NOPAT)

Independent Variable	Co-efficient	t	Multiple R	R-Square	Adjusted R Square	Std. Error of the Estimate	Durbin-Watson	F Value
Commercial Vehicles :								
NOPAT	3.044	1.231	0.348	0.12	0.04	618.02	0.74	1.52
Passenger Cars and Multiutility Vehicles:								
NOPAT	3.295*	2.568	0.612	0.38	0.32	437.47	1.33	6.59
Two and Three Wheelers:								
NOPAT	10.870*	7.896	0.922	0.85	0.84	238.99	1.21	62.34
Whole Industry:								
NOPAT	4.034*	4.698	0.817	0.67	0.64	198.68	1.52	22.08

* - Significant at 0.05 level   Source: Computed

Table 22.5

MVA – RONW: Linear Regression Analysis

Dependent variable - Market Value Added (MVA)

Independent variable – Return On Net Worth (RONW)

Independent Variable	Co-efficient	t	Multiple R	R-Square	Adjusted R -Square	Std. Error of the Estimate	Durbin-Watson	F Value
Commercial Vehicles :								
RONW	29.044*	2.209	0.554	0.31	0.24	548.61	1.39	4.88
Passenger Cars and Multiutility Vehicles:								
RONW	3.364	0.266	0.080	0.01	-0.08	551.48	1.97	0.07
Two and Three Wheelers:								
RONW	-62.75*	2.943	00.664	0.44	0.39	461.56	1.19	8.66
Whole Industry:								
RONW	20.59**	1.874	0.492	0.24	0.17	299.95	1.48	3.51

* * - Significant at 0.10 level

* - Significant at 0.05 level

Source: Computed

whole industry the relationship between MVA and RONW is fairly significant. However, in case of passenger cars and multiutility vehicles, Table 22.5 provides the value of R, R-square and adjusted R-square are 0.08, 0.01 and -0.08 respectively. It sounds that there exists poor relationship between MVA and RONW in passenger cars and multiutility vehicles sector. The t and F statistics also give identical results but both of them lead to insignificant association between the variables under reference. The overall analysis showed that RONW is negatively association with MVA only in case of two and three wheelers sector during the study period.

Conclusion

A research idea has been evolved in this study to find out the industry-wise and sector-wise trends in the EVA and traditional financial variables that affect MVA. The regression analysis has been carried out and the succeeding outcomes that have been arrived revealed that NOPAT and RONW are the most significant variable with MVA followed by EVA, ROCE and EPS. In almost all cases, the positive relationship through correlation model has been established between the variables under reference. Thus, revealing the influence of this tool for rummaging the financial potency of Indian corporate comprising an industry and Indian industries comprising the particular sector may be measured as the need of the hour for all such companies that have not Started reporting their financial position in terms of EVA and MVA.

References

1. Stern, Joel (1990), "One way to build value in your firm, Executive compensation", Financial Executive, pp. 51-54.
2. Stewart, G. Bennet, (1994), "EVATM Fact and Fantasy", Journal of Applied Corporate Finance, pp. 71-84.
3. Grant, J. (1996). "Foundation of EVA for investment managers: Just in time, EVA", Journal of Financial Management, Vol.23, No.1, p.41(8).
4. Luber, R. B. (1996), "Who are the real wealth creators". Fortune, pp.2-3.
5. Banerjee, Ashok (1997), "Economic Value Added (EVA): a better performance measure", The Management Accountant, pp.86-88.
6. Ethiraj, Govindaraj (1998), 'The EVA feather in the market cap", The Economic Times, p. 1.

7. KPMG- BS, (1998) " Corporate India: An Economic Value Scoreboard", The Strategy, Jan-March, 1998, pp.22-25.
8. Anand, Manoj, Garg, Ajay and Arora, Asha (1999), "Economic value added : Business performance measure of shareholder value", The Management Accountant, pp.351-356.
9. Bao, B.H. and Bao, D.H., 'The Association between firm Value and Economic Value Added', Indian Accounting Review, Vol.3, No.2, pp.161-164.
10. Harihar,T.S.(1999), "EVA prorating Myths", Chartered Finance Analyst, pp.8-9.
11. Thenmozhie, M. (1999), "Economic value added as a measure of corporate performance", The Indian Journal of Commerce, Vol.52, No.4, pp. 72-85.
12. Banerjee, Ashok (2000), "Linkage between Economic Value Added and Market Value : An Analysis", Vikalpa, Vol.25, No.3, July-September, pp.23-36.
13. Riceman, S.S. and Cahan, S.F. (2002), "Do Managers Perform Better under EVA Bonus Schemes", Social Science Research Network Electronic Paper Collection, at http://oaoers.ssrb.cin.
14. Mangala, Deppa and Joura Simpy, "Linkage between Economic Value Added and Market Value: An Alaysis in Indian Context", Indian Mangement Studies Journal, June 2002, pp.53-65.
15. Bardia, S.C. (2002), "Economic Value Added: Overall Consideration", Economic Challenger, pp. 1-7.
16. Stern, Joel (2003), "Workshop on Value – based Management," Organised by the ASCI, Hyderabad, pp. 21-22.
17. Balachandran and Sriram (2005), Economic Value Added: A Case Study of M/S Lakshmi Machine Works Ltd, Coimbatore, Management and Accounting Research, pp. 113-122.
18. Ali, M. Ghanbari and Narges Sarlak, (2006), Economic Value – Added; An Appropriate performance Measure in the Indian Automobile Industry, The Icfaian Journal of Management Research, Vol.V, No.8, pp.45 – 61.

PART - VI

SOCIAL PERFORMANCE

23

APPRAISAL OF SOCIAL PERFORMANCE OF TASCO

The value of a business enterprise to the Society is called social performance. Business enterprises are directly concerned with the society. The business resources should be used for the betterment of society. It emphasize that business undertakings have social responsibility and that their performance should be evaluated in this context. Traditionally, accountants have valued the efficiency of an enterprise in terms of profitability or return on investment. But now considerable interest is given in the use of value-added approach to measure the prosperity of a business. The reason is that the performance of an enterprise is now evaluated from the society point of view.

Value-added indicates that net value created by the enterprise during a particular period. An enterprise may survive without making profit, but it cannot survive without adding value. The value-added is an excess of turnover plus income from services. Further, it has been distributed to employees, providers of Capital and Government who have created the value. Thus, the concept of value-added is wider than the concept of profits. The Value Added Statement (VAS) can be defined as a statement of presenting the value created by a business during an accounting period.

Hence value added statement is an indicator of a business enterprise to the society. An attempt has been made in this chapter to read the financial statements of Tamil Nadu Sugar Corporation (TASCO), in the respective of value-added concept.

Appraisal of Social Performance

The generation of value-added and application of value added of the Tamil Nadu Sugar Corporation has been given in the Table 23.0 and Table 23.1 respectively.

Table 23.0 reveals that the total revenues including the revenue from other services, marked an increasing trend throughout the study period except during 1990-91. On an average, 97 per cent revenue was added by sale of goods and 3 per cent was added by other services.

Table 23.0

Generation of Value-Added

(Rs. in lakhs)

Particulars	1985-86	1986-87	1987-89	1989-90	1990-91
Operating Revenues	1846.73	2865.10	3996.04	4027.76	2946.25
	(90.04)	(96.15)	(98.08)	(98.41)	(97.32)
Non-Operating Revenues	116.67	114.78	78.27	65.04	81.15
	(5.96)	(3.85)	(1.92)	(1.59)	(2.68)
Total Revenues (A)	1963.70	2979.88	4074.31	4092.80	3027.40
	(100)	(100)	(100)	(100)	(100)
Cost of Goods and	1140.38	2084.10	2659.15	2657.08	1935.82
Services (B)	(58.07)	(69.94)	(65.27)	(64.92)	(63.94)
Value-Added (A–B)	823.32	895.78	1415.16	1435.72	1091.58
	(41.93)	(30.06)	(34.73)	(35.08)	(36.06)

The proportion of cost of goods and services to the total revenues ranged from 58.07 per cent in 1985-86 to 69.94 per cent in 1986-87. It increased in 1986-87 as compared to the year 1985-86, but afterwards the trend was towards decline, which is an indication of good performance. The result is that the generation of value-added in the TASCO was to the tune of Rs.823.32 lakhs in 1985-86, which increased to Rs.1435.72 lakhs in 1989-90. It decreased to Rs.1091.58 lakhs in 1990-91. The proportion of value-added was 41.93 per cent in 1985-86, which declined to 30.06 per cent in 1986-87 but showed an increasing trend from 1987-89 to 1990-91 and finally it reached 36.06 per cent. Thus, there has been an increasing trend in the percentage of value-added during the study period.

It is evident from the Table 23.1 that the proportion of value added belonging to employees increased continuously during the first three years from 27.40 per cent to 35.09 per cent, but thereafter it decreased to 24.40 per cent (the lowest) in 1989-90. The table also showed the highest percentage (40.21 per cent) in 1990-91. The proportion of value added belonging to the Government fluctuated from 39.75 per cent in 1985-86 to 51.72 per cent in 1990-91. It should be mentioned here that the largest single distribution of value-added goes to the Government. It was due to the imposition of heavy excise duty and tax. The share paid to the providers of capital (in the form of interest and dividend) ranged from 3.75 per cent in 1987-89 to

9.08 per cent in 1990-91. It showed an increasing trend except in the years 1987-89. A major part of this proportion went to financial institutions, which provided debt capital. Due to a conservative policy regarding distribution of dividends, the TASCO has not paid any dividend from 1985-86 to 1987-89. It was also due to the lower profitability during earlier years. The TASCO had paid dividend to the tune of Rs.77.92 lakhs in the year 1989-90 only which was 5.44 per cent of value added.

Table 23.1
Application of Value-Added of TASCO

(Rs. in lakhs)

Particulars	1985-86	1986-87	1987-89	1989-90	1990-91
Applications					
To Employees	225.59	225.10	496.55	350.33	438.98
	(27.40)	(28.48)	(35.09)	(24.40)	(40.21)
To Government	327.32	434.10	700.66	621.46	564.58
(including excise duty & Tax)	(39.75)	(48.46)	(49.51)	(43.28)	(51.72)
To Providers of Capital					
Interest to Financial	46.82	52.93	53.05	34.78	99.10
Institution	(5.69)	(5.91)	(3.75)	(2.42)	(9.08)
Dividend	---	---	---	77.92	---
				(5.44)	
To Re-invested	156.35	144.55	188.88	153.10	338.15
Depreciation	(19.00)	(16.13)	(13.35)	(10.66)	(30.98)
Retained Earnings	67.24	9.10	- 23.98	198.13	- 349.23
	(8.16)	(1.02)	(- 1.70)	(13.80)	(- 31.99)
Total	**823.32**	**895.78**	**1415.15**	**1435.72**	**1091.58**
	(100)	**(100)**	**(100)**	**(100)**	**(100)**

Re-invested value of the TASCO in the form of depreciation was Rs.156.35 lakhs in 1985-86, which increased to Rs.338.15 lakhs in 1990-91, while in the form of profit it was Rs.67.24 lakhs in 1985-86, which declined to Rs.23.98 lakhs in the negative in 1987-89 and finally it was Rs.349.23 lakhs in the negative. The percentage of depreciation varied from 10.66 per cent to 30.98 per cent during the study period. While the percentage of profit retained was 8.16 per cent in 1985-86, which slipped down to 1.70 per cent in the negative and finally it was 31.99 per cent in the negative.

Conclusion

On the basis of the foregoing analysis, it may be concluded that the TASCO generated sufficient value-added and could thus be considered as a healthy unit from this point of view. The largest share of value-added has gone to the Government followed by its employees and providers of capital. It is also inferred that value-added statement certainly gives a better picture and appears to be more useful indicator of the performance of TASCO. Therefore, it is suggested that the TASCO has included value-added statement in their annual reports. To conclude that the management has succeeded in fulfilling, in part, its responsibility towards the society at large, but a conservative policy regarding the distribution of dividends and net losses in 1987-89 and 1990-91 created a bad impression especially in the share-holders of the Corporation at large.

References

1. M.C. Gupta, (1989) Profitability Analysis – An Empirical Approach, Pointer Publishers, Jaipur.
2. A.N. Agarwal, (1991) Corporate Performance Evaluation, Pointer Publishers, Jaipur.
3. Dr. K.K. Sharma & R.K. Agarwal, Value-Added concept in Road Transport. *The Management Accountant,* Vol.22, No.5, May 1987, p.337.
4. Jagadish Prakash and Vinod Kumar Shukla, Value-Added Analysis with special reference to SAIL, *The Management Accountant*, Vol.24, No.11, Nov. 1989, p.679.

PART - VII

IMPACT OF LIBERALISATION, PRIVATISATION AND GLOBALISATION

24

PRIVATISATION OF PUBLIC SECTOR ENTERPRISES—ISSUES AND PROSPECTS

Privatisation has become a hallmark of market-oriented reforms in many countries across the globe especially in those countries where experimentation with socialism and public sector has not yielded bountiful returns. The PEs in most of the countries, share substantially in national saving/investment accounts, Balance of payment accounts and government receipts and payment accounts. Thus their performance at a micro or firm level has significant impact at macro or national level. The public sector in many countries including India has become an epitome of low profitability, low rate of return, over employment, unnecessary burden on exchequer, and political manipulation. The multi-dimensional objectives of public sector gives enough room for criticism. Whatever the justification is given for public enterprise, the state of economy, state of public sector with colossal loss and resource crunch call for improvement in the performance of public sector.

However, privatisation as a measure being experimental in different countries to solve the problems with regard to the resources of public enterprise or to increase efficiency of them as an economic necessity. Hence, in this paper, an attempt has been made to study the various issues and constraints involved in the process of privatisation and suggest suitable measures for improvement of public sector enterprise efficiency.

What is Privatisation?

Privatisation is an idea like communism or socialism. It means different things to different people. It means the gradual exit of the government from owing and running industries to only regulating them. In other definition, privatisation has been used to mean sale through public offer of a part or whole of the capital by government out of its total holding of shares at a fair and reasonable price. Thus, underlying idea of privatisation is to transfer the control of the government companies to non-government management. The broader perspective being advocated for privatisation are:

- ❖ End of demarcation of the areas of activity for public and private sectors.
- ❖ Closure of non-viable unit is on the same line as they could be in case of private sector units.

The two dimensions of privatisation are one with regard to future policy for new investments in private sector formerly confined to public sector alone, and the other with regard to the existing enterprises whose shares could be transferred to private sector either wholly or partially.

Global Development

It was in the eighties that the concept of privatisation attracted the attention of policy-makers, planners and politicians throughout the world, due to economic compulsions like the failure of various public enterprises, high pressure on government budgets, slow rate of economic growth and so on. Margaret Thatcher of Britain was the first to implement the idea of privatisation in Britain's economic life 15 years ago. In order to solve the problems of inflation, unemployment, declining productivity, powerful labour unions, she curbed the role of government in economic and personal life by way of privatisation. Thereafter, America, France, European countries, Brazil, Mexico, Turkey, Malaysia, Korea, African countries etc., have adopted privatisation as the lever to improve the efficiency and competitiveness of their economics. Even in the former communist countries like East Germany, Romania, Poland, China, the process of privatisation have started. Thus, there is a global development and expansion of the concept of privatisation.

Which one to privatise and how?

There can be three alternatives before the Government.

- ❖ Whole public sector
- ❖ Profit-making units
- ❖ Loss-making units

Privatising whole public sector remains outside the purview of consideration as it defeats the welfare objective of the Government. Thus, the choice left is either profit-making or loss-incurring units. The profit-making unit is call for privatisation when government wants to have surplus state by selling away such units. In rest of the cases the loss-making units, which became a burden on budget and ultimately on economy are opted for privatisation.

After deciding which one to privatise the next issue crops in 'how to privatise.' The choice is between:

- Complete de-nationalisation, or
- Partial de-nationalisation.

Complete de-nationalisation can be done by out right sale of public enterprise. Partial de-nationalisation can be worked out by any of the following ways:

- Issuing share to the public.
- Opening up areas for private sector, hitherto reserved for public sector.
- Private management with public ownership.
- Providing environment of autonomy and accountability similar to that of private sector.
- Concentrating on core activities and contracting other activities to private sector or co-operatives.

Either of the two is resorted on the basis of its implication on the affected parties. Some common trends of privatisation around the globe are:

(1) It has been embedded in a programme of broad liberalisation and reform.

(2) The second trend is to divide state owned enterprises into different groups, and to pursue separate and specific privatisation goals for each group of enterprises.

(3) The third trend is largely a corollary to the first two, includes special programmes for small enterprise privatisation, enterprise liquidation scheme with asset sale or auction, leasing arrangements for state assets management/employee buy-out/buy-ins, restitution to previous owners and mass privatisation.

Among the three, the third one is the broad mix of privatisation tools used by most countries.

Why Privatise the Public Sector in India?

Over the last four decades, the public sector in India has phenomenally grown and spread into every conceivable industrial and commercial enterprises as modern temples. These temples are now being offered take-over by the private sector for sale privatisation as the process is otherwise called—under the country's new industrial and commercial for revamping and restructuring the economy. The public sectors in India may be thought for privatisation for reasons like:

- Need for funds for other developmental activities.
- In efficiency of public sector units.
- Withdrawal of government from economic activities.
- To do away with the burden, of Public Sector, in the form of budgetary subsidies.

The economic survey of India mentioned that public sector will not only need to maintain financial discipline in their operations but the budgetary support to them will also need to be scaled down. It also mentioned that this sector should be exposed to competitive pressure wherever possible. As such privatisation is advocated for increasing efficiency. It will create new work culture and improve efficiency.

Arguments for Privatisation

The following are the advantages we had by way of privatizing the Public Sector Enterprises.

(1) Economic Efficiency

The greatest advantage that is claimed in favour of privatisation is economic efficiency. In fact, a number of efforts have been made in India to create an atmosphere for the concept to take its roots. Concepts such as planning, programming, budgeting systems, zero-based budgeting, management by objective, worker incentives, performance budgeting, centralising-decentralising, productivity councils, computerisation, operations research, etc., have been introduced in the public sector. But the impact of all these on the efficiency of the government has been modest in India.

(2) Cut Down Budget Deficits

A weighty argument in favour of privatising these enterprises is that it would help a fiscally strapped Government to cut down on its deficits. This could serve as a boon to an economy facing a resources crunch and enable it to get out of the trap.

(3) Increasing Operational Efficiency

Another benefit stemming from privatisation is stated to be the potential increase in the operational efficiency of the enterprises. Improved efficiency of the enterprises comes through changes in objectives, higher incentives, and reduction of operational constraints, greater accountability and measurability of performance at various levels.

Issues and Constraints

Privatising state owned enterprises usually involves a number of economic, financial and legal issues (hurdles), as well as conflicting goals and interests that frequently impose constraints and make trade-off inevitable.

(1) Supply of Social Services Curtailed

One of the argument put forward against privatisation is that the supply of social services of a public nature will be severely curtailed. It is true that of privatisation were introduced on a large scale, the prices of these services would increase dramatically. it would be essential in this background that the government ensure that health and other services should be provided to the poor at subsidized rates, even if privatisation was introduced.

(2) Mass Retrenchment

One serious problem facing privatisation is resistance from the man-power sector. If fair play has to be given a chance, mass scale retrenchment is out of question. There are no social security schemes operative in India. Hence, likely lay off consequent upon immediate privatisation, is bound to lead to privatisation and therefore strong resentment.

(3) Jobs Redundant

With the large backlog of unemployment in the country, there is now all the more need to preserve as many jobs as possible. Computerisation, as it is, has rendered millions of jobs redundant. As for the "golden handshake scheme" for PSU employees who have completed 10 years of service, it involves a mind-boggling amount that can't be raised over night.

(4) Unfair Labour Practices

Furthermore, the pricing policy in certain sectors like oil is too politically sensitive to be left suddenly in the hands of commercial operators. The private sector also carries the stigma of black-marketing, tax evasion and unfair labour practices.

(5) Low Prices

A frequent criticism of privatisation is that they are merely a give-away of public property at prices for below the fair valuation of the assets. One reason for the low prices companies fetch is the large risks that private investors have to take, besides price controls exercised by the Government that can prevent a fair return on capital.

(6) Poor Financial Capacity

Another important question concerns capital. The private sector in India does not have the capacity to buy the shares of PSU's on a large scale. This sector has already taken up many mega projects and hence may not be in a position to finance the takeover of public sector projects. It needs to be noted that many of these mega projects are also financed through the public sector financial institutions.

(7) Loss of Revenue

The opponents to privatisation raise fears also about loss of revenue and strategic supplies as also the survival of uneconomic socially necessary services.

(8) Remedy not for all

In a developing country like India, privatisation can't serve as a remedy for all the ills of public enterprises as they are expected to serve as powerful instruments for achieving social and economic justice. Mere changes of ownership from public to private sector alone does not guarantee efficiency or effectiveness in the production and delivery of public goods and services.

(9) Budgetary Trade-offs

According to economic theory, privatisation without efficiency gains does not improve a country's fiscal stance. This is because when a state owned enterprise is sold at a fair market price, the value of sales proceeds should more or less equal the net present value of further after-tax earnings. Hence, when a profitable state-owned enterprise is privatised, the state obtains sales proceeds but forgoes further earnings; the opposite is true when a loss-making state-owned enterprises is privatised. In either case, all that takes place is a trade-off between current and further net proceeds.

In Government accounts, net proceeds from privatisation should preferably be treated as a long repayment, but alternatively may be treated as capital revenue. Developing on what the government actually does with these proceeds, i.e., whether it reinvests them, uses them to retire outstanding public debt or simply uses them as an opportunity to increase government spending or reduce taxes, the fiscal stance would at best be unaffected.

(10) Policy Trade-offs and Constraints

In practice, policy-makers wish to achieve a broad number of policy objectives, which may or may not be compatible with enhancing efficiency. Such objectives include privatising the economy in the shortest possible time; maximising privatisation proceeds; selecting the right buyers; safeguarding employment, and obtaining investments. To meet all five objectives—proceeds, ownership, employment, and new investment—the number of independent policy tools should equal the number of policy goals. Clearly not all objectives can be achieved at once, and trade offs and compromises are inevitable.

Suggestions

The following suggestions are offered to improve the impact of privatisation of public sector enterprises.

(1) But just privatising enterprises is not enough, entire industries have to be restructured to ensure competitiveness; even for natural monopolies it will be necessary to introduce regulation and supervision to reproduce effective competition. Otherwise, privatised enterprises may be able to reap substantial monopoly profits, leaving consumers worse off. Hence, improvements in efficiency do not follow from privatisation *per se*, but from the benefits that increased competition can bring to the market place if it is accompanied by industrial restructuring.

(2) One alternative is to allow foreign capital to bid when the public sector concerns are put up for sale. The foreign investors would be in a position to bring in additional technology or management skills. Foreign investment may partly cease the current scarcity of foreign exchange. But a possible area of concern could be the element of control exercised by foreign interests on important sectors of the economy.

(3) To remove the loss of revenue and the survival of uneconomic socially necessary services, special provisions to be incorporated in various legislations.

(4) Economics privatising their public sector must bear in mind that they do not commit the seven sins of privatisation. They are:

   (a) Confused objectives

   (b) Lack of transparency in the privatisation process.

(c) It should not result in a greater concentration of assets.

(d) Financial strategy should be sound.

(e) It can't be based on an unrealistic labour strategy.

(f) It should not be the vehicle for bridging budgetary deficits.

(g) Finally, the lack of political consensus.

Conclusion

To conclude, liberalisation should not mean indiscriminate privatisation, but efficiency and competitiveness in industry. The debate of privatisation is not a question of government or private control. It is essentially a question of competitiveness. It is a formidable task requiring shared political leadership and vision. Evidence suggests that efficiency gains that are needed for improving a country's fiscal stance will only materialise if privatisation is accompanied by extensive industrial restructuring. This revolution will be best served if it is allowed to evolve in a phased manner over a period of time.

25

GLOBALISATION AND INDIAN INDUSTRY-PERSPECTIVE AND IMPLICATIONS

The term 'Globalisation' has infact become the magic term of the recent years. It has attracted the attention of the people both at home and abroad. Indian economy is faced with serious problems in the beginning of 90's—large trade deficits, huge foreign debt, sharp decline in the external value of rupee, low economic efficiency, recession. All the above factors led to fiscal and external imbalances, inflation, chronic unemployment and such other related consequences. Considering the graveness of the situation, the government came with a package of comprehensive economic reforms. It has often been characterised as an attempt to globalize our economy in the sense of its being moved closer to an effective integration with the world economy. Initiated in July 1991, liberalization of trade and free enterprise aims at globalization of Indian economy with a view to improve efficiency of production through infusion of competitiveness amongst the Indian traders and producers.

It has been considered as a panacea to solve all the problems of our economy, because it will promote competition, globalization, efficiency, productivity, cost-effectiveness, technological upgradation, modernization and growth. This marks a shift in the attitude of our policy-makers in favour of a more liberal and more open economic system as against the system of controls that prevailed for four decades. It must be argued that the process of globalization has completed already 5 years of its tenure and maturity period and hence its performance and achievements must be evaluated to justify the usefulness of this policy package in terms of hopes and cheers extended to the people through it and also giving some guidelines of the future to the policy-makers.

In this paper, an attempt has been made to review briefly the area and phasing of the reform package in the context of the period of 5 years with a view to discuss the outcome of the reform process implemented in the Indian Industry.

Economic Reforms and Indian Industry

A good response of Industrial sector can be visualized since the inception of reform package with regard to its production scenario. The trends in the industrial growth during the study period could be seen from Table 25.0.

Table 25.0

Index Numbers of Industrial Production

(Base: 1980-81 = 100)

Particulars	1990-91	1991-92	1992-93	1993-94	1994-95
General Index	212.6	213.9	218.9	231.1	250.6
	(8.2)	(- 0.1)	(2.3)	(5.6)	(8.4)
Mining and	221.2	222.5	223.7	231.2	245.8
Quarrying	(4.5)	(0.6)	(0.6)	(3.4)	(6.3)
Manufacturing	207.8	206.2	210.6	222.3	241.8
	(8.9)	(- 0.8)	(2.2)	(5.5)	(8.8)
Electricity	236.8	257.0	269.9	290.0	314.6
	(7.8)	(8.5)	(5.0)	(7.4)	(8.5)

Figures in brackets show the growth percentage.

Source: RBI, Annual Report, 1994-95, p. 137.

It becomes evident from Table 25.0 that the industrial production has suddenly shown a negative rate of growth during 1991-92, in which year the globalization measure was initiated. This is due to a severe recession. The trends relating to the post-globalisation period have shown some recover. The industrial production during the fiscal year 1994-95 was marked by consolidation of the revival process that began in the second quarter of the financial year 1993-94. The index of industrial production recorded a growth rate of 8.4 per cent during 1994-95 as compared with a modest growth of 5.6 per cent during 1993-94. The acceleration of industrial growth in the year under review was spearheaded by 8.8% rise in the Manufacturing sector (5.5% last year). Mining and Quarrying as well as the Electricity sectors also posted better performance over the previous year with growth rates of 6.3% (3.4% last year) and 8.5% (7.4% last year) respectively.

The relative contribution of the manufacturing sector to the overall growth of Index of industrial production during 1994-95 was placed at over 77.1 per cent, followed by electricity sector and mining and quarrying sector with relative contributions placed at 14.4 per cent and 8.5 per cent respectively. The overall industrial performance in 1994-95 not only showed a remarkable revival from the low growth of the preceding three years, but also surpassed the average growth of 7.4 per cent p.a. recorded during the 'eighties.'

The robust industrial growth reflects the contemporaneous and impact of globalization measures at work beginning in July 1991. These include the reduction and rationalization of excise duties as well as customs duties over the last four years, the delicensing of several drugs and pharmaceutical products, the ready access to imports of raw-materials and capital goods at affordable costs, and opening up of telecommunication services to the private sector, etc. These measures not only stimulated industrial activity and rendered the output cost-effective but also facilitated export growth.

Trend of India's Trade Balances

The trend of exports and imports over all the years seems to be fluctuating but the trade balance is always negative in character (Table 25.1)

It is evident from Table 25.1 that Indian Export during 1994-95 stood at 26763 US $ million against 22700 US $ million last year reflecting the growth of 18 per cent. Imports during the same period were 30709 US $ million against 23985 US $ million showing a growth of 28 per cent. The acute deficit had been experienced during 1990-91, i.e., 9437 US $ million. This crisis to same extent had been minimized due to the various globalization measures from 1991 onwards till recently. The trade deficit had declined to 3946 US $ million in 1994-95. It is one-third of the deficit in 1990-91. It shows that despite the lowering of import duties, and liberalization of trade policy there had been no flood of imports.

In consonance with the robust growth of exports during 1993-94 and 1994-95, the share of exports in GDP rose to 9.2 per cent, indicating the growing confidence of the Indian Economy to interface with the international trading community and the significant influence of exports on overall economic activity in the years to come. With the share of imports in GDP remaining stable, except for a spurt in 1994-95, export and import would move to a closer alignment with regard to their relative importance in economic activity. The degree of openness of the Indian economy as measured by the ratio of exports and imports to GDP has been showing a rising trend over the last five years, indicative of greater degree of integration with the world economy.

The import purchasing power of exports proxie by the income terms of trade has improved considerably since 1990-91 and is estimated to have risen sharply in 1994-95. This points to the

TABLE 25.1
India's Overall Balance of Payments and Key Indicators

(US $ Million)

Particulars	1990-91	1991-92	1992-93	1993-94	1994-95
1. Exports f.o.b	18477	18266	18869	22700	26763
2. Imports c.i.f.	27914	21064	23237	23985	30709
3. Trade Balance	- 9437	- 2798	- 4368	- 1285	- 3946
Key Indicators					
(a) Degree of Openness					
(i) Exports/GDP(%)	6.2	7.3	7.8	9.1	9.2
(ii) Imports/GDP(%)	9.4	8.3	9.8	9.6	10.6
(b) Indicators of Sustainability					
(i) Import purchasing Power of Exports (Base 1978-79=100)	212.2	249.3	283.8	373.0	428.0
(Annual growth rate)	(0.3)	(17.5)	(13.8)	(31.4)	(14.7)
(ii) Current receipt/ Current payment (%)	71.5	94.3	87.3	98.0	94.3
(iii) CAD/GDP	- 3.2	- 0.4	- 1.8	- 0.1	- 0.7

Source: RBI, Annual Report, 1994-95, p. 72.

emergence of a self-equilibrating character in the merchandise trade account. The ratio of current receipts to current payments has moved up appreciably over the past three years. Current receipts financed as much as 94.3 per cent of current payments in 1994-95. The Current Account Deficit (CAD) as a proportion to GDP was 0.7 per cent in 1994-95, notwithstanding growing import liberalization. This indicates that the recovery and acceleration of the growth process in 1993-94 and 1994-95 has essentially been sustained indigenously.

Thus, the distinct resilience acquired by the external sector has assumed a new significance as the pace of economic recovery is gathering momentum. The sharp reduction in external imbalance in the last two years reflected certain intrinsic strengths.

Impact of Globalisation on Indian Economy

As a result of introduction of globalization measures in July 1991, the performance of the economy was not satisfactory up to 1993. This is due to the time lag involved in the policy implementation and it's yielding of results. The performance of the Indian economy since 1993 has been beyond expectation.

Besides retrieval of BOP crisis, this exercise is essentially devoted to integration of Indian economy with the world. As a result of these changes, there has been a general improvement in key economic indicators. These include fall in the imports weighted tariffs, which have been slashed from 87% in 1990-91 to 64% in 1992-93 and 47% in the year 1993-94. The growth of GDP increased 1.2% in 1991-92 to 5.3% in 1994-95. India's foreign exchange reserves rose from US $ 19,245 million as at the end of March 1994 to US $ 25,186 million as thc end of March 1995. The inflation rate has fallen from a peak of 17% in July 1991 to below 5% now. There was considerable success in reducing the fiscal deficit in the first two years when the gross fiscal deficit was reduced from 8.3 per cent in 1990-91 to 5.9 per cent in 1991-92 and then to 5.7 per cent in 1992-93. However, the fiscal deficit rose sharply in 1993-94 to 7.7 per cent and is estimated to be around 6.2 per cent in 1994-95.

Further foreign direct investment has risen to an all time high. Foreign investment through direct equity participation registered an increase from US $ 620 million during 1993-94 to US $ 1,314 million during 1994-95. This reflected the unwinding of approvals for such investments which amounted to US $ 11.4 billion between July 1991 and March 1995. USA was the largest direct investors in India followed by the U.K. and Japan. The inflow of Foreign Direct Investment has gone into critical industries such as chemicals and allied products, engineering, domestic appliance, finance, service, electronics and electrical equipments, food processing and dairy products.

Evaluation

The major benefit claimed for our Globalisation is that we have been able not only to overcome foreign crisis but also build foreign exchange reserves quite fast. The other important benefits of Globalisation includes:

(i) Increasing confidence of our creditors, foreign Investors and NRI's.

(ii) Entry of more MNC's and DFI in our country giving rise to enhanced economic growth.

(iii) Better capacity utilisation and efficient use of resources.

(iv) Increase in exports and decrease in imports, thereby leading to reduction in balance of payments deficits.

(v) Helps in gaining new knowledge.

(vi) The foreign competition in the domestic market will stimulate local producers to minimize their production cost.

(vii) The Free Trade and free foreign investment will add greatly to India's competitive strength in world markets.

(viii) It will enhance the competitiveness of Indian exports and improve the par value of Indian rupee and India's credit worthiness in the international community.

But, however, the opponents of globalisation have severely criticised it is a variety of ways. The fears expressed by the economist, social thinkers, politicians and host of others about the globalisation of the Indian economy includes:

1. Globalisation would lead to entry of MNC's into our country in a big way. The market for such industries is very large in India and they offer quick and high profits. The repatriation of these profits would put strain on our foreign exchange resources. This problem will not be felt so long as inflow of fresh investment is larger than the outflow of profits.
2. Foreign investments should be permitted only in high technology industries for which domestic entrepreneurs are not capable and which would kill indigenous technology.
3. The attainment of technological dynamism and international competitiveness requires that enterprises must be enabled to swiftly respond to fast changing external

conditions. But the Indian industrialists instead of concentrating on increasing their competitiveness have resorted to the strategy of join them if you can't beat them. The result is a number of mergers. Brook Bond and Lipton, Hindustan Lever and Tata Oil Mills (TOMCO), Gillette, the Malhotra Brothers and Indian shaving products Ltd., Bajaj Auto and LML, Parle and Coco-Cola and TTK Pharma and Kiwi.

4. Globalisation attempts could have been initiated after adequate strengthening of the domestic economy. Without initiating steps towards strengthening the domestic competitiveness, an attempt to increase global competitiveness is a disastrous move ultimately lead to the collapse of the Indian Economy.
5. Globalisation will lead the developing countries to cut-throat foreign competition which will weaken their political, social and economic independence. MNC's might be in a position to manipulate things to their advantage, which will prove detrimental to the interest of the developing nations.
6. Foreigners think that investment climate in India is not conducive, as even today a lot of bureaucratic controls, delays, etc. are very much present. In this situation, it will be very difficult for India to attract huge Foreign Direct Investment.
7. Our industries are required to face global competition no doubt, big hand technically modernised industries will compete and survive but what will be of small and less technically modernised industries. There will be question of their survival in the global market.
8. With regard to employment, increase in investment and inflow of foreign capital will lead to increased production and ultimately will have a high demand for human resources. But, foreign investors may prefer automation as well as sophisticated machinery which create unemployment problems in our country.

Conclusion

The objections raised against the globalisation measures are not acceptable cent per cent because no one can deny a difference of better recovery between the economic scenario of June 1991 and the present economic soundness. It gives frequent positive signals for smooth running of this reform package such as agricultural production increased, inflation remained well under control, exports started boosting up, buoyancy of capital market, upward swing in foreign exchange reserves; they are in progress. Improvement in the segments of the economy after Globalisation measures indicates that economy has already market towards recovery and advancement. Though the questions have been raised about its political acceptability, impact, scope, speed and sustainability. On balance, it can be remarked that the performance of Indian Globalisation measures appears to be more satisfactory.

But one thing is quite convincing that success of any scheme of development rests upon hard work, culture, dire honesty and strict discipline for which, we both the policy-makers and the policy-holders are responsible. Unfortunately, for the Indian economy, non-economic factors and issues like Khalistan, Ayodhya, Bombay holocaust, Pakistan's inference in J & K, unaccounted money in the hands of a few people and Hawala scandal occupy the centre-stage and impose unconquered challengers in the process of economic development. It can be removed through the development of sense of nationality. Thus the success of the policy can not be judged only on economic considerations.

References

1. K.R. Gupta, (1995). Liberalisation and Globalisation of Indian Economy, Atlantic Publishers and Distributors, New Delhi.
2. George, P.V., "Liberalisation and NIP in India in Search of an Analytical Framework," *The Indian Economic Journal,* Vol.40, October-December 1992, No.2, pp. 9-21.

   Reform—Liberalisation and Globalisation, Special Issue, Southern Economist, Vol.35, No.1, May 1996.